GOOD IDEAS
Vol. 2

to Help Young People Develop Good Character

Lessons and Activities for Bringing the Six Pillars of Character to Schools, Youth Groups and Communities

**Produced by the Department of Publications
Josephson Institute of Ethics**

Wes Hanson
*director
and editor*

Steve Nish
*associate editor
and webmaster*

John Fritz
*special projects
editor*

Acknowledgments

The publications department at the Josephson Institute thanks all the teachers and youth-service professionals who shared their ideas with us, as well as the Institute's CHARACTER COUNTS! department for helping to contact Coalition members for their ideas. We are also grateful to those who granted permission to reprint or adapt previously published material. Thanks to Josephson Institute volunteers Carl Flegal (for his fundraising research) and Ruby Graupner (for helping with the bibliography). Finally, a special thanks goes to photographer Keith Gaynes, school principal Megan Cassette and the students of El Segundo Middle School (California) for the photograph used on the book's cover.

CHARACTER COUNTS!

JOSEPHSON INSTITUTE OF ETHICS SM

TRUSTWORTHINESS • RESPECT
RESPONSIBILITY • FAIRNESS
CARING • CITIZENSHIP

DEPARTMENT OF PUBLICATIONS

Josephson Institute

4640 Admiralty Way, Suite 1001
Marina del Rey, CA 90292-6610
(310) 306-1868 • cc@jiethics.org
www.charactercounts.org

Cover Photography: Keith Gaynes Photography
Printing: Pace Publication Arts

GOOD IDEAS
to Help Young People Develop Good Character
VOL. 2

SECTION ONE: Good Ideas for Bringing CHARACTER COUNTS! to Your Community

What People Are Doing: Samples of CHARACTER COUNTS! Events
and Activities from Around the Country ... and Beyond

SECTION TWO: Lesson Plans and Activities

Good Ideas to Help <u>4- TO 6-YEAR-OLDS</u> Develop Good Character

Good Ideas to Help <u>6- TO 9-YEAR-OLDS</u> Develop Good Character

SECTION TWO
Lesson Plans and Activities

Good Ideas to Help 9- TO 11-YEAR-OLDS Develop Good Character

SECTION TWO
Lesson Plans and Activities

Good Ideas to Help <u>11- TO 13-YEAR-OLDS</u> Develop Good Character

SECTION TWO
Lesson Plans and Activities

Good Ideas to Help __TEENAGERS__ Develop Good Character

MORE A Good Ideas for Character Educators

Once scorned as a burden on teachers, a usurpation of parental prerogative and a foray into politics and religion, character education is now seen simply as smart. It just makes sense to teach young people right from wrong, in the classroom, living room and locker room. We want to be surrounded by good people, people we can trust to make decisions according to principle rather than expediency. Wariness about "agendas" that might lurk behind this desire has given way to weariness with deceit and violence and incivility. After all, what are education, coaching and child-rearing supposed to be about ... developing good people who can live healthy, happy lives of purpose — or just clever people who can pass a ball or a test?

Diverse communities seeking a workable character-education model start by developing consensus on shared values — values that are clear and unequivocal but do not trample on political, religious, racial/ethnic, socioeconomic or gender sensibilities. The **CHARACTER COUNTS!** youth education project has found that there are at least six such values that can and should be taught to all age groups (even adults). These are known as the "Six Pillars of Character": trustworthiness, respect, responsibility, fairness, caring and citizenship.

The **CHARACTER COUNTS!** Coalition of over 400 schools, communities and youth-serving organizations promotes the Six Pillars in programs and materials for kids, teachers, coaches, youth coordinators and parents. As the Coalition has grown (from Connecticut to Siberia), so has the demand for practical teaching ideas, such as the lesson plans created and assembled for this book.

This volume follows another of the same name first published in 1997. Some ideas in this volume (as in its predecessor) were submitted by teachers in schools that have adopted **CHARACTER COUNTS!**; other ideas were developed by the editors from a variety of sources. These lessons are not intended as an add-on to an already busy school day. They are meant to enhance what educators are already doing by using a common, consistent language to heighten awareness of ethical duties and opportunities.

Words, of course, are not enough. Lessons of integrity, personal responsibility and compassion must be taught by *personal example*. That's the hard part. What makes it easier is creating an environment where it is safe to be of good character, where multiple institutions vocally support and reward good behavior.

To help the reader build or sustain such an environment, this book starts by presenting some of the Coalition's fundamental documents along with information about its projects and programs. This is followed by a lengthy section summarizing some of the activities and achievements of communities nationwide. The first section also offers suggested community- and school-wide activities, as well as pointers for parents and tips for involving the business community, garnering local political support, working with the media and arranging speaking engagements. Sample documents — a suggested governmental declaration, a media advisory, a speech and various letters to prospective supporters — are provided here to help you get started. We also supply a list of key Internet and bibliographical resources.

Feel free to adapt the lesson plans to your needs. For instance, an idea for 6- to 9-year-old children might work, with a little tinkering, with 4- to 6-year-olds or 9- to 11-year-olds. Or you might find that a lesson on "trustworthiness" can be tailored to emphasize "responsibility." As you come across or develop your own creative ideas, please share them with us so we might continue to share them with others.

The Aspen Declaration

In July 1992, the Josephson Institute of Ethics convened in Aspen, Colorado, a diverse group of ethicists and educators to find ways to work together and boost their character-education efforts. The declaration that concluded this meeting would form the intellectual foundation for the CHARACTER COUNTS! movement, started by the Institute the following year.

1. The next generation will be the stewards of our communities, nation and planet in extraordinarily critical times.

2. The present and future well-being of our society requires an involved, caring citizenry with good moral character.

3. People do not automatically develop good moral character; therefore, conscientious efforts must be made to instruct young people in the values and abilities necessary for moral decision making and conduct.

4. Effective character education is based on core ethical values rooted in democratic society, in particular, respect, responsibility, trustworthiness, caring, justice and fairness, and civic virtue and citizenship.

5. These core ethical values transcend cultural, religious and socioeconomic differences.

6. Character education is, first and foremost, an obligation of families and faith communities, but schools and youth-service organizations also have responsibility to help develop the character of young people.

7. These responsibilities are best achieved when these groups work in concert.

8. The character and conduct of our youth reflect the character and conduct of society; therefore, every adult has the responsibility to teach and model the core ethical values and every social institution has the responsibility to promote the development of good character.

The Six Pillars of Character

(Definitions for Young People)

TRUSTWORTHINESS
- Be honest.
- Don't deceive, cheat or steal.
- Be reliable — do what you say you'll do.
- Have the courage to do the right thing.
- Build a good reputation.
- Be loyal — stand by your family and friends.

RESPECT
- Treat others with respect; follow the Golden Rule.
- Be tolerant of differences.
- Use good manners, not bad language.
- Be considerate of the feelings of others.
- Don't threaten, hit or hurt anyone.
- Deal peacefully with anger, insults and disagreements.

RESPONSIBILITY
- Do what you are supposed to do.
- Persevere: keep on trying!
- Always do your best.
- Use self-control; be self-disciplined.
- Think before you act — consider the consequences.
- Be accountable for your choices.

FAIRNESS
- Play by the rules.
- Take turns and share.
- Be open-minded; listen to others.
- Don't take advantage of others.
- Don't blame others carelessly.

CARING
- Be kind.
- Be compassionate and *show* you care.
- Express gratitude.
- Forgive others.
- Help people in need.

CITIZENSHIP
- Do your share to make your school and community better.
- Cooperate.
- Stay informed; vote.
- Be a good neighbor.
- Obey laws and rules.
- Respect authority.
- Protect the environment.

The Arizona Sports Summit Accord

Athletic competition is a powerful means of character development. To explore issues in sports that affect athletes and young people, nearly 50 sports leaders met in Scottsdale, Arizona in May 1999 at a conference called "Pursuing Victory With Honor." At the end of their summit (sponsored by the Josephson Institute, the **CHARACTER COUNTS!** Coalition and the coaching division of the United States Olympic Committee), they issued the "Arizona Sports Summit Accord" to provide a framework of principles for sports organizations to adopt (and practice). This version of the Accord was prepared for high school and youth sports organizations; the original, intercollegiate version is available from the Institute or online. If you or your organization would like to be a signatory to the Accord, or if you would like printed copies of this document, please contact the Institute.

At its best, athletic competition can hold intrinsic value for our society. It is a symbol of a great ideal: pursuing victory with honor. The love of sports is deeply embedded in our national consciousness. The values of millions of participants and spectators are directly and dramatically influenced by the values conveyed by organized sports. Thus, sports are a major social force that shapes the quality and character of the American culture. In the belief that the impact of sports can and should enhance the character and uplift the ethics of the nation, we seek to establish a framework of principles and a common language of values that can be adopted and practiced widely. It is therefore agreed:

1. The essential elements of character-building and ethics in sports are embodied in the concept of sportsmanship and six core principles: trustworthiness, respect, responsibility, fairness, caring and good citizenship. The highest potential of sports is achieved when competition reflects these "six pillars of character."

2. It is the duty of school boards, superintendents, school administrators, parents and school sports leadership — including coaches, athletic administrators, program directors and game officials — to promote sportsmanship and foster good character by teaching, enforcing, advocating and modeling these "six pillars of character."

3. To promote sportsmanship and foster the development of good character, school sports programs must be conducted in a manner that enhances the academic, emotional, social, physical and ethical development of student-athletes and teaches them positive life skills that will help them become personally successful and socially responsible.

4. Participation in athletic programs is a privilege, not a right. To earn that privilege, student-athletes must abide by the rules and they must conduct themselves, on and off the field, as role models who exemplify good character.

Legendary UCLA basketball coach John Wooden signs a banner at the conference where the Arizona Sports Summit Accord was drafted and issued. Universities and interscholastic and youth sports programs have adopted the Accord as a guide for conduct on and off the field.

5. School boards, superintendents, school administrators, parents and school sports leadership shall establish standards for participation by adopting and enforcing codes of conduct for coaches, athletes, parents and spectators.

6. All sports participants in high school sports must consistently demonstrate and demand scrupulous integrity and observe and enforce the spirit as well as the letter of the rules.

7. The importance of character, ethics and sportsmanship should be emphasized in all communications directed to student-athletes and their parents.

8. School boards, superintendents, school administrators, parents and school sports leadership must ensure that the first priority of their student-athletes is a serious commitment to getting an education and developing the academic skills and character to succeed.

9. School boards, superintendents, principals, school administrators and everyone involved in sports program governance must maintain ultimate responsibility for the quality and integrity of those programs. Such individuals must assure that education and character development responsibilities are not compromised to achieve sports performance goals and that the academic, social, emotional, physical and ethical well-being of student-athletes is always placed above desires and pressures to win.

10. All employees of schools must be directly involved in and committed to the academic success of student-athletes and the character-building goals of the school.

11. Everyone involved in competition — including parents, spectators, associated student body leaders and auxiliary groups — has a duty to honor the traditions of the sport and to treat other participants with respect. Coaches have a special responsibility to model respectful behavior and the duty to demand that their athletes refrain from disrespectful conduct,

including verbal abuse of opponents and officials, profane or belligerent trash-talking, taunting and inappropriate celebrations.

12. School boards, superintendents and school administrators must ensure that coaches, whether paid or voluntary, are competent to coach. Training or experience may determine minimal competence. These competencies include basic knowledge of: 1) the character-building aspects of sports, including techniques and methods of teaching and reinforcing the core values comprising sportsmanship and good character; 2) the physical capacities and limitations of the age group coached, as well as first aid; and 3) coaching principles and the rules and strategies of the sport.

13. Because of the powerful potential of sports as a vehicle for positive personal growth, a broad spectrum of sports experiences should be made available to all of our diverse communities.

14. To safeguard the health of athletes and the integrity of the sport, sports programs must prohibit the use of alcohol, tobacco, drugs and performance-enhancing substances, as well as demand compliance with all laws and regulations, including those relating to gambling and the use of drugs.

15. Schools that offer athletic programs must safeguard the integrity of their programs. Commercial relationships should be continually monitored to ensure against inappropriate exploitation of the school's name or reputation. There should be no undue interference or influence of commercial interests. In addition, sports programs must be prudent, avoiding undue financial dependency on particular companies or sponsors.

16. The profession of coaching is a profession of teaching. In addition to teaching the mental and physical dimensions of their sport, coaches, through words and example, must strive to build the character of their athletes by teaching them to be trustworthy, respectful, responsible, fair, caring and good citizens.

Training Courses: Character Development Seminars

In addition to sharing resources and curricular materials, the **CHARACTER COUNTS!** Coalition conducts training sessions for teachers, administrators, youth-service professionals and community leaders. These three-day courses, known as Character Development Seminars (CDS), provide practical strategies and materials for teaching and reinforcing the Six Pillars. Municipalities nationwide have brought community members together for on-site training sessions. Individuals whose communities are not prepared to host an on-site CDS may attend an open-enrollment session (held in various cities around the country).

Learn how to:

- develop effective character-building strategies and techniques.
- design character-building activities for integration into existing curricula and extracurricular activities.
- respond effectively to questions and challenges — including political and ideological objections — from students, parents and colleagues.
- use and modify lesson and activity ideas.
- network with teachers, coaches and other professionals to learn from their experience.

Benefits include:

- experienced trainers
- personal attention through small classes
- evening reception, several common luncheons
- one-year Josephson Institute membership
- roster of all CDS graduates (for networking)
- certificate of completion

National trainer Mary Jane Aguilar of New Mexico works the room at a Character Development Seminar in Bridgeport, Connecticut.

- license to reproduce copyrighted materials
- extensive training materials:
  - "pre-course" readings
  - on-site manual
  - CD-ROM with 1,500 + presentation slides
  - lesson plans
  - "Making Ethical Decisions" booklet
  - numerous handouts, activity sheets, etc.

Ethics in the Workplace seminars are intensive, three-day programs focusing on the needs of ombudsmen, consultants, executives, human resource directors, ethics officers and compliance officers to develop more ethical workplaces. To learn more, please visit www.josephsoninstitute.org or call (800) 711-2670 for a brochure.

American Youth Character Awards

Do you know a young person (10- to 18-years-old) who embodies the Six Pillars of Character? Communities everywhere are filled with young exemplars of trustworthiness, respect, responsibility, fairness, caring and citizenship — young people who go beyond what is compulsory or convenient to help others, who overcome obstacles and otherwise live with integrity and purpose.

Winners of the first local AYCA (at the Westchester YMCA in Los Angeles): Lorena Montenegro, Jeanna Duff and Arturo Alvarez

This makes them worthy candidates for an American Youth Character Award (AYCA). The AYCA program is run locally in communities nationwide. The **CHARACTER COUNTS!** national office supports these programs with special "implementation kits," which include certificates, nomination forms, guidelines and other useful tools.

Why not get an award program going in your area? It's a great way to bring a diverse community together around common values and goals. An AYCA program is also a great way to generate awareness of, and enthusiasm for, your group's character education efforts.

The implementation kit also makes it possible to nominate adults or institutions for "character-builder" awards. (After all, character isn't just kids' stuff.)

Schools, youth organizations, and community groups may obtain authorization and an "implementation kit" from the national office of **CHARACTER COUNTS!** to present an American Youth Character Awards local program. This kit includes the following:

- Nomination forms and certificates for award winners and all young people nominated.

- Judging forms and instructions for evaluating nominees.

- Fliers and a sample press release to publicize your program and the awards ceremony.

- An awards ceremony outline, including tips and an itinerary for recognizing award winners.

- Two compact discs and sheet music for staging musical performances and providing a soundtrack for the awards ceremony.

Terry Duffy, national director of the AYCA program, applauds Seth Witte, an AYCA winner in Iowa. (From left: the state's Lt. Gov. Sally Pederson and former Gov. Robert Ray)

CHARACTER COUNTS! Sports
Projects, Programs and Training

CHARACTER COUNTS! Sports

One of the best ways to reach kids, of course, is through sports. And sports is a natural place to talk about and emphasize character education, with teamwork, courage and personal perseverance being key to success. The **CHARACTER COUNTS!** Sports project aims to help restore the ennobling tradition of amateur athletic competition with specific programs for players, officials and coaches. All programs are designed to:

* encourage athletes to exhibit good character — on and off the field.
* help coaches and other responsible adults instill and reinforce in young people a commitment to develop and exhibit good sportsmanship.

In May 1999, nearly 50 sports leaders issued the "Arizona Sports Summit Accord" to emphasize the ethical and character-building aspects of athletic competition. **CHARACTER COUNTS!** Sports is also creating an ethics training course for coaches of all 41 Olympic sports.

Pursuing Victory With Honor Sports Seminars

Ideal for coaches, athletic directors, counselors, sports officials and administrators, this training seminar focuses on building and demonstrating character through sports. Among the topics covered:

* the ethical aspects of sport and sportsmanship
* practical decision-making techniques
* professional responsibilities of coaching

The program's extensive training materials include activity guides, presentation materials and strategies for coaches, officials, parents and players. Graduates also receive:

* certifications of completion
* rosters of graduates
* licensing agreements to reproduce and distribute **CHARACTER COUNTS!** copyrighted materials
* discounts on **CHARACTER COUNTS!** materials

The CHARACTER CAROUSEL ℠

Responsibility
Ansvar the Elephant

Trustworthiness
Shinrai the Camel

Caring
Karina the Kangaroo

Fairness
Guisto the Giraffe

Citizenship
Kupa the Bear

Respect
Austus the Lion

The **CHARACTER COUNTS!** Coalition created "The Character Carousel" to help teach young children about the Six Pillars of Character in a fun, adventurous way. The Carousel features a diverse group of six animals whose names are derived from different languages but whose values are universal.

SHINRAI (from the Japanese for "trust") is the Camel who always keeps her promises, always does what she says she'll do and is loyal, honest and punctual.

AUSTUS (from the Estonian for "respect") is the Lion who is confident that respect is one of the highest qualities one can have — for nature, for others and for oneself.

ANSVAR (from the Norwegian for "responsible") is the Elephant with colorful ribbons tied around his trunk and tail to help him remember his responsibilities.

GUISTO (from the Italian for "fair") is the Giraffe who always tries to do what's right. Guisto uses his long neck to see all sides of any issue and has a gentle way of helping others do the same.

KARINA (from the Spanish for "caring") is the Kangaroo who has a seemingly endless supply of "things" inside her pouch, including a special box of little hearts for children she meets on her travels.

KUPA (from the Hawaiian for "citizen") is the Bear who considers herself a citizen of the world. A philosopher and poet, she believes that we are all part of the same family and must do our share to help each other.

The Carousel animals are featured in various educational aids available from CHARACTER COUNTS!. Please see the lesson plans in the four- to six-year-old age group for samples.

Other Six-Pillar Programs

Paul Tracey's "Your Character Counts" Show

Paul Tracey performs seven different musical assemblies for schools and youth groups. The most popular of these is his "Your Character Counts" program, which focuses on the Six Pillars of Character and on making good choices. A great way to kick off or rejuvenate a school-wide CHARACTER COUNTS! program, this educational and entertaining program includes packets of materials for teachers to use in the classroom. The CC! national office also offers sets of his materials, including an audio cassette, student workbooks and a teacher's guide. A talented singer, song writer, instrumentalist, storyteller and folklorist, Paul has written songs for Jim Henson's "Muppets" and has appeared on Broadway and on the Tonight Show. He donates part of his earnings from the "Your Character Counts" show to the CC! Coalition.

For more information and links:
www.charactercounts.org/paultracey.htm

Primary Focus "Choices Count!" Assemblies

Primary Focus is a nonprofit organization that coordinates assemblies for thousands of children each year. Teams of eight young adults travel the United States, performing at elementary schools and at conventions, theme parks, churches, synagogues and community centers. With music, choreography, drama, costumes, props and audience participation, their "Choices Count!" assemblies provide an entertaining way to help children learn about the Six Pillars of Character — and to make these core values ground rules for life. The program includes materials (based on various CHARACTER COUNTS! resources) to help teachers conduct character-building activities throughout the year.

Effective character education requires commitment, consistency and a strong personal example. It doesn't require that you buy "stuff." To the extent that it helps you in your important work, however, the Coalition has developed a variety of age-appropriate resources, from curricula and posters to audio and video tapes. Please call toll free (800) 711-2670 for a free catalog or visit CHARACTER COUNTS! online: www.charactercounts.org.

GOOD IDEAS

SECTION ONE: GOOD IDEAS FOR BRINGING CHARACTER COUNTS! TO YOUR COMMUNITY

What People Are Doing:
Samples of CHARACTER COUNTS! Events and Activities From Around the Country . . . and Beyond

Communities around the country are finding creative, effective ways to reach people of all ages with the message that their character really counts. Although character education is a year-round, life-long commitment, many of these communities build awareness and enthusiasm by participating in National **CHARACTER COUNTS!** Week (the third week of October). *We want to share your stories on the CC! website, in newsletters and in future editions of this book. Please keep us informed by sending e-mail to publications@jiethics.org.*

ARIZONA

The national office of **CHARACTER COUNTS!** is designing and administering a five-year statewide character-education program. By 2004, the program will make **CC!** an active part of over 350 schools and nonprofit organizations through: training courses for educators and youth-service professionals; curricular materials for schools; materials and workshops for parents; an evaluation component; and sports programs for coaches and athletes. The initiative comes from the office of Governor Jane Hull.

CALIFORNIA

■ *Tulare County*

Ground-breaking work with gangs and at-risk youth in special schools has spread to the entire school system in this central California county. Civic leaders have dedicated "Pillar Square" to underscore the community's commitment to the Six Pillars of Character (see photo).

"It's making a tremendous difference in the way the schools run," says John Forenti, whose full-time job is to coordinate **CC!** throughout the school system. The community has noticed, and is supportive. For instance, the local news-

paper, the *Visalia Times-Delta*, runs front-page stories throughout the year profiling exemplary young people who embody one of the Six Pillars of Character. The program is run by the County Office of Education, which has carried the message to over 15 other California counties and facilitated the endorsement of **CC!** by the California Teachers Association and its nearly 300,000 members. Other local highlights include:

• The Six Pillars provide a common language for the curriculum of the Court/Community Schools, which serve over 550 at-risk teens who have been expelled from school or are on probation.

Tulare County, California, has built a monument to the Six Pillars of Character. Called "Pillar Square," the new structure enshrines the rural area's commitment to reaching every young person with the message that a healthy community must count on the character of all its members. Here, John Forenti, the full-time coordinator of Tulare's **CHARACTER COUNTS!** program, waves at the dedication ceremonies (April 1997).

- Since October 1996 over 2,200 educators, parents and community members have attended CC! seminars in Tulare County.

- In October 1996 on "CHARACTER COUNTS! Day" at Sunkist Stadium in Visalia, over 100 students were honored as "Kids of Character" with 1,100 people present. This has become an annual tradition, with increasing numbers of young people receiving honors, and increasing numbers of residents attending ceremonies.

- The Friday Night Live Program uses CC! to reach out to 750,000 students with an anti-drug, -alcohol, -tobacco and -gang message.

- The Tulare County CC! program sponsors weekly features on a local TV station recognizing the area's "kids of character."

Six Pillar Success Stories From Tulare County

Maybe the best thing that could have happened to Liz Molina was getting busted for that pocketknife in her backpack after she was caught fighting at another school. That, finally, got her expelled.

She landed at Mid-County Community School, which like other schools working with problem and delinquent kids in Tulare County, uses CC! to ask kids what kind of people they want to be and how good decisions are made. Liz started to think about it, and a new world opened up for her.

"I never realized I have so many choices," Liz says. "I never thought about anyone's feelings. I'm more responsible and respectful now."

Seeing an old friend showed her the distance she's traveled. "She was the same, still getting into trouble. She's all mean. She asked me what was going on with me. I told her. I told her how to change."

Liz, who volunteers as a teacher's assistant and wants to be a police officer, says she enjoys talking to kids about their "trouble." ("There's fighting trouble, grades trouble, family trouble," she explains.) She knows about trouble: "I would fight with girls, street stuff," she recalls. But she's moved on. "You gotta think twice," she says.

Other good news from Tulare:

- A gang member, upon learning of a plot by her gang to ambush and shoot into a school bus, went to her probation officer and school officials to warn them. Dangerously informing on her own gang, she said she cared about all those who might be hurt, and she helped avert a potential tragedy. She is referred to by one sheriff as "the CHARACTER COUNTS! girl."

- An alternative school student who was a member of a gang called off a retaliatory drive-by shooting, which his "homeboys" had planned. Telling a school counselor later about his action, he said a CC! lesson had made him think about the importance of doing the right thing.

- A student with a history of theft at a court/community school turned in the custodian's lost set of keys. "If I hadn't, the custodian might have lost his job," explained the boy, who cited a CC! decision-making lesson as the inspiration for his choice.

- A school principal reports that, among his nearly 300 sixth-grade students, suspensions decreased almost 30 percent during the first six months of the 1999 school year and 22 percent for the entire year. At another school, a sixth-grade teacher reports that discipline referrals have decreased by nearly 50 percent since implementing CHARACTER COUNTS!.

■ Los Angeles

The Venice Community Housing Corp. (VCHC) is helping students at Mark Twain Middle School beautify their community with a Six Pillar mural, creatively using a Los Angeles County grant normally dedicated to graffiti abatement. Committed to providing low-income housing in the Los Angeles area, VCHC also runs a program to employ at-risk young people as ceramic artists. Called "Clay-Works," this three-year-old program recently received a $150,000 grant for its project at Mark Twain. As a **CHARACTER COUNTS!** Coalition member, Mark Twain had a ready-made theme for its mural, which covers an outside wall with clay medallions designed by students in Cheryl Townsend's seventh and eighth grade art classes. The medallions represent the students' self-portraits and their favorite Six Pillar values. The students prepared themselves for their medallion-making by discussing the everyday applicability of the values in classic fables. At the end of the school year, when all the medallions were finished, students helped ClayWorks artists install the elaborate 2,000-square-foot mosaic.

• • •

All 24 branches of the Los Angeles Metropolitan YMCA are integrating the Six Pillars into after-school, child-care and youth sports programs.

There is never enough beauty in San Clemente, where young people of various ages are involved in CHARACTER COUNTS! programs, as here on the beach.

■ San Clemente

Preparing young people for a productive future is the duty of parents and teachers. But through **CHARACTER COUNTS!**, law-enforcement officials around the country are making this part of their beat. Take Leslie Mowers, crime prevention specialist for the Orange County Sheriff's Department in San Clemente. In 1998 she brought **CC!** to the sheriff's department, various local youth-service organizations and 22 district schools. The sheriffs work with these groups as part of a program to recognize youngsters who demonstrate good character. When two teenage boys nonviolently detained a robber and contacted police, they were recognized in front of the city council and given prizes donated by local businesses. She sees this type of activity as a step toward crime prevention and fostering trust between local youth and the police.

■ Mission Viejo

Think about all the things high school students talk about with each other. Would "character" be on the list? Well, it was for students at several high schools in Mission Viejo and Worthington, Ohio. They linked up via video conference in November 1999 to discuss such topics as getting parents and teachers to be more accepting of character development and moving character education from the classroom to the community. An Orange County **CC!** enthusiast, Bill Klimek, organized the event at the Ohio and

Pacific Palisades (near Los Angeles) celebrated **CC!** Week 1996 in a park with different sectors of the community representing each of the Six Pillars of Character.

Children entertained a crowd of over 2,500 with skits and songs about the Six Pillars during Hartford's **CC!** Week 1995.

California facilities of Liebert Corp., an electronics firm from which he recently retired. His goal: to help local kids who haven't had much exposure to **CC!** hear from peers in an area active in **CC!**. He worked with his friend Jan Elliott, executive director of the Partners for Citizenship & Caring in Worthington.

▪ *Anaheim*

Anaheim's school district is working to help teachers make **CC!** an active part of every classroom in this Orange County city, host to one of the **CC!** Coalition's three regional conferences in 2000.

CONNECTICUT

▪ *Bridgeport*

Both the Bridgeport Police Department and Police Activities League have embraced **CHARACTER COUNTS!** as a community policing tool. The Coalition's character-building materials are used in training new officers, and ethical decision making based on the Six Pillars is part of the police department's Youth and Violence program.

▪ *Hartford*

The **CC!** Week 1995 celebration drew bus-load after bus-load, ultimately packing Hartford's Bushnell Memorial Auditorium with close to 2,700 youngsters. In all, some 75 school districts were represented at the rally, attracting students from all corners of Connecticut, and making theirs the first state on the east coast to implement **CC!** statewide.

Volunteer Power: California Woman Makes a Difference

CHARACTER COUNTS! is powered by the passionate commitment of so many volunteers that it might seem unbalanced to single one out. But in this case it's hard to resist, as irresistible as the person herself. Her name is Vicki Middleton and when she's not working for international human rights causes, the Pacific Palisades homemaker gives her time and resources to advance **CHARACTER COUNTS!** and the improvement of humanity in her own backyard. Her many contributions to **CC!** include: orchestrating elaborate musical programs for middle schools in Hawthorne (near Los Angeles); forming a leadership council in her neighborhood; sponsoring newspaper ads; organizing nature walks for kids and parade entries on the Fourth of July, Central American Independence Day and Constitution Day. She even once caught up with President Bill Clinton on the Santa Monica beach to tell him about **CHARACTER COUNTS!** .

Volunteer extraordinaire Vicki Middleton helped organize **CC!** Week 1998 programs at three middle schools in the Hawthorne School District in Los Angeles County. She even arranged for a professional photographer and a local cable station to capture the colorful events.

Joining CC! President Michael Josephson and Coalition Spokesman Tom Selleck were Connecticut Governor John Rowland, Hartford Mayor Michael Peters and prominent educators and state and community leaders.

But the students brought the event to life, showing off original artwork, receiving awards, and providing entertainment with songs and videos they had made about good character.

FLORIDA

▪ *Leesburg*

R-E-S-P-E-C-T!

Aretha Franklin's musical plea is practically irresistible, especially to the karaoke set. Now, finally, it looks like they can give it a rest — and add another version to their repertoire, courtesy of some spirited fifth graders.

Performing their original rap song "Respect," the 5th-grade class of Fruitland Park Elementary School injected a little CHARACTER COUNTS! soul into the Oct. 1995 meeting of the local Leesburg Area Chamber of Commerce.

Developed by school guidance counselor Cheryl Moser, the activity is one of several ways these Floridians are championing the cause of good character. In coordination with the Chamber, Mrs. Moser's 1,000 schoolchildren — along with students at surrounding schools — actively promote one of the Six Pillars each month.

But it isn't just kids who are getting out the word. Leesburg city officials adopted a resolution declaring CC! Week, and the city's economic development director, Leslie Little, says that one only has to take a drive around this town of 15,000 to see how the locals have taken to it. In front of a local chiropractor's office reads a sign admonishing the passerby to treat others with respect. A large marquee at the electric company's office building also displays the "value of the month" (one of the Six Pillars) followed by definitions. In November and December, to coincide with Thanksgiving and Christmas, a billboard near a major thoroughfare reminded residents that "Caring Counts in Leesburg."

▪ *Jacksonville*

Two major television stations recorded Jacksonville's spirited Character Youth Awards Luncheon during CC! Week 1999. In front of 200 attendees, six youths and six adults received awards and recognition for displaying the Six Pillars of Character in their daily lives.

ILLINOIS

▪ *Lombard*

Good character may be the embodiment of timeless qualities, but what relics of character education will stand the test of time? Lombard is going to find out. The city's Peck Museum filled a 50-year time capsule with CHARACTER COUNTS! items donated by organizations and individuals to commemorate CC! Week 1999. There is a lot to commemorate in this Chicago suburb, where local citizens of good character are profiled in the local newspaper, *The Lombardian*, and where special events keep interest high (American Youth Character Awards, a fundraising pancake breakfasts, football game shows, signs of police vehicles, etc.). The city was also host to the largest of the Coalition's three regional conferences in 2000.

▪ *Bloomingdale*

A town gazebo — with columns in the Six Pillar colors of blue, yellow, green, orange, red and purple

In Lombard, Illinois, the CHARACTER COUNTS! logo is emblazoned on police squad cars.

— was constructed in 1999 as a site for student skits and other activities on character, to be performed each year during **CC!** Week. Westfield Junior High School used **CC!** Week 1999 to collect donations for survivors of earthquakes that had recently struck Turkey and Taiwan.

Bloomingdale's Westfield Junior High School builds character as well as muscles in its gym classes. During these classes, groups of students discuss trustworthiness before performing activities that require trust and reliance on one another.

Most of the town of Anderson took to the streets during **CHARACTER COUNTS!** Week 1999, symbolically crossing a bridge to a better tomorrow.

INDIANA

■ *Anderson*

A former professional vocalist, Don Peslis now sings of **CHARACTER COUNTS!** — and everyone in Anderson has heard him. Inspired by what he had learned at a Character Development Seminars training class in August 1998, by October he had built a local organization capable of holding its own multi-day training class and press conference as well as staging a family celebration attended by thousands. But, Mr. Peslis said at the time, "if all we did is have a big parade and eat a lot of hot dogs we've failed."

Less than a year later, all of Anderson's elementary schools had signed on to the Six-Pillars framework for character development and were making a concerted effort to teach children these core ethical values.

For **CC!** Week 1999, Mr. Peslis, who is now a national **CC!** trainer, rounded up 7,000 of his neighbors and had them dance the "Six Pillar Shuffle" at a hometown rally. Festivities also featured school assemblies, a visit by the governor and a presentation for business.

IOWA

■ *Des Moines*

"Sesquicentennial" is not exactly a word that rolls off the tongue, but Iowans proud of their 150 years of statehood know it well through the efforts of the Legacy 150 Institute (now known as the Institute for Character Development at Drake University). The words "character counts" are also becoming better known because of the group's focus on character education as the key to securing the state's next century (and a half). For CC! Week 1998, Legacy 150 hosted an all-day event for 240 elementary students at the State Historical Building, with a performance from the Des Moines police department rock band "Legal Limit," a proclamation from the governor, a performance by Clegg Park School students and a visit from Ronald McDonald and his Six Pillar- based show "On the Inside." Libraries and elementary

Police officers in Iowa entertain students with a CHARACTER COUNTS! performance.

schools throughout the state also showed the CC! Coalition's "Kids for Character" children's video, co-ordinated litter-removal activities and displayed books focusing on ethics and character.

The Institute for Character Development has cultivated partnerships between schools, communities and civic organizations through the Iowa Youth Character Awards and various character-development training seminars. As of June 1999, over 25 districts and communities in Iowa were working directly with ICD and the CC! program.

KENTUCKY

Concerned with displays of bad character in sports, the University of Kentucky selected 26 freshmen student-athletes to participate in its fall 1999 inaugural CC! Sports program. Representatives from the school's athletic department who had graduated from CC!'s "Pursuing Victory With Honor" seminars taught the course. Lessons included service projects and discussions on sportsmanship.

LOUISIANA

As it has in other states, the 4-H service club has taken the lead in cultivating Louisiana for CHARACTER COUNTS!. Each parish (or county) sets up a committee, including representatives from the

---

Survey of Parents, Students and Staff at Clegg Park Elementary School, Iowa

PARENTS (114 responses)
■ Have you seen any changes in your child's behavior that might be the result of CHARACTER COUNTS!?
94 percent said "yes"

■ Does the CHARACTER COUNTS! program seem like a worthwhile effort to you?
99 percent said "yes"; 85 percent said "a lot"

■ Has your child mentioned any of the Six Pillars of Character . . . in conversation at home?
98 percent said "yes"; 51 percent said "a lot"

■ Have you participated in CC! home projects?
62 percent said "yes"

STUDENTS
■ Do you think that learning about character traits such as T.R.R.F.C.C. [the Six Pillars] has been important to you?
89 percent said "yes"; 67 percent said "a lot"

■ Do you think the other students' behaviors have changed as a result of CHARACTER COUNTS! ?
83 percent said "yes"; 28 percent said "a lot"

FACULTY/STAFF (29 responses)
■ Do you think CHARACTER COUNTS! has had an impact on you personally?
93 percent said "yes"; 7 percent said "no"

---

business community, clergy, court system, prison system (adult and juvenile), parish school system, youth-serving agencies, parenting programs and other organizations. Fifty-eight of the state's 64 parishes participated in the program in 1999, with 48 parishes reportedly reaching 94,000 children. Participation varied from parishes that piloted the program in a few schools to those that had the program in every school. Other highlights:

- A survey indicated that 75 to 80 percent of 735 teachers observed "some" to "very much" improvement in classroom behavior after the **CHARACTER COUNTS!** "Exercising Character" lessons were taught.

- More than 2,700 adults and 2,100 teens have been trained to deliver "Exercising Character."

- In schools using **CHARACTER COUNTS!**, policies and rules reflect Six-Pillar language and teachers are trained to reinforce Six-Pillar behavior. Six or more assemblies per year focus on one of the Pillars. Student organizations conduct at least one presentation on each Pillar at their regular meetings. Athletes focus on one Pillar per month (five minutes per week with coach, guest or student motivational talk) and Six-Pillar guidelines are displayed at sports events, along with announcements on Pillars at games. At least three hours of training per year is given to administration, parents, volunteers, faculty, clerical, maintenance, cafeteria and bus staff. Schools recognize exceptional students each month for demonstrating the Pillar of the month.

- Schools involve parents with orientation packets and special activities.

- Louisiana has pioneered the use of specialized curriculum, not only using the Coalition's "Exercising Character" but producing its own lesson plans called "Exercising Character in Schools." Louisiana **CC!** trainers also wrote the "Showing Character" lesson plans related to raising live-

stock, and a 4-H official developed a set of Six-Pillar stories for youngsters called "Character Critters" to be distributed through the statewide Head Start program.

- **CC!** volunteers contact businesses to make them aware of the Six Pillars. Many businesses display and promote the Six Pillars in the workplace, provide financial support for character education in schools and throughout the community and use Six-Pillar language in advertising.

- Clergy incorporate Six-Pillar language into their sermons, programs and materials.

Teens perform a "character rap" at this Louisiana ceremony.

- **CC!** volunteers train local public servants to help them support character education in their communities. News releases from school boards, law enforcement and elected officials include Six-Pillar language. School board members support **CHARACTER COUNTS!** in the schools.

- Louisiana State Police troopers are trained to present Six Pillar-based programs. Department of Corrections officers have also been trained and have conducted programs for thousands of inmates. The 4-H plans to work with the Department of Corrections to develop a series of lessons to be used in prisons. "Safe and Drug-Free Schools" and "School to Work" personnel are working to support character education in the school system.

Evaluating CC! in Louisiana

Louisiana Cooperative Extension Service surveyed teachers in 47 parishes (counties) regarding their perception of behavioral change in students who had used the CC! Coalition's "Exercising Character" lesson plans. They received responses from 735 teachers throughout the state.

- Has behavior improved related to the Pillar of *trustworthiness*?
  78.4 percent reported "some" to "very much" improvement.

- Has behavior improved related to the Pillar of *respect*?
  78.4 percent reported "some" to "very much" improvement.

- Has behavior improved related to the Pillar of *responsibility*?
  79.5 percent reported "some" to "very much" improvement.

- Has behavior improved related to the Pillar of *fairness*?
  77.2 percent reported "some" to "very much" improvement.

- Has behavior improved related to the Pillar of *caring*?
  81.6 percent reported "some" to "very much" improvement.

- Has behavior improved related to the Pillar of *citizenship*?
  74.7 percent reported "some" to "very much" improvement.

Thirty-eight percent of teachers responding indicated that, apart from teaching lessons on the Six Pillars, they spent an additional five to 15 minutes per day on character education. Only 5.4 percent of respondents indicated that they did not spend any additional time on character education.

MARYLAND

- ### *Gaithersburg*

This Washington, D.C. suburb, host site of the 1999 CC! national convention, quickly became a CHARACTER COUNTS! leader after local educators discovered the program in 1995. This was due in no small part to the commitment of the city's late mayor, Edward Bohrer, Jr. By February, 1996, the city had passed a resolution declaring Gaithersburg a CHARACTER COUNTS! community.

Over the ensuing months trainers introduced CHARACTER COUNTS! into the curricula of 21 public schools. The new program was integrated into various city and community programs and special events including the Olde Town Festival, Festival of Many Cultures, City Recreation Camps activities and Teen Center activities. The mayor even decreed that "the City of Gaithersburg logo will not appear without the CHARACTER COUNTS! logo alongside."

By October, 1996, Gaithersburg had become a partner in the national Coalition. The business community had started sponsoring various character education projects and the religious community agreed to stress character development using the language of shared values. National CHARACTER COUNTS! Week was celebrated with a city-wide "graffiti paint-out" and a poster contest at the mall. The city's "vision statement" was revised to read: "In the 21st century, Gaithersburg will be a city that lives by the Six Pillars of CHARACTER COUNTS! (trustworthiness, responsibility, caring, respect, citizenship and fairness)." Its "mission statement" also was updated: "We are a CHARACTER COUNTS! city that serves as a catalyst for the involvement of residents, business and organizations to ensure that Gaithersburg is a great place to live, work and play." And its "guiding principles" now affirm: "We are guided by the Six Pillars of CHARACTER COUNTS!."

"What we did and the scale on which we did it has had a powerful impact even far beyond our city borders," says Linda Morgenstein, the Gaithersburg police department's director of citizen services. She predicts that all schools in Maryland will soon have character education programs. "This is the most important thing I have ever done in a job," she says.

The test of CC! is not in proclamations, of course, but in how well it works at school. The Mental Health Association of Montgomery County has lauded Gaithersburg Middle School "for providing an exceptionally supportive environment for students and families through its CHARACTER COUNTS! program." Features of the school's program:

- Students sign pledges related to good character and turn in periodic self-evaluations based on the Six Pillars.

- Guest speakers discuss such topics as "Heroes: How Do You Select Them?" and "Getting and Keeping Guns Off Our Streets."

- Local businesses are recruited to help (e.g., restaurants have offered contest awards).

- The monthly PTA newsletter features a "CHARACTER COUNTS! Corner" to keep parents abreast of activities and to provide tips for character building at home.

- Parent groups are encouraged to share ideas related to character development.

"We were really pleased that this was something everybody got behind right away with lots of enthusiasm," says Principal David Steinberg, who comments on character in his daily morning announcements to students and staff.

■ Easton

In 1997, the year before CHARACTER COUNTS! was introduced to Moton Elementary School in Easton, teachers reported 115 incidents of classroom disruption. In 1998, the number fell to 36 incidents.

■ Frederick County

Schools in Frederick County collaborate routinely on CHARACTER COUNTS! projects. Staff members from each school meet regularly to share information about activities at their individual schools, and teachers throughout the county contribute to a "Best Practices CHARACTER COUNTS! Handbook," which is updated annually.

Teachers nominate students in each of Frederick County's "feeder systems" (a high school, middle and elementary schools within a district) for exhibiting exemplary character. These students are recognized at a high school play, concert or athletic event in their district. All students throughout the county who are nominated are invited with their parents to a celebration picnic at the end of the year. Corporate sponsors provide food, T-shirts and other incentives for students. More than 1,000 people attend the picnic each year.

At Ballenger Creek Elementary School the theme is "CHARACTER COUNTS! Every Day." Since introducing CC! to the school, referral rates have been cut by more than 50 percent, incidences of violence are rare and attendance averages are in the upper 90th percentile.

As part of its CC! program, the school has organized and hosted two Walk/Run fundraisers for the needy. The Frederick Keys Baseball organization hosted two nights at the ball games where students participating in CHARACTER COUNTS! programs were recognized in front of the crowd prior to the game. The Keys also distributed free tickets to Frederick County students who are peer mediators.

Students at Middletown Elementary School sponsor various programs to benefit the community though their CHARACTER COUNTS! program. The school raised more than $7,000 for the American Heart Association though its annual Jump Rope for

In 1998, one of the CC! Week events in Gaithersburg, Maryland, was "International Games Day," which emphasized respect for diversity and allowed community members to participate in activities from a variety of cultures.

Students at St. Michael's High School in Easton, Maryland, pose with two of the six murals they painted on their campus. Each represents one of the Six Pillars of Character.

Heart. Students also participated in the Heart Campaign for Homeless Children and Youth by collecting school supplies and toiletry items. Newsletters are sent home monthly from the school counselor highlighting current CC! activities and goals.

• • •

The three elementary schools in the Walkersville "feeder system" award students for showing good character. Local businesses display honorary bricks with students' names on them. All schools use CHARACTER COUNTS! in the morning announcements.

MICHIGAN

Michigan State University Extension offers Six Pillars training and curriculum for adults and teens in several locations across Michigan. To help those working on the moral development of youth, MSU has also created resources on media and values, citizenship and courtesy.

■ *Greenville*
The Career Preparation Advisory Council, made

up of representatives from a dozen or so local businesses in this rural bedroom community of Grand Rapids, seems to be echoing a major concern of companies nationwide: the need for more trustworthy and responsible managers, employees, vendors and customers. Consequently, the public school district and their county's CC! coordinator, April Petersen, have been working to teach character to a broader audience than just the elementary and middle school students. In February 2000, they targeted parents and high school athletes with a series of presentations given by Dr. Michael Thomson, host of the video series "In Search of Character" and author of *Getting Your Parents Off Your Back ... And On Your Side.* His message reiterated the community's call for individuals to be more accountable for their choices.

MINNESOTA

■ *Bloomington*
The Rotary Club of Bloomington Daymakers works in partnership with several schools and community organizations to promote CHARACTER COUNTS!. In addition to producing materials to raise awareness in the community, the Daymakers provide classroom materials, conduct workshops and address educational leaders on the issue of character education. They have received the support of the Bloomington City Council, and the Bloomington Parent-Teacher-Student Association (PTSA), and are conducting community-wide activities in coordination with Healthy Communities – Healthy Youth, the Minnesota Center for Corporate Responsibility, and the Minnesota Alliance With Youth.

NEBRASKA

When Gary Heusel says it would be "remarkable" to find someone involved with 4-H in Nebraska who is not familiar with CHARACTER COUNTS!, he's not kidding. Dr. Heusel, a professor of education at the University of Nebraska at Lincoln and a CC! Advisory Council member, has used his position as director of the statewide 4-H to make sure CC! has a presence in each of the state's 93 counties. Now the goal is to make that presence pervasive; a three-day conference in February 2000 brought together legislators and business groups to spur new developments in the state's character-education efforts. Members of the legislature are now proposing a resolution to support the use of CC! throughout the state. They have a strong base to build on already:

- About 2,000 youth and adults have been trained to teach the CHARACTER COUNTS! approach.

- CHARACTER COUNTS! programs have reached more than 31,000 youth, each of whom have been exposed to at least 15 program hours.

- 128,000 youth have been through other programs using CHARACTER COUNTS!, including day camps, one-on-one contact with Kiwanis members, Family Community Education clubs, religious school classes, employees participating in workforce training programs.

Six Pillars Unite Diverse Communities

Multi-ethnic communities and schools involved with the CHARACTER COUNTS! youth ethics movement recognize that, for all our diversity, agreeing to a shared set of core ethical values is not beyond us.

Whether in Navajo, Vietnamese, Khmer, Spanish, or even English, six principles (*trustworthiness*, *respect*, *responsibility*, *fairness*, *caring* and *citizenship*) are being employed nationwide as the basis for promoting a shared moral sense. These values, or "Pillars of Character," are the foundation of the CHARACTER COUNTS! youth values movement.

"We really haven't had any resistance to the [CHARACTER COUNTS!] program up here," reports Phyllis Guile of Salem-Keizer Public Schools, Oregon's second largest district where over 30 languages are spoken. "In fact, the only questions we've been faced with are from non-English-speaking parents who want to know when more materials will be available in their language. When they show interest like that, we've got to respond in kind." The campus walls now feature hundreds of posters displaying the "Six Pillars of Character" in five languages.

ХАРАКТЕР
УЧИТЫВАЕТСЯ!
(Russian)

ចរិតដែលគួរធ្វើ
(Khmer)

DÊM CHƯ!
(Vietnamese)

T'ÁÁ HÓ HAZHÓ
Í ÁJÍT' ÉEGO ÍLĮ́
(Navajo)

¡EL CARÁCTER
CUENTA!
(Spanish)

CHARACTER COUNTS! *any way you say it.*

In the northwestern New Mexico town of Farmington, Navajo Preparatory School recently created posters with these consensus values in Spanish and Navajo. Principal Anslem Davis says using these core ethical values to help build character in young people isn't far removed from traditional Navajo teachings.

"We can teach the Six Pillars to our students as an extension of what is already theirs," says Dr. Davis, "rather than as something that is new being imposed upon them." In Navajo tradition, he says, the maturation process is fundamentally about learning core ethical values and taking responsibility for teaching them to others.

The school uses the traditional model of "concentric circles," which teaches that each individual has an "internal universe," and that "circle" is expanded as one grows. "So these Six Pillars," he explains, "first need to be an essential part of who you are, then you must share these with your immediate family, then with members of your clan, then the Navajo nation at large, then the country, and finally with the whole global community."

- Media information about character education has reached an estimated 700,000 youth.

More importantly, being exposed to **CHARACTER COUNTS!** appears to be changing the way young people behave. In a recent survey, 85 percent of Nebraska teachers and facilitators who are using the program reported an overall positive difference in the children they teach, 73 percent reported students using the language of the Six Pillars and 75 percent reported changing their own behavior as a result of teaching **CHARACTER COUNTS!**. Sixty-one percent reported increased frequency of seeing students help each other; fifty-five percent reported seeing few instances of students blaming others; and 50 percent reported seeing more instances of students being truthful.

The teachers noted that they now had a greater awareness of themselves as models for desirable behavior and that **CHARACTER COUNTS!** had enabled them to focus more on students' positive behavior.

- ■ *Boys Town*

Boys Town USA has been providing care to abused, abandoned and handicapped children for over 80 years and helping those who care for them to become effective parents. Seeking to supplement its own resources for parents, the **CC!** national office approached the famous charity to forge a more active collaboration. While Boys Town has been a member of the **CC!** Coalition for years, the new dialogue has familiarized the Omaha-based institution with **CC!**'s resources, says Bobbie O'Conner, Boys Town's director of family services. She says **CC!** materials and programs that focus directly on character development can augment her nonprofit's more indirect efforts at moral development (such as teaching independent living and social skills). Even more exciting for the **CC!** national office is the prospect of Boys Town incorporating the Six Pillars of Character into new materials for the home.

In Beatrice, Nebraska, community members volunteered during **CC!** Week 1997 to help young people learn about the Six Pillars of Character. Local theaters also held free screenings of the **CC!** Coalition's "Choices Count!" children's video.

NEW JERSEY

Gov. Christine Todd Whitman announced a character-education initiative in January 2000 to assist public school educators. **CHARACTER COUNTS!** was selected as one of the state "programs of merit" deemed capable of meeting students' developmental needs. **CC!** impressed state educators with its ability to provide proven training programs and student assessment surveys. School districts adopting a "program of merit" will receive state funding to implement a character-development program for 2001.

- ■ *East Brunswick*

Tom Selleck told the throng of cheering students at East Brunswick's Hammarskjold Middle School's **CHARACTER COUNTS!** Week '95 rally that they would do well to place less emphasis on celebrity status as a criterion for choosing heroes and role models. Parents and teachers, said this original **CC!** spokesperson, are often better suited than actors and sports stars for emulation and exaltation.

Showing support with their presence were several public officials, including a member of the governor's cabinet, the mayors of East Brunswick and New Brunswick, members of the New Jersey State Assembly, the local board of education president and the local superintendent of schools.

Hundreds of students attend a special rally in New Jersey during CC! Week 1995.

Hammarskjold became involved with **CHARACTER COUNTS!** at the beginning of the 1994-1995 school year. Since then, the Six Pillars have been celebrated in student essays, speeches, artwork — and behavior.

"Everybody is much more considerate of other people," seventh-grader Julie Kreisman told a local newspaper. "At first, a lot of people thought it was stupid and boring, but now most people think it's a good idea."

NEW MEXICO

- ### *Albuquerque*

CHARACTER COUNTS! has virtually swept the state of New Mexico, but it is especially strong in Albuquerque, which pioneered many of the ways CC! develops in communities nationwide. It all started at the city's Bel-Air Elementary School, which adopted CC! in September 1993. In four months, official reprimands at the school dropped to 17 from 64 (with the number of fights dropping from 25 to six). The numbers stayed low. Bel-Air's success prompted the Albuquerque Public School system, one of the nation's largest, to adopt the program throughout the district in the spring of 1994. The media took notice, and so did the state's senior U.S. senator, Republican Pete V. Domenici, who joined with Albuquerque's Democratic mayor, Martin Chavez, to lead a citywide **CHARACTER COUNTS!** initiative. They chaired a diverse task force of community activists, teachers, business people and public servants. Later that year,

the Josephson Institute's Michael Josephson arrived in Albuquerque to train 35 people in effective organizational and teaching techniques — and to train them to train others. Today thousands of Albuquerque residents have gone through the multi-day training classes (now known as "Character Development Seminars"). To secure funding and coordinate events, the task force established "Albuquerque **CHARACTER COUNTS!**" as a 501(c)(3) nonprofit corporation (as required by the national **CC!** Coalition). Funding came from local donations and a federal grant. Today, Albuquerque **CHARACTER COUNTS!** is a growing partnership of employers, government institutions and all the city's schools. The original task force has matured into a "Leadership Council" of 32 citizens, with subcommittees for marketing, communications, resource development, program development, training and membership. Here are some highlights of Albuquerque's journey:

- Parents are supportive. In a 1998 survey, 94 percent agreed that "it is important to teach character education in the public schools." And 73 percent (83 percent at the elementary level) agreed with the statement "I believe the character education program at my child's school has made a difference in student behavior."

- **CHARACTER COUNTS!** can make a dramatic difference in a short time, even in the most challenging environments. For example, during the first 20 days of the school year before it adopted **CHARACTER COUNTS!**, gang-plagued Garfield Middle School recorded 91 incidents of physical violence among its 570 students. The next year, Garfield recorded 26 such incidents.

- In 1997, Albuquerque started a "Workplace Partner" program to reach adults with the message that their character counts too. The program provides a systematic way to critique current practices and set goals for improvement, in everything from hiring to advertising to securing customer feedback.

- One of the Albuquerque area's largest employers, Sandia National Labs, has distributed to all elementary schools 2,000 copies of the "Kids for Character" video, which was produced by the national Coalition. Other businesses have sponsored billboards and public service announcements, while the student council of Taft middle school invites businesspeople to explain to students why, and how, good character is important in the workplace.

Selling links as a CC! fundraiser and creating a "Chain of Character" in Roswell, New Mexico, has become a CC! Week tradition.

- The Albuquerque **CHARACTER COUNTS!** Leadership Council produced a workbook to help participants in its "Workplace Partner" program in making customer, personnel and vendor decisions based on the Six Pillars. The workbook was initially distributed to 100 small- and medium-sized businesses in the area.

- Kirkland Air Force Base personnel mentor students at Wilson Middle School, helping them with their homework, and their character. According to Wilson principal Tim Thomassen, Wilson students with character mentors have better attendance, fewer discipline problems, more homework completion, a more positive outlook and better self-esteem. In another partnership, Zuni Elementary students exchanged letters on character with the crew of the U.S.S. Albuquerque.

- The public school system developed a guide for grades kindergarten through 8, offering lessons based on each of the "Six Pillars of Character" usable in various settings and tied to the school system's "core curriculum competencies" and to state standards. The guide also offered sample assessment tools; a section for parents; sample "awareness-building" materials (certificates, buttons, ribbons, posters, etc.); and

Teen winner of achievement award at an Albuquerque YMCA **CC!** Week event

age-appropriate bibliographies for each Pillar. In 1996-1997 a small group of high school teachers, developed a guide for teaching character in grades 9 through 12, with a collection of "best practices" gleaned from local programs, lesson plans, a section on athletics, a section for parents, a bibliography, and assessment information. It was distributed to all high schools the following year.

- In 1995, the New Mexico department of education submitted a grant application to the U.S. Department of Education, and used the monies received in part to fund character education in Albuquerque public schools, creatively boosting the money the school system had already dedicated to **CHARACTER COUNTS!**.

- The Albuquerque Leadership Council produced two video presentations to build awareness locally, and to share with other communities in and outside state; distributed a newsletter; and set up a website with a calendar of community events and other information. The Albuquerque website links to the national **CHARACTER COUNTS!** website, which offers resources, articles, photos, tips & guides, separate "message boards" for parents, teachers and community activists, and more.

CC! Week 1998 in Santa Fe

- Surveys may find that teenagers are naturally idealistic, but reaching this age group can be challenging. One of the best ways is to involve them in mentoring younger kids or through art projects (like murals). Albuquerque's "Character Comics" combines elements of both. Teenagers make and distribute comic books "with a message" for other kids. When the project started in 1996, 16-year-old artist Leander Morgan said, "Comic books have a huge influence on young people. There is a responsibility to influence them in a positive way."

- The district's "Middle School Athletics" program was re-cast to feature Six-Pillar lessons; for instance, children who do not act "responsibly" by doing their homework are not allowed to participate. The school system also developed an "Athletics Character Code" and distributed it to every high school for display on customized banners.

- Schools and youth groups are endlessly creative in finding ways to highlight the Six Pillars. One school "color-codes" books in the school library (with a color representing a value somehow addressed or reflected in the book), while another (Cibola High) hosted a public forum on character education and held retreats for parents, students and staff to plan its character education program. Los Ranchos Elementary has a program for fifth graders to raise plants (learning lessons about science and responsibility), then sell them and use the money to purchase blankets for the homeless (citizenship and caring).

- Starting in 1996 the Albuquerque Public Schools Indian Education department distributed materials to show how the Six Pillars could be integrated in the Indian culture's traditional concept

Innovative Albuquerque: The Mountainside YMCA

With its 12 local branches, the YMCA (a founding member of the Coalition) has helped spread CHARACTER COUNTS! throughout the Albuquerque metropolitan area.

Case in point: the Mountainside YMCA's "Fade to Reality" program, which uses a documentary video project to offer emotional support and volunteer opportunities for young people. Written and produced by teenagers, the video (a new one each school year) spotlights issues relevant to young people, such as peer pressure and integrity. The final video airs on several local TV stations and is shown at an Oscar-style film "premiere" at the YMCA.

Since 1991, the program has sought to help teens make the right choices, but according to Y's Stephanie Browne, CHARACTER COUNTS! gave kids, counselors, teachers and parents a common language with which to address values and morality, she explains. "Before, we weren't talking about the same issues with the same language, and no, I don't think with the same depth. Now there's a language to it and a family motto, if you will. Everything comes back to those six words."

Becky Voccio, an 18-year-old graduate of "Fade" who now volunteers as a mentor for younger children, credits CHARACTER COUNTS! and "Fade" with motivating her to make a difference in the lives of others. "I never would have gotten involved with the community if it hadn't been for [our focus on] the citizenship [Pillar]," she says. "I live my life in a whole different way because of CHARACTER COUNTS!. Every choice I make revolves around it."

of "wellness." By 1998 character education was included in the curriculum guide for the Indian Education division. Farmington, with a heavy Navajo population, is among the many New Mexico communities Albuquerque has inspired. "We can teach the Six Pillars to our students as an extension of what is already theirs," says Anselm Davis, principal of Farmington's Navajo Preparatory School.

■ *Roswell*

Sierra Middle School has an entire structure devoted to character development: the first-ever **CHARACTER COUNTS!** outdoor classroom. Students were involved in its construction. Math students measured the placement of sprinklers and trees. Honor society students placed the benches and tables and special education students created and maintained the garden. Today, the space hosts various Six Pillar-based skits, discussions and activities.

• • •

A key sponsor of the outdoor classroom, the Future Homemakers of America has organized a recycling program to benefit needy families and a women's shelter. The group also sponsored a fundraising activity called the "Chain of Character" to "link" local schools (students sold paper links which were then connected).

OHIO

■ *Akron*

A member of the national **CC!** Coalition, the city of Akron has worked steadily since 1996 to make **CHARACTER COUNTS!** pervasive throughout the school system and the community at large. Hundreds of school teachers, counselors, community members and city officials have gone through character education training; graduates make presentations throughout the community. Local institutions such as the Peace Education Foundation and other community groups emphasize the Six Pillars in their activities or their materials. Now the public schools are working to integrate character education into the statewide proficiency test. Other highlights include:

• The 3,500 employees of Akron Public Schools

(APS) started the 1997 school year with a special **CC!** orientation, where they each received a character-development resource guide along with **CC!** pencils, bookmarks, magnets and stationery.

• The *Akron Beacon Journal* has been very supportive of **CC!** The paper provided refreshments and manpower for the back-to-school kick-off and worked with Children's Hospital to select and recognize a "Kid of Character," profiled each week in the newspaper.

• The Akron police department's "Do the Right Thing" program recognizes 10 students each month with a city council ceremony. The mayor and police chief make presentations, and the students receive plaques, T-shirts and other donated gifts.

• A local Presbyterian church works with a nearby elementary school to implement a six-week evening **CC!** program for youth and parents. The church provides dinner and a play focusing on the "Pillar of the night" for each session. The play is followed by a class for students and a separate class for adults on the given Pillar.

The Junior League of Fargo Moorhead in North Dakota brought Ronald McDonald's Six-Pillar show to a local elementary school in 1999.

SIX PILLARS
CARING
CITIZENSHIP
FAIRNESS
RESPECT
RESPONSIBILITY
TRUSTWORTHINESS

CHARACTER COUNTS! is a service mark of the CHARACTER COUNTS! Coalition, a project of the Josephson Institute

Akron Public Schools in Ohio designed and distributed refrigerator magnets to help publicize its CC! program.

- The city bus service has placed CC! signs (with Pillar definitions) in all buses for the beginning of the school year.

- Thousands have attended special CC! events, from "Community Awareness Day" in 1997 to "**CHARACTER COUNTS!** Day" in August 1998 (which drew 9,000 and was held to coincide with a baseball game).

- In addition to fruits, vegetables and other comestibles, one of Akron's Acme grocery stores now displays portraits of local notables whose lives exemplify the Six Pillars of Character. It's part of an effort to recognize and promote the **CHARACTER COUNTS!** program in the schools. The nine honorees were chosen by a committee of business and community leaders and their portraits unveiled by APS students. The portraits, paid for by Acme's parent firm, the F.W. Albrecht Grocery Co., were created by University of Akron art professor Neil Sapienza. Those honored included: Judith Resnick, the astronaut who died in the 1986 Challenger space shuttle explosion, and Edward Davis, the first African-American president of the Akron City Council. The store also sells a poster of the honorees for $25, with proceeds benefiting the local **CHARACTER COUNTS!** program.

▪ Toledo

Toledo has been very active with **CHARACTER COUNTS!**, thanks in no small part to the energy of Ken Newbury, the local school system's director of student assistance. He reports:

- Every week of the school year, students, teachers and parents engage in "word of the week" activities related to one of the Six Pillars of Character. In many schools, parents are partners with teachers in the effort to reinforce good character. Parents receive "family homework" assignments that correspond to weekly in-class lessons. The focus on character is further integrated into the district's high school leadership, conflict-mediation, violence-prevention and drug-education programs. In several elementary schools, known as the "Golden Rule Schools," discipline strategies linked to the Six Pillars of Character are incorporated into the daily school routine.

- Numerous **CHARACTER COUNTS!** programs and activities have been created for students. The district's successful "Speak No Evil" campaign addresses disrespectful and hateful speech. In this campaign, students and staff both wear "Speak No Evil" stickers or buttons for a day. They may continue to wear their button or sticker as long as they do not engage in negative or disrespectful speech.

- Other creative endeavors include school char-

Brookridge Elementary School brought the Six Pillars of Character to its community's Memorial Day parade in Brooklyn, Ohio (1999).

acter carnivals, assemblies, Six-Pillar games, and a "Got Character?" campaign. Another community event featured a giant "Characterland" game board in a local mall. As part of the Characterland game, students traveled around and explored different lands of character. Older students served as guides in the game for younger students.

- The Ohio National Guard teaches good character to Toledo Public School high school students. In two programs, Guard members relate the Six Pillars through curriculum and activities. Positive evaluations of the program were recorded in a review of the program by Miami University.

- Toledo Public Schools operates a special character-education program for the district's youngest students. The "Courtesy Counts" program reinforces important skills with family lessons on the value of common courtesies. The program operates as a partnership with parents and kindergarten teachers and is sponsored by a bank.

- Believed to be more important than academic or athletic achievement, the highlight of all CC! activities is the annual recognition of students of character. Local businesses offer prizes for students of character and their parents.

- Extensive training is provided to staff, community members and parents. A local CC! advisory board provides leadership and direction to the district and community. A special partnership between the Toledo Federation of Teachers and the school administration provides resources and coordination related to CC! in each elementary school.

- Examples of Toledo's success are numerous. In a much publicized story, students from an urban elementary school returned stolen money dropped by a bank robber weeks after CHARACTER COUNTS! lessons. Parent involvement is also increasing. Parents have taught thousands of school-designed lessons about courtesy and character to their children at

Akron Public Schools' Statement of Purpose

Vision:
A community where all citizens personally embrace the principle that positive character counts and where all citizens, no matter their age, role model the positive character traits of *trustworthiness*, *respect*, *responsibility*, *fairness*, *caring* and *citizenship*.

Mission:
The mission of the CHARACTER COUNTS! Akron Steering Committee is to provide leadership and coordination which will promote and encourage character development in Akron. The committee will place character at the forefront of our community's agenda.

Goals:

1. Raise the consciousness and commitment of all members of the community, youth and adults, so that all embrace the principle that *character counts*.

2. Involve the youth and adults of Akron in the promotion of character at home, in the schools, in the workplace and in the community.

3. (a) Empower community organizations, businesses and schools to integrate character education into new and existing programs.
(b) Encourage families and the entire community to adopt and model the Six Pillars of Character: *trustworthiness*, *respect*, *responsibility*, *fairness*, *caring* and *citizenship*.

4. Build and maintain a proactive approach to character education at home, at work, in athletics, in the religious community and in the media, as a way to create a safe, healthy community.

5. Establish a long-term commitment to the concept that CHARACTER COUNTS! by providing current and future leadership to CHARACTER COUNTS! Akron.

6. Develop specific result-oriented objectives which will indicate the improvement in Akron due to community implementation of character education.

home. School suspensions are also significantly lower after CHARACTER COUNTS! and other district programs were implemented. Finally, the integration of character education into anti-violence and drug-prevention strategies appears to have reduced substance abuse rates district-wide.

OKLAHOMA

■ Sapulpa

Most people know that the CC! framework isn't supposed to be confined to classrooms, but it takes planning and foresight to effectively spread the Six Pillars throughout a community. Iris James and Teresa Edwards are two character-education catalysts who will never be accused of being myopic. In 1998, these Sapulpa Middle School teachers graduated from CC!'s Character Development Seminars and quickly established the framework in their district's schools.

Then plan to go community-wide: First, they presented workshops on CC! for Sapulpa's civic leaders. Then they sent letters to the chamber of commerce, all churches and all parents in the district. Next, they arranged for the civic leaders to present the program to these and other groups, including law enforcement, youth-service, sports and civic organizations, and faith communities. These diverse sectors now work together to make character development everyone's business.

OREGON

■ Grants Pass

CHARACTER COUNTS! of Josephine County is waging an ongoing "awareness" program to ensure that character development becomes and remains a community-wide commitment. Presentations are given for schools; youth groups such as Boys & Girls Clubs, Little League, AYSO; civic organizations; churches; businesses — "wherever anyone will listen," reports a local organizer.

■ Coquille

It doesn't take a wizard to figure out that character education takes time and many forms — and that it can be a fun journey of self-discovery. These are lessons well known to Elizabeth Swinea, principal of Lincoln Elementary School in Coquille, Oregon. As part of her creative approach to teaching values, Ms. Swinea plays Dorothy in "The Wizard of Oz," which at Lincoln takes on a distinctly CC! cast. Off stage, she sees to it that CC! is integrated into classroom life, with a curriculum that recognizes heroic citizens in the community. To help students become heroes themselves, they are required to perform three hours of volunteer service outside school each grading period. And to help parents participate effectively, Ms. Swinea offers a seminar on new ways to model positive values. Also, an after-school program called "Character Plus" offers children the chance to develop their character through the arts — and gives peace of mind to working parents who can't be with their children when school ends.

SOUTH DAKOTA

South Dakota State University has adopted the CC! framework as a means of promoting social responsibility on campus. Each freshman is exposed to this framework in a required life-skills course. Residence halls, athletic programs and student clubs promote the Six Pillars while administrators are considering a proposal to recognize students at graduation ceremonies for being socially responsible.

Mark Britzman, a CC! Character Development Seminars national trainer and a faculty member at South Dakota State University, is chairperson of a new university program on school safety that uses the CC! framework. At the request of Sen. Tim Johnson, this program is developing an elaborate website (supported by a grant from the South Dakota governor's office) and is conducting training throughout South Dakota.

South Dakota's 4-H Extension has been a leader in helping communities, schools and youth organizations form partnerships to teach young people about the Six Pillars. Using CHARACTER COUNTS! materials, 4-H trains teens to be mentors and "ethics teachers" to children throughout the state.

TENNESSEE

In 1997, Gov. Don Sundquist mandated that all Tennessee schools teach character education. By February 1998, each of the state's nine regional human resource agencies had received a $20,000 grant to run **CHARACTER COUNTS!** programs.

In a league of their own: student athlete Krista Mostek, martial arts instructor Larry Hoover (and his bodyguards) and volunteer coach Gene Carr

South Dakota's Team Players

The spitting, biting and throat-throttling millionaire athletes who often make headlines could take a few pointers from some *real* sports heroes in South Dakota.

Take Krista Mostek, a high school varsity basketball player who, because of her good character, was selected to appear on the front of a collectible card — one in a series of 26 being talked about and traded at youth sporting events and other recreational gatherings.

Distributed by the Sioux Falls YMCA and the local **CC!** program, the cards include the featured player's thoughts and a few discussion questions on a given ethical value, such as caring or respect.

"We ask [the kids] to take five minutes out at practice or after games to distribute the cards and talk about character," says Joel Hathaway, development director at the YMCA.

Initially introduced to the state by Judge Steven H. Jones of Sullivan County, **CC!** spread quickly after the Tennessee Association of Human Resource Agencies (TAHRA) adopted the **CC!** mission and urged other organizations to get involved.

The Upper Cumberland Human Resource Agency (UCHRA) provided the model by which **CC!** has spread throughout the state: first in the local human resource agency, then in schools, then in the community at large. Some of UCHRA's highlights:

- **CC!** has been introduced to all agency employees and into 68 service programs.

- All 450 UCHRA employees have participated in two- and three-day **CC!** workshops.

- Young people learn of good character through the Summer Youth Employment and Training program administered by UCHRA.

- At-risk teens learn about making good choices in the In-School Career Training program.

- The UCHRA's Community Intervention Service programs teach youth who have been sentenced by local general sessions judges about making choices and about consequences as part of a **CC!** program.

- Recipients of public assistance learn the basics of ethical decision making through the "Fresh Start" program taught by UCHRA staff.

- Mentors for parents on public assistance partner with **CC!** trainers to incorporate ethical decision making into home life.

To move the program to schools, 14 Tennessee superintendents were invited to participate in a **CC!** training. The program is now being used, at some level, in 12 of their 14 districts. Teachers have received **CC!** training from certified trainers. School programs include special events, contests and lesson plans emphasizing violence prevention.

To move the program to the community, **CC!** trainers have hosted events at local schools to introduce the schools' character-education programs to civic leaders and representatives from local businesses, churches and law-enforcement agencies. As these community groups became involved, they

Tennessee's Upper Cumberland Human Resource Agency works with a local marketing company and the CC! national office to produce this publication on character development.

formed CC! subcommittees to administer budgets, event planning and public relations. This led to a regional CHARACTER COUNTS! kick-off held in Cookeville (Putnam County) in July 1998. Entertainer Lee Greenwood and Judge Steven Jones spoke to the group of 800, including local Boy and Girl Scouts, church youth groups, local government officials, state legislators, chambers of commerce, state and local law-enforcement and local business leaders.

As this coalition grew, local county CC! coalitions were formed, each holding similar kick-off celebrations. With the sponsorship of local businesses, CC! groups collaborated to produce a guide called "Protect Our Children," which includes tips on building character in young people. Distributed to elementary schools throughout Tennessee, this free publication has helped introduce parents to CC!.

CC! groups also have collaborated to produce local and regional radio and television spots and programs focusing on character education and ethical decision making. Local judges, civic and business leaders and government officials have delivered "Character Minutes" over the air, and CC! trainers have spoken with public television interviewers and civic organizations about how core ethical values are being taught in local schools.

■ *Humphreys County*

The Humphreys County Alliance for a Drug-Free Tennessee and local law-enforcement groups have led efforts to bring CC! to this part of the state. Squad cars of the Waverly Police Department and Humphreys County Sheriffs — along with school buses and

other city vehicles — sport CC! license plates and logos. The Waverly Wal-Mart sells these items to help raise funds for character-education activities, such as the "CHARACTER COUNTS! in the Classroom" elementary schools program developed by the Waverly Police Department. As word spread about the program, various groups in the community became involved and worked together to create resources and activities such as:

- CC! calendar and CC! brochure.
- CC! website (**www.geocities.com/Athens/ Thebes/9804**), including general information, a photo album and a monthly calendar.
- E-mail group (charactercounts@egroups.com) to facilitate communication about CC! activities and character education.
- CC! information and articles in each issue of the *News-Democrat* and *Shopper's Guide* newspapers.
- 4-H essays on the Six Pillars in newspapers.
- Bumper sticker contest coordinated by Humphreys County 4-H.
- Renaming of hallways at Waverly Elementary to emphasize the Six Pillars (e.g., Respect Way, Trustworthiness Blvd., etc.)
- CC! saying of the day announced each morning at Waverly Central High School and at Lakeview School.
- Local business professionals visited schools to speak about ethical decision making.
- CC! flag flown at the Dixie League Field. (Due to high demand, more CC! flags were produced

Honk if you believe character counts. This license plate is sold in Humphreys County, Tennessee, to raise funds for — and awareness of — the local CC! program. It appears on law-enforcement vehicles and city buses.

and distributed to residents.)

- Six Pillars of Character colored banners displayed at the check-out area in Wal-Mart.

■ *Knox County*

In July 1997 a CC! leadership council was formed and the Knoxville CC! coalition was chartered. Three pilot schools were selected for the 1997-1998 school year: West High, Halls Middle and Norwood Elementary. Principals and three teachers from each school received CC! training in November 1997 and were made responsible for training other teachers and implementing the Six-Pillars character-education framework in their schools.

Students at Cedar Bluff Primary School in Knoxville add to their Six-Pillar bulletin board.

Thirty-five community trainers were trained in November 1997 by the CC! national office, with each agreeing to train at least 50 additional people.

Among those who received training were attorneys who work with the high schools' Moot Court program. They are using CC! to teach ethical decision making in these juvenile justice programs. Juvenile court officers, probation officers and many police officers also have received CC! training, and a curriculum has been written to begin a CC! program for first offenders through the juvenile court system. Also, D.A.R.E. officers with the Knoxville Police Department use CHARACTER COUNTS! in their school programs.

The Knoxville Bar Association (KBA) and its board of governors has integrated the Six Pillars into KBA-sponsored public-service programs that serve students and adults. They also have developed a CC! section on their website (www.knoxbar.org). "As one who usually can only react to the bad decisions made by our youth," said a Knoxville judge, "it is rewarding to be involved with a proactive program to change the way decisions are made. CHARACTER COUNTS! is such a program."

In August 1998, the Knox County School Board unanimously endorsed CHARACTER COUNTS! and agreed to make CC! materials available to every school in Knox County. Community groups such as the Downtown Rotary Club have supported this effort by helping to pay for materials.

Around the community many nonprofit and youth-service organizations (e.g., YMCA, Boy Scouts and United Way) have incorporated the Six Pillars into existing programs.

Pat Summitt, head coach of the five-time national championship ladies' basketball team at the University of Tennessee, agreed to be the spokesperson for CC! in Knox County. She has made seven public service announcements, which have aired on local TV and radio stations.

Mission Statement of the Tennessee Association of Human Resource Agencies

"The Tennessee Association of Human Resource Agencies (TAHRA) is a nonprofit organization dedicated to the promotion of good character and positive values. We will work with individuals, families, schools, communities, businesses and other organizations to build a solid foundation of good self-esteem, trustworthiness, respect, responsibility, fairness, caring and citizenship. We will provide the tools necessary to develop good character for a more productive future."

CC! organizers have held training sessions to help daycare and preschool professionals learn about teaching the Six Pillars to young children, and in 1999 CC! in Knox County purchased CC! videotapes for every daycare and preschool program in the county (over 400 classrooms).

In 2000, the Coalition's seventh annual conference was split into three regional meetings. In Knoxville, over 150 people attended the May meeting, which included a tour of local schools along with panels and workshops on teaching techniques and challenges.

TEXAS

Under the terms of a two-year $900,000 state grant, CC! has teamed up with the Texas Education Agency to develop materials and programs designed to help young people learn about the Six Pillars in what amounts to the nation's largest and most comprehensive character-development program.

In all, more than 40 training programs and seminars are being developed for about 5,000 Texas educators, coaches and other youth-development professionals. In addition, a series of booklets are being developed for parents and a special training will be offered to state agencies to help them integrate character-building strategies into all state programs dealing with youth.

Teens at a YMCA-sponsored CC! rally in Dallas during CHARACTER COUNTS! Week in 1996

■ *Dallas*

The diverse metropolis of Dallas finds common cause in CHARACTER COUNTS!, the focus of citywide education campaigns and celebrations. The Dallas Coalition on Character and Values works with the YMCA to teach the Six Pillars to the city's youth.

Seeds for the Dallas Coalition were planted in 1995 when more than 200 community members participated in a two-day forum coordinated by then School District President Sandy Kress, then-Mayor Steve Bartlett, and Dallas County Judge Lee Jackson. In the same year, 35 representatives of the Dallas public schools and 35 community leaders took the next step by gathering for a three-day Character Development Seminar to learn how to train teachers, youth workers and business leaders to build character in students and employees.

The Dallas Coalition on Character and Values held a joint luncheon with the Downtown Dallas Rotary to recognize local schools' commitment to the Six Pillars. The YMCA of Metropolitan Dallas also handed out tokens of "character appreciation."

■ *El Paso*

For CHARACTER COUNTS! Week '99, students at the Carlos Rivera School performed the "Six Pillar Shuffle," collected items for the Child Crisis Center and coordinated a CHARACTER COUNTS! Walk (parents, teachers and students walked past performing school children). The collaboration inspired organizers to submit a proposal the next week to the El Paso Community Foundation. The result: a $3,000 grant.

■ *Houston*

CHARACTER COUNTS! materials serve as valuable teaching tools for officers of the Houston Police Activities League.

VIRGINIA

■ *Northern Virginia*

High school seniors in Fairfax County attend one-day ethics seminars where volunteers from the business community discuss character themes with the students. The sessions break into groups of six to eight per business volunteer, and each group spends the day working through ethical dilemmas, applying

The International Language of CHARACTER COUNTS!

■ RUSSIA

To Westerners, Siberia might suggest frozen tundra and prison camps. But to Nat Cooper, the forbidding landscape is fertile territory for **CHARACTER COUNTS!**.

Over the last several years, Dr. Cooper has made several trips from his home in Lubbock, Texas, to train teachers at over 400 schools in Siberia and Tartarstan, using Russian-language **CC!** materials.

A Biblical scholar and vice president of Lubbock Christian University, Dr. Cooper finds the nonsectarian, nonpartisan approach of **CC!** the key to its success in a land that not long ago abandoned rigid indoctrination.

Dr. Cooper does not reserve his character education efforts for outposts of the former Soviet empire. He and seven colleagues also have trained some 2,000 teachers in Texas. And in Belfast, Northern Ireland, of which he is a native son, Dr. Cooper introduced **CC!** to a charitable foundation that brings Protestant and Catholic schoolchildren together. "I grew up with all this hate," he says of his own upbringing. "If character isn't taught to the children, they don't have the basis for a healing community."

Teachers in the Altai Region of Siberia have lined up behind the nonpartisan values of CHARACTER COUNTS! (spelled here in the Cyrillic alphabet). Nat Cooper, in glasses, is seated front and center.

■ BRAZIL

Teachers and school children in several Brazilian municipalities are learning about the "seis pilares do caráter" thanks to Gary Heusel and a nonprofit organization that teams U.S. states with countries in Central and South America. Dr. Heusel, a member of the **CC!** Council of Advisors who directs Nebraska's 4-H program, first met with Brazilian educational authorities in 1997 after delivering an address on **CHARACTER COUNTS!** at a United Nations conference. The Brazilian **CC!** effort is also led by Dennis Shaw — a Character Development Seminars alumnus, retired U.S. diplomat and volunteer with the nonprofit Partnership of the Americas — who has conducted several trainings with **CC!** materials newly translated into Portuguese.

Lithuanian President Valdas Adamkus (left) receives a **CHARACTER COUNTS!** necktie from CC! Chairman Lloyd Hackley.

■ LITHUANIA

To the long list of tasks performed on behalf of the character-education movement he chairs, Lloyd V. Hackley can now add typing in Lithuanian. "Then I put in the little [accent] marks with a pen," he laughs. "That takes *forever*."

But it was worth it to bring **CHARACTER COUNTS!** materials to a country small in size but big on values instruction (its new constitution even spells out teachers' and parents' moral responsibilities toward children). In the summer of 1998 Dr. Hackley, chairman of the **CHARACTER COUNTS!** Coalition, was invited to deliver a series of lectures in the Baltic land. He then had training materials translated (at his own expense) and kept in touch with visits and calls. "You should see my phone bill!" he gasps.

the Six Pillars and the CC! decision-making model.

The program has expanded to five high schools. "I'm kind of like Johnny Appleseed," says local businessman and CC! organizer Chuck Veatch. "I go to these schools and every time somebody expresses an interest I set one up." He's also working with schools so that character is stressed throughout the year, and emphasized in earlier grades, too.

• • •

In Reston, national CC! trainer Nancy Van Gulick and other CC! leaders have used the local Autumnfest celebration to dispense character education information to the community. They also have plans for training sessions open to all residents and a chamber of commerce-sponsored seminar to teach ethical decision making to teenagers.

• • •

The town of Herndon has extended its CC! programs beyond its elementary schools to its middle and high schools and provided a two-day training for police and community center staff.

■ **Virginia Beach**

This community has promoted its involvement with **CHARACTER COUNTS!** with such activities as:

• the decoration of City Hall with Six-Pillar collages made by children at 52 recreation centers.

• emphasis on the Six Pillars in sports and physical fitness activities during the "Family Fun and Fitness Fest."

• "Caring" food drives and Six Pillars painting activities by the public pool.

• Story-telling at the public library with a **CHARACTER COUNTS!** theme, including instructions for parents on how to build character when reading to their kids.

• "Good citizenship" litter-removal campaigns.

"Sure, there's a lot of fun and games," said CC! Committee Chairperson Marcie Sims. "But we think we can combat violence and make our youth part of a positive society by highlighting these [Six Pillars]."

WEST VIRGINIA

■ *Jefferson County*

The following is from a Jefferson County Schools report summarizing the implementation of CHARACTER COUNTS! *in the 1998-1999 school year.*

• CHARACTER COUNTS! was implemented at the beginning of the 1998-99 school year. Each of the system's more than 800 employees received training in the program. Each of the system's 13 schools has introduced the program in classroom studies, in special awards/incentive programs for students and through hallway and classroom displays.

• The faculty of Jefferson High School presented the first CHARACTER COUNTS! scholarship to a 1999 graduate this year. The award, a $600 scholarship collected through teacher donations, was presented to senior Patrick Flanagan during graduation ceremonies for the Class of 1999.

• A CC! Employee-of-the-Month program was implemented. The monthly award is given to a professional staff member and a service personnel staff member. Each school department nominates employees based on actions that stress one or more of the Six Pillars of Character. A committee of employees from each school department makes the selection. Winners are presented to the Board of Education at the first regular meeting each month. Business partners, including a local department store, several area banks, local restaurants and a telephone company, provide gifts to the winners, including savings bonds and gift certificates.

• A CHARACTER COUNTS! newsletter is sent to each school periodically throughout the year so teachers and staff can share ideas.

• Students present special programs incorporating the CHARACTER COUNTS! program. At T.A. Lowery Elementary School, sixth grade students wrote and presented speeches on the Six Pillars. Two sixth graders were selected to present their speeches to the Board of Education during a regular meeting.

- At North Jefferson Elementary School, as an example of implementation, the guidance counselor presented activities on sharing, taking turns and being responsible to students in pre-kindergarten. Kindergarten students did lessons on honesty and fairness while second grade students discussed the importance of telling the truth after reading "The Boy Who Cried Wolf."

- Blue Ridge Elementary School staff has prepared units of study for all grade levels centering on one of the Six Pillars. Each unit focuses on a Pillar through different activities and lessons for a period of six to eight weeks. All grades study the units on the same day at the same time. By the time kindergarten students reach the sixth grade, they will have studied an in-depth unit on each of the Six Pillars.

WISCONSIN

■ **Beaver Dam**

Not content to leave character education in the school room, Beaver Dam's **CHARACTER COUNTS!** Steering Committee challenged businesses, service organizations and individuals to perform 2,000 hours of community service throughout the Week. The response: 5,000 service hours performed, recorded on a thermometer-like chart for all to see at a Week-ending community festival.

■ **Tigerton**

After deciding in 1997 that values were not being sufficiently taught to young people, Tigerton's public schools joined with local churches and the

A Wisconsin Town's CC! Goal

- **To Inform** . . . All citizens in the Tigerton area that values (both good and bad) guide us in our everyday lives.
- **To Emphasize** . . . Good values which provide the foundation for positive character.
- **To Apply** . . . Each of the Six Pillars of Character on a month by month basis during the school year.

Shawano County Extension Office of the University of Wisconsin to evaluate character-education programs for possible adoption. **CHARACTER COUNTS!** was chosen. To prepare for the **CC!** roll-out, local citizens participated in a two-day training the previous spring and formed a local coalition, which consists of a steering committee and seven standing committees (business, church, civic & service, local government, media, parents, school, senior citizens and youth). Teaching teams of adults and students visit classrooms, preschool to eighth grade, introducing one Pillar a month starting in November and ending in May.

Wisconsin's CC! group in Beaver Dam challenged businesses, service organizations and individuals to perform 2,000 hours of community service for CC! Week '99. After having donated more than twice that amount of time, residents celebrated at a festival, which included musical entertainment such as the fellow at right.

Did we miss your community's story (or get something wrong)? Please contact the publications department at the Josephson Institute to let us know what, and how, you're doing. We want to share your success with others. Send e-mail to: publications@jiethics.org. Send newsletters and photos to: Publications Dept., Josephson Institute, 4640 Admiralty Way, Suite 1001, Marina del Rey, CA 90292

Membership in the CHARACTER COUNTS! Coalition

Bringing **CHARACTER COUNTS!** to your community means adopting a framework for voluntary citizen action — not imposing a rigid structure on schools and youth organizations. Signing on as a Coalition member allows a nonprofit group to join forces with other organizations and to benefit from the sharing of ideas as well as discounts on products and services. Coalition members make three commitments when they join:

1. To seek opportunities to integrate character education into new and existing programs and to encourage young people and their families to live in accordance with core ethical values (the "Six Pillars of Character").

2. To participate in and encourage community involvement in local and national **CHARACTER COUNTS!** public-awareness programs.

3. To contribute ideas for context- and age-appropriate methods and materials to be used in educational environments and/or in the home.

In addition, Coalition members are expected to use their own communication channels to publicize local, statewide, or national **CHARACTER COUNTS!** activities and the impact of character education in their communities.

Membership in the Coalition is broken down into three categories:

1. *Youth-service organizations and schools.*

2. *Local affiliates of a <u>national</u> Coalition member organization.* Local affiliates of a national organization that is a member of the Coalition may choose to be listed independently on the roster and receive information directly instead of having the national organization share information with them. (This also applies to local schools and school districts.)

3. *Communities.* Cities or communities that join the Coalition make all local schools, civic and youth organizations, churches and local government agencies eligible to receive the benefits of membership.

Becoming part of this alliance means making a serious commitment. If you wish to join the **CHARACTER COUNTS!** Coalition, please contact the national office for an application packet.

Steps to Bringing CHARACTER COUNTS! to a Community

STRUCTURE

I.   Core Leadership Task Force
Raise awareness; unite various constituencies

II.   CHARACTER COUNTS! Leadership Commission
Lead, plan, implement, monitor, evaluate

PROCESS

III. Community Development
Get buy-in and support; address criticism/skepticism

IV.   Comprehensive Plan
Develop a plan with specific, measurable objectives and implementation strategies

V.   Implementation Committees
Sub-groups to elaborate on general plan and implement program; fund development and marketing functions included

VI.   CHARACTER COUNTS! Handbook
Create a local source book outlining your mission, strategy, structure and other important information

VII. Community Training and Speakers Bureau
Continuous training of teachers and administrators by local leaders

---

To help ensure long-term success, a community-based character development movement should develop programs and materials not just for the classroom but for the workplace, where parents spend much of their time and where their children will soon spend theirs. Albuquerque has developed this manual along with other business-oriented materials and programs.

CHARACTER COUNTS!
·ALBUQUERQUE·

RESPECT · CITIZENSHIP · CARING
TRUSTWORTHINESS · FAIRNESS · RESPONSIBILITY

CHARACTER COUNTS!
In the Workplace

LEADERSHIP COUNCIL
of
ALBUQUERQUE CHARACTER COUNTS!
P.O. Box 289
Albuquerque, NM 87103-0289
http://www.abqcharactercounts.org
Phone: (505) 345-6000

Character Counts! is a service mark of the Character Counts! Coalition, a project of the Josephson Institute of Ethics.

Copyright © 1997 by Albuquerque Character Counts, Inc.

Community Development Process

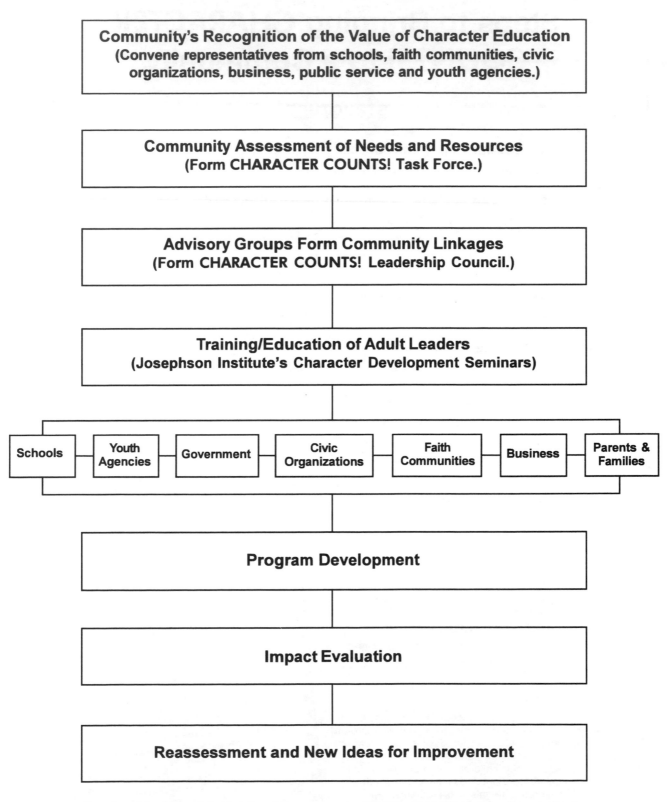

Community's Recognition of the Value of Character Education
(Convene representatives from schools, faith communities, civic organizations, business, public service and youth agencies.)

Community Assessment of Needs and Resources
(Form CHARACTER COUNTS! Task Force.)

Advisory Groups Form Community Linkages
(Form CHARACTER COUNTS! Leadership Council.)

Training/Education of Adult Leaders
(Josephson Institute's Character Development Seminars)

Schools → Youth Agencies → Government → Civic Organizations → Faith Communities → Business → Parents & Families

Program Development

Impact Evaluation

Reassessment and New Ideas for Improvement

Developed by Mary Jane Aguilar, Albuquerque CHARACTER COUNTS! community coordinator

Charting the Introduction of CHARACTER COUNTS! to Your Community

STEP 1   Assess the community's problems.

STEP 2   Build a team to tackle the problem. Use this checklist as a guide to involve the community:

Name	Neighborhood	Ethnicity	Youth	Parent	Other Adult	Expertise												Other team members needed
						media	financial management	public relations	education	parenting	counseling	business/industry	fundraising	community	youth groups	religious groups	government	

STEP 3   Create a common vision for your community with the people listed above.

STEP 4   Put your plan on paper, making sure to cover the following issues:

	where we are	what we want to be	necessary changes/goals	actions to take	person responsible	committee	deadline
Schools							
Youth Groups							
Businesses							
Local Government.							
Families							
Media							

STEP 5   Use this chart to help you share the vision with decision makers:

	decision makers	interest	how CCI can promote those traits	message	medium	person to convey message	deadline
Schools							
Youth Groups							
Businesses							
Local Government.							
Families							
Media							

Created by trainer Peggy Adkins for "Promising Practices in Character Education," edited by Phillip Fitch Vincent (New View Publishing, 1996)

Steps to Implementing CHARACTER COUNTS! in Schools

Step One: Needs Assessment (School Climate Assessment)
- Survey what your school is currently doing to encourage good character.
- Determine the contact person for consultation, training and resources.
- Develop a timeline for creating and implementing a character-education program.
- Assess trust/confidence of the staff to determine what percentage will commit to character-building efforts.
- Review school rules in light of the Six Pillars of Character.
- Develop baseline statistics for measurement of improvement. (Use records of referrals, detention, suspension and other disciplinary actions.)

Step Two: Putting a Team Together
- Introduce CHARACTER COUNTS! to established program/curriculum review committee(s) (e.g., School Restructuring Council).
- Develop a volunteer task force (e.g., CC! Leadership Council).
- Create and assemble information packets (pamphlets, brochures, fliers, etc.)
- Arrange study groups before and after school.
- Coordinate with mediation/conflict resolution efforts in the school.

Step Three: Consultation/Training
- Invite a trainer from the CC! Coalition.
- Determine whether presentation will be to administration, staff, parents and/or students.
- Determine length of presentation (minimum of one presentation).
- Training begins the implementation.
- CC! Leadership Council members assist and consult with parents and community groups.

Step Four: Parental Involvement
- Have CC! trainer or staff contact person introduce the framework to parent groups (PTA, parent advisory committees, etc.).
- Arrange meetings with parents to discuss their contributions/responsibilities in relation to school activities.
- Link discussions with what parents are already doing at home.
- Draw connections to the Six Pillars of Character, and how these ethical values transcend cultural differences.
- Discuss CHARACTER COUNTS! in your school/parent newsletter.
- Define the Six Pillars at an open house or general meeting; showcase related student creations (e.g., artwork, essays, etc.).
- Devote a page in the student/parent handbook to CHARACTER COUNTS!.

Step Five: Student Involvement
- Make presentations to student government/leadership groups.
- Encourage student groups to pass resolutions endorsing CHARACTER COUNTS!.
- Develop community-service goals for school clubs using CHARACTER COUNTS! as a focal point.
- Develop goals for school organizations focusing on and making reference to the Six Pillars.

Step Six: Staff/School Involvement
- Explore the foundations of CHARACTER COUNTS! (curricular and extracurricular)
- Activities should be developed to provide:
  Autonomy: Independently recognizing what is right in a given situation
  Cooperative Learning: Working as a group toward a common goal
  Transcendence: Embracing ideals rather than rewards/punishments
- Responsibilities should be assigned to:
  1. Administrators
     - *Discipline, staff issues*
     - *Extracurricular activities (athletics and service learning*
     - *Leadership groups (student government and honor societies)*
  2. Teachers
     - *Classroom management*
     - *Interdisciplinary planning in core content areas and business education, English as a Second Language, art/music, home economics, industrial arts*
  3. Parents
     - *Community service*
     - *Parent/teacher conferences*
     - *Newsletters*
  4. Counselors
     - *Conflict resolution/mediation; self-esteem*

Step Seven: Evaluation
Funding is available to help schools develop their own surveys or methods of evaluation. Data obtained from these evaluations will provide an indication of the overall effectiveness of the project and provide recommendations for changes and improvements.
- Discipline/suspension statistics
- Portfolio assessments
- Surveys (staff/students/parents)
- Anecdotal accounts (teacher/staff stories of improved character)
- Reduced incidence of fighting/vandalism

Assessing Your Program

Is your character-education program making a difference? It is difficult to quantify the effectiveness of efforts to teach ethical values, but it is important to monitor your progress to determine what is working and what needs improvement. Ideally, implementing a character-education program should begin with a discussion of goals and expectations among all adults involved: teachers, youth-service workers, counselors, coaches, administrators and parents. These groups should meet periodically to discuss challenges and obstacles as well as strategies and success stories.

In addition to these anecdotal reports, many schools and organizations have found it helpful to measure variables such as:

- *Attendance and drop-out rates*. Are students more responsible about showing up on time and staying in school?

- *Completion of homework assignments*. Are students showing more responsibility in this area?

- *Discipline problems*. Measure changes in the rates of office referrals, detention and expulsions/suspensions. Do teachers find students more or less trustworthy, respectful, responsible, caring, fair and supportive of others? Are young people working more cooperatively?

- *School pride*. Have incidents of vandalism and graffiti increased or decreased? Ask the custodian if he or she has noticed any changes.

- *Harassment, physical aggression*. Have there been changes in the number of student reports of harassment and bullying?

- *Theft*. Have there been changes in the number of student reports of locker break-ins and other thefts?

- *Use of controlled substances*. Have instances of tobacco, alcohol and drug use/ possession increased or decreased?

- *Student attitudes*. Do they feel differently about the school/organization environment?

To measure these variables, schools and youth groups often administer surveys to students, staff and parents *before* the adoption of CHARACTER COUNTS!, and then periodically as the program takes hold and develops. For this purpose, attendees of Character Development Seminars (*please see page 6*) receive assessment instruments (among other materials).

Good Ideas for Character-Builders:
What an Effective Program Is . . .

■ **Purposeful.** Clear and explicit objectives should be articulated and all elements of the program should be purposefully designed to influence values and behavior.

■ **Pervasive.** Messages encouraging and reinforcing the Six Pillars of Character should be visible throughout the school or organization and in all aspects of its activities.

■ **Repetitive.** Messages about the meaning and importance of the Six Pillars should be frequently and conspicuously repeated using common language and definitions.

■ **Consistent.** Attitudes, words and actions must be consistent with and supportive of the Six Pillars, regardless of how inconvenient or costly it might be. The most powerful and lasting lessons about character are taught by making tough choices when the cost of doing the right thing is high.

■ **Creative.** The program must go beyond moralizing; it should employ a variety of direct and indirect teaching/learning strategies to actively engage the imagination.

■ **Concrete.** The values should be expressed explicitly and directly in the context of concrete, realistic and relevant situations.

Entertainer Eddie Coker performs for young people in a scene from the CHARACTER COUNTS! Coalition's "Choices Count!" video.

Good Ideas for School-Wide Activities

Community-wide **CHARACTER COUNTS!** programs often begin with one or two teachers or school counselors who introduce the Six Pillars of Character to their students. As more kids and staff catch on, the message becomes more pervasive, visible and consistently reinforced. Creating this school-wide or organization-wide environment is an important part of the **CHARACTER COUNTS!** approach; character-building lessons, like all educational activities, are most effective when young people are continually reminded of what they have learned.

Many teachers and administrators report that **CHARACTER COUNTS!** has helped get parents involved in school activities. Reinforcing these lessons at home is crucial, and a concerted effort should be made to bring parents into the fold. Do this by speaking to them individually about your approach and by inviting all parents to regular programs coordinated by students and teachers. Also, be sure to solicit parental participation in **CHARACTER COUNTS!** after-school activities.

The following are ideas for large groups (e.g., entire schools). Variations on some of these activities appear as separate ideas in Section Two.

• *Pillar of the Month/Week*: Designate a monthly or weekly value and coordinate activities that emphasize that trait.

• *Morning Announcements*: Share a daily message (over an intercom, for instance) about good character with the whole group.

• *Mottos/Slogans*: Have young people write and display "catch-phrases" based on the Six Pillars.

• *Quotations of the Week*: Display Six Pillars-related quotes on marquees or other prominent places. *Visit www.josephsoninstitute.org for hundreds of quotes about ethics and character.*

• *Good Sportsmanship Programs*: *Read about the* **CHARACTER COUNTS!** *Sports project on page eight of this book.*

• *Ceremonies and Rituals — the American Youth Character Awards*: Organize an American Youth Character Awards program to recognize young people who model the Six Pillars of Character. This program could be established as an annual event. *For more information on the AYCA, see page seven of this book. Related articles and updates are posted at www.charactercounts.org.*

• *"Recognition Wall"*: Periodically have young people nominate their peers using criteria based on the Six Pillars. Frame the photos of honorees on a special wall designated for this purpose.

Students at Kawean High School in Exeter, California, go out on a limb to give their campus some character. The roots of this creation are the Six Pillars of Character, which branch out to form expressions of these core values.

- **Contests with Awards and Prizes**: (essays, art, music, poetry, speeches, plays, etc.)

- **Posters**: Give hallway, cafeteria and gymnasium walls some character with student-designed posters. *Various posters are also available from the* CC! *national office.*

- **Six Pillars Wallpaper**: Line walls with newsprint or butcher paper and have kids cover the paper with artwork, slogans or famous quotes about character.

- **Student Newspaper**: Help young people create a publication focusing on ethical living and "local heroes," including student commentary, reporting, photography and artwork.

Children at Birmingham Elementary School in Toledo, Ohio, spell out what counts for the crowd during a performance about the Six Pillars of Character.

- **Library Exhibits and Book Lists**: Create wall decorations about books that promote good character; develop a list of recommended books with lessons about good character; and arrange library events focusing on character and ethical living. Invite community members to give readings from relevant books.

- **Codes and Rules of Conduct**: Design rules based on the Six Pillars for adults and young people.

- **Pledges**: Have children create and sign pledges to "practice the Pillars."

- **Six-Pillar Assemblies**: Have new guests address a different core value every month.

- **Cafeteria "Table Tents"**: Have students design small folded cards with quotes, ethical dilemmas, or other messages. Place these on cafeteria tables and encourage

everyone to discuss them during lunch.

- **Six Pillars Clubs**: Design six clubs — one for each Pillar — and have children rotate club affiliation every week or two.

- **Faculty/Staff Training and Discussion**: Incorporate the Six Pillars into the training of youth leaders and teachers. Provide a list of "examples of how to be an example."

- **Parent Meeting/Workshops**: Bring parents together to discuss the importance of teaching the Six Pillars at home.

- **Parent/Faculty Task Force**: Designate a group of parents and teachers and/or other youth leaders to design and administer CC! activities.

- **Student/Faculty Task Force**: Have students work in coordination with teachers to design, administer and carry out CC! activities.

- **Peer Counseling/Mentoring**: Designate young people with leadership skills to serve as peer counselors and mentors. Incorporate the Six Pillars into their training.

- **Cross-Age Tutoring/Mentoring**: Arrange for pre-teens and teenagers

To celebrate CC! Week 1999, elementary school students in Idaho Falls, Idaho, enlisted the help of local firefighters and merchants in collecting 290 pounds of recyclable tabs from soda cans (at right). The students donated monies from this fundraiser to the Ronald McDonald House charities.

to counsel and tutor younger children.

• *Landscaping and Gardening Project*: Cultivating and maintaining a community vegetable or flower garden is a great way to teach young people about responsibility, caring and teamwork. The America the Beautiful Fund offers free seeds to support these endeavors. *Contact information is listed under "Resources" at the end of this book.*

• *Public Area Beautification*: Have young people

Elementary school students in Dunn, North Carolina, sign pledges to be "Kids for Character" during **CHARACTER COUNTS!** Week 1999.

organize and carry out a cleanup of a playground, park or other neglected area.

• *Clothing Drive*: Collect items of clothing and donate them to an agency that serves the needy.

• *Cooking for Neighbors*: Bring food to people who are homebound with illnesses.

• *Caring for the Homeless*: Organize groups of young people to serve food at a homeless shelter.

• *Charity Service*: Participate as a group in a charitable event (e.g., a walk-a-thon) or organize your own fundraiser (e.g., an auction, bake sale or car wash) and donate the money to a charitable organization.

• *Sponsoring an Impoverished Child*: Hold a fundraiser to sponsor children in developing countries.

• *Book/Magazine Drive*: Collect reading materials to donate to a hospital or nursing home.

• *Student-Designed T-Shirts*: Hold a contest to design a local Six Pillars mascot.

• *Murals*: Help young people paint the Six Pillars or the **CHARACTER COUNTS!** logo in a prominent location on school grounds or on a banner to place in front of your organization (permission to use the **CC!** logo is required). To replace and deter graffiti, they might paint — and maintain — a mural of good character on a wall that is commonly targeted by "taggers." (Be sure to get authorization from the owner of the property!)

• *"Chain of Character"*: Have various youth groups or elementary schools sell paper "links" as a fundraiser. Designate a color for each group if you want them to compete to sell the most. Then display the chain at a large gathering. (In Roswell, New Mexico, a "Chain of Character" circled the field twice at a football game between rival high schools.)

• *"Kids In Nature's Defense" (KIND) Clubs*: The Humane Society's education division publishes "KIND News" and maintains a website (**www.kindnews.org**) with activities and articles to help kids "develop values of kindness toward people, animals, and the Earth." Also available: a "Student Action Guide" for teens (**www.nahee.org/teenscene/sag**). *Contact information is listed under "Resources" at the end of this book.*

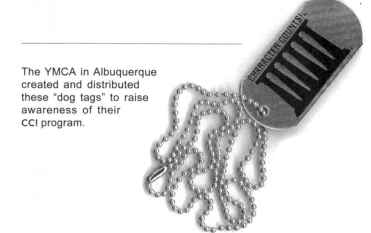

The YMCA in Albuquerque created and distributed these "dog tags" to raise awareness of their CC! program.

Art Projects Are Easy, Educational and Fun

Stay in Touch With Your Community!

Schools, youth organizations and municipalities with successful **CHARACTER COUNTS!** programs often have effective newsletters that publicize their activities and offer articles and tips on building character.

Six-Pillar Tips for Building Character Through Sports

Coaches and others working with youth sports programs might find these Six-Pillar tips useful for promoting character and good sportsmanship in young athletes.

TRUSTWORTHINESS

Always pursue victory with honor ■ Demonstrate and demand scrupulous integrity ■ Observe and enforce the spirit and letter of rules ■ Don't compromise education and character-development goals ■ Don't engage in or tolerate dishonesty, cheating or dishonorable conduct

RESPECT

Treat the traditions of the sport and other participants with respect ■ Don't engage in or tolerate disrespectful conduct including verbal abuse of opponents and officials, profane or belligerent "trash talking," taunting or unseemly celebrations ■ Win with grace and lose with dignity

RESPONSIBILITY

Be a positive role model on and off the field and require the same of your athletes ■ Further the mental, social and moral development of athletes and teach life skills that enhance personal success and social responsibility ■ Maintain competence including basic knowledge of: 1.) character building; 2.) first aid and safety; and 3.) coaching principles, rules and strategies

FAIRNESS

Adhere to high standards of fair play ■ Treat players fairly according to their abilities ■ Never take unfair advantage ■ Be open-minded

CARING

Assure that the academic, emotional, physical and moral well-being of athletes is always placed above desires and pressures to win

CITIZENSHIP

Avoid gamesmanship and promote sportsmanship by honoring the rules and goals of the sport ■ Establish codes of conduct for coaches, athletes, parents and spectators ■ Safeguard the health of athletes and the integrity of the sport by prohibiting the use of alcohol and tobacco ■ Demand compliance with all laws and regulations, including those relating to gambling and the use of drugs

Good Ideas for Character-Builders: *The "T.E.A.M." Approach*

TEACH

Teach children that their character counts — that their success and happiness will depend on who they are inside, not on what they have or how they look. Tell them that people of character know the difference between right and wrong because they guide their thoughts and actions by six basic rules of living (the "Six Pillars of Character"): *trustworthiness*, *respect*, *responsibility*, *fairness*, *caring* and *citizenship*. Explain the meaning of these words. Use examples from your own life, history and the news.

ENFORCE

Instill the "Six Pillars of Character" by rewarding good behavior (usually, praise is enough) and by discouraging all instances of bad behavior by imposing (or, in some cases, allowing others to impose) fair, consistent consequences that prove you are serious about character.

Demonstrate courage and firmness of will by enforcing the core values when it is difficult or costly to do so. Character building is most effective when you regularly see and seize opportunities to: 1) strengthen awareness of moral obligations and the moral significance of choices (*ethical consciousness*); 2) enhance the desire to do the right thing (*ethical commitment*); and 3) improve the ability to foresee potential consequences, devise options, and implement principled choices (*ethical competency*).

ADVOCATE

Continuously encourage children to live up to the "Six Pillars of Character" in all their thoughts and actions. Be an advocate for character. Don't be neutral about the importance of character nor casual about improper conduct. Be clear and uncompromising that you want and expect your children to be trustworthy, respectful, responsible, fair, caring and good citizens.

MODEL

Be careful and self-conscious about setting a good example in everything you say and do. Hold yourself to the highest standards by honoring the "Six Pillars of Character" at all times. You may think you are be a pretty good model now, but you can always do better. Everything you do, and don't do, sends a message about your values. Be sure your messages reinforce your lessons about doing the right thing even when it is hard to do so. When you slip (and we all do), act the way you want your children to behave when they act improperly — be accountable, apologize sincerely and do better.

Good Ideas for Involving the Business Community

A mall in Martin County, Florida, displays young people's artwork and other CC! materials.

Just as they are urged to bring ethics training into the workplace, businesses are encouraged to support character development beyond the company walls. Johnson & Johnson, Metropolitan Life and State Farm Insurance, for instance, have generously supported **CHARACTER COUNTS!** at the national level, while other companies have sponsored community forums and countless activities in schools and youth organizations. In addition, various businesses have underwritten Character Development Seminars programs in their home towns.

Cultivate relationships with business leaders who want to exhibit a sense of responsibility to the communities in which the operate. Activities associated with the Six Pillars have wide appeal.

You could help familiarize the staff of a company with your group's activities and your need for community support by having the management place an informational sheet — about the Six Pillars and something specific about your activity — in each employee's pay envelope. Or, when soliciting the support of a business for an activity, you might provide tips from this book and suggest that they share these with employees who,

in turn, can take them home or to youth organizations to which they belong.

Clearly identify your needs to those whose help you're soliciting. Is it money? Publicity? Materials? Food? A venue? Also, try to estimate the costs of your program. Then identify the people who could authorize the contribution you seek and speak to them if possible. Follow up with a compelling and clearly written letter spelling out the nature of your request and why your activity warrants sponsorship. After a few days, make a friendly reminder telephone call to check the status of your request.

When you've got a firm commitment of support, make sure everyone in your organization knows about it. Also, it's a good idea to have the young people who benefited from the donation write thank-you notes. (You could turn this into a character-building exercise in itself.) Of course, you should also write a letter thanking them for their generosity.

Give credit — publicly, if possible — to businesses for helping you. Give the stores and companies **CHARACTER COUNTS!** posters, stickers, buttons or other display items. This is a way to simultaneously acknowledge the donor's generosity and boost public awareness.

Commercial buildings show support for CHARACTER COUNTS! Week in Philadelphia.

- For your contests, competitions and raffles, solicit the support of booksellers, video and music stores, toy stores, restaurants and any other merchants who could offer prizes for young people.

- Various large corporations may underwrite your activity if funds are the issue. Usually there is one person in charge of corporate giving. Find out who this person is and what the company's guidelines are for giving before you send your letter.

- A local newspaper may provide free advertising of an event or ongoing activity.

- Businesses may explicitly support CHARACTER COUNTS! in their advertising and make reference to an event or ongoing activity. They may sponsor a newspaper ad or billboard sign.

- A local newspaper, print shop or copy shop may donate printing and typesetting services to a community newspaper produced by young people.

- A print shop or copy shop may donate its services to reproduce and bind materials to make a collection of essays on the Six Pillars or a student newspaper focusing on character.

- An office supplies store may donate materials (e.g., paper, notebooks, pens) for a journal-writing activity.

- A local chain of grocery stores, restaurants or other businesses may display posters or include information on marquees or billboards at all of their locations.

- Local grocery stores and restaurants may make contributions to food drives.

Allied Signal Aerospace in Torrance, California took the lead to get CHARACTER COUNTS! going in its community by "adopting" a local middle school. Among other activities, the company has sponsored an essay contest for the children, with select entries displayed at the firm's annual "Integrity Day" celebrations — a great way to integrate character education, community involvement and employee development.

- Office and art supplies stores may contribute materials for arts and crafts projects focusing on the Six Pillars.

- Fabric stores may donate materials for a CHARACTER COUNTS! or "Pillar of the Month" banner (permission to use the CHARACTER COUNTS! service mark and logo is required). Various other businesses should be encouraged to make an ongoing commitment to sponsor activities celebrating the "Pillar of the Month."

- CD and tape stores may provide music for activities involving song and dance.

- Video stores may provide free video rentals, and supermarkets might donate snacks, for a movie night focusing on character development.

- Hardware stores, car/truck rental lots, and refuse haulers may donate materials for community service endeavors such as school painting and other maintenance projects, park cleanup projects and recycling activities.

Integrity Awareness Week Essay Contest

How can integrity help you make the world a better place?

If everyone had integrity, the world would be a better place to live. Integrity is very important. I choose friends with integrity. I want to play on soccer and basketball teams with integrity. If my friends have integrity, I won't get hit in games. They are honest and I can trust them. People with integrity are good to the environment too. I wish everybody had integrity.

Please use this form for all entries.

Name: Luke Saville
Grade: Second   Age: Seven
Employee Name: Marshall Saville
Work Location: AES/TORR
Extension: 4541

Contest Rules

- Eligibility limited to children of AlliedSignal Aerospace employees assigned to Torrance, Rancho Dominguez and Bandini facilities only.
- Choice of savings bond or gift certificate to the first-place winners in the following categories:
  > Grades K thru 3   > Grades 4 thru 6   > Grades 7 thru 9   > Grades 10 thru 12
- Deadline for entry: Friday, Oct. 13, 1995. Winners announced Wednesday, Oct. 18, 1995.
- Submit entries to: Jeanie Buckner, AlliedSignal Aerospace Public Affairs, 38-0-1434, ext. 2638.

Good Ideas for Fundraising

FUNDING FOR EDUCATIONAL ORGANIZATIONS

■ **Safe & Drug-Free Schools Program**
www.ed.gov/offices/OESE/SDFS
(202) 260-3954
The Safe and Drug-Free Schools Program is the federal government's primary vehicle for reducing drug, alcohol and tobacco use, and violence, through education and prevention activities in schools. Staff are available to provide technical assistance on administering programs and applying for grants.

FUNDING FOR COMMUNITY ORGANIZATIONS

■ **"Promising Initiatives to Improve Education in Your Community"**
www.ed.gov/pubs/promisinginitiatives
This guide to selected funding opportunities with detailed information on specific programs, including "21st-Century Community Learning Centers" (*www.ed.gov/21stcclc*). The complete guide, which includes descriptions of exemplary projects and links to related resources, is available online and may be downloaded as a .PDF file or as a Word document.

■ **National 4-H Council Youth Grants Program**
www.fourhcouncil.edu/programs/grantinfo.htm
The Youth-Corporate Connections team of National 4-H Council offers grants for youth in communities, counties, and on the state level. These grants seek to help young people take a leadership role in improving their communities: they design the project, write proposals, implement and evaluate the projects.

■ **Office of Juvenile Justice and Delinquency Prevention – Grants & Funding**
ojjdp.ncjrs.org/grants/grants.html
The OJJDP offers grants to community organi-

zations working with at-risk youth. Updates on funding opportunities are available on its website.

GENERAL TIPS ON FUNDRAISING

■ **The Grantsmanship Center**
www.tgci.com
This website includes information on training, articles from the Center's magazine, tips on grant-writing and samples of successful proposals.

■ *Grassroots Fundraising Journal*
www.chardonpress.com
This publication provides practical information on "funding the work of social justice and social change." Articles and other resources are available online.

■ **National Youth Development Information Center – Funding Opportunities for Youth Development Programs**
www.nydic.org/funding.html
This extensive website includes information on finding funds for youth-development programs, with links and listings of resources, including local, state and national foundations.

■ **The Foundation Center**
www.fdncenter.org
The Foundation Center collects, organizes, analyzes and disseminates information on foundations, corporate giving and related subjects.

■ *The Chronicle of Philanthropy* **Internet Resources**
http://philanthropy.com/free/resources/fresources.htm
This website includes a vast collection of links to useful sites. Pages are organized by such categories as "General Information on Fund Raising," "Using the Internet to Seek Donations," "Online Charity Shopping Malls" and "Organizations for Fund Raisers."

Good Ideas for Getting the Support of Local Government

CHARACTER COUNTS! and the Six Pillars of Character have been endorsed by about 40 states and 500 cities, counties, school districts and chambers of commerce (not to mention the president and both houses of Congress). Community activists have secured the support of hundreds of national and local elected officials for National CHARACTER COUNTS! Week (every third week of October) and other celebrations. Political pronouncements don't solve problems, of course. But generating community-wide support and awareness is easier if public officials endorse your work.

Encourage your mayor, city council, state legislators, school board members and other community leaders to introduce a resolution endorsing the Six Pillars of Character and proclaiming the third week in October "CHARACTER COUNTS! Week." Other awareness-raising events — Knoxville's "CHARACTER COUNTS! Days" is a good example — also benefit from proclamations.

To secure these endorsements, contact the office of your elected officials, either in writing or by telephone. Provide a background sheet on the activities of your school or organization and why you feel they should support CHARACTER COUNTS!. Urge them to commit to sponsoring character-development programs based on the Six Pillars in local schools and other youth programs.

During CHARACTER COUNTS! Week, local governments can also participate by draping a banner in front of City Hall or in another prominent position (permission to use the CHARACTER COUNTS! service mark and logo is required). Provide a local contact phone number along with the Coalition's main number and website on the banner for information on how to get involved.

Encourage local officials to hold a CC! town hall meeting in the city council chamber. Invite a broad cross section of community members to discuss the Six Pillars and acknowledge individuals who exemplify them. Local elected officials can give these individuals certificates or plaques.

Good Ideas for Raising Awareness: Working With the News Media

The press is a useful vehicle for promoting CHARACTER COUNTS! events and ongoing activities — or broader ideas related to character education. If you have your own newsletter or other media outlet, use it to publicize these ideas and your activities. Gaithersburg Middle School in Maryland, for instance, has a "CHARACTER COUNTS! Corner" in its school paper. Also, encourage other community organizations to publicize your events and activities in their newsletters. Consult www.charactercounts.org if you would like to reprint an article or general information. (Please contact the national office for permission.)

The key to all outside media relations is to think like a journalist. Tell the reporter, editor or producer why your event or character-building campaign is newsworthy and what the broader implications of the story are. Remember, the media are bombarded with all sorts of ideas every day. The following pages outline how to access the media with press conferences, "opinion-editorial" articles, radio and television talk shows, and public service announcements (PSAs).

The following guide will help you plan and carry out a press conference, write and place an article for the commentary section in your newspaper, get on radio or television talk shows, and place public service announcements.

Planning a Press Conference

A news conference is a convenience for reporters, but not a guarantee of getting the press to cover your event. Reporters must have good reason to show up. If you have a notable spokesperson, a big event, or if you live in a small media market, then a news conference may be appropriate. Here are some tips for planning one:

■ *Find a credible spokesperson.* A well-recognized and respectable figure can help attract attention to your event. The CHARACTER COUNTS! Coalition was fortunate to have the late congresswoman Barbara Jordan and actor Tom Selleck as its original national spokespersons. Entertainer Lee Greenwood has also served as a spokesperson for the Coalition.

VENTURA COUNTY STAR
Seminar on sports ethics finds them missing too often

Fallon Park Elementary program could become model for state
'Character Counts' at Roanoke school

The Washington Post
METRO
THURSDAY, FEBRUARY 4, 1999
Students Learn the Six 'Pillars' of Character

■ *Choose an appropriate date* for the press conference. Make sure your conference doesn't coincide with a presidential campaign stop in your community or another overshadowing news conference. If your press conference is related to a CHARACTER COUNTS! Week celebration, you should choose a date near the beginning of October so the media have the whole week to cover your activities. Remind them to continue to track your CC! activities throughout the year.

■ *Choose a convenient time* for the press. A good time to schedule a news conference is 10:00 a.m. This allows time in the morning for the assignment editor to review the story options for the day and to assign a reporter to your event. Remember, TV and radio producers need time to edit the story for broadcast, and newspaper reporters need time to write. That's why the morning hours are preferable.

■ *Identify a site* for your news conference. Is it where you will be doing a community service project? Is it where art projects are on display? Will it be where you hold your event? Remember that TV tells its story in pictures, so make your site as visually appealing as possible.

■ *Write a media advisory* using the "who, what, where, when and why" basics (see the following sample). Keep it brief — a media advisory is not a press release. Include crucial information such as directions, a map, where to enter the building, and parking instructions.

■ *Develop a "media list"* for recipients of the advisory. Include the names of assignment editors and reporters for print, radio, television and wire services. (Associated Press is the ubiquitous newswire; your community may also have a local one.)

■ *Fax or e-mail the media advisory* to those on your media list. Most assignment editors do not look in the mail for media advisories. Send it as early as two days before the event, then follow up with a phone call to confirm that each newsroom has received it. Send it again the day before and the morning of the event. Be sure to make follow-up calls to sell your story to the assignment editor. Remember, they are constantly bombarded with advisories, so don't let yours get lost in the shuffle.

■ *Have your materials prepared* and ready to be distributed to the attendees. You should include a press release (see the following sample), a CC! brochure and fact sheet, information on your organization (a brochure, number of members, key contact person, etc.) and its participation in year-round character-development activities.

■ *Have the site of the conference well prepared.* Post decorative signs or other visuals in advance. Also, post directional signs to guide journalists to the site.

■ *After the press conference,* send materials to those who were unable to attend.

DuPage COUNTY
■ More local news on Pages 5, 6, 7, 8 and 9 and in Neighbor

DuPage gets 'Character' boost

Daily Herald
Sunday, February 6, 2000

Survey suggests S.D. teens improving ethical choices

VISALIA TIMES-DELTA

OPINION

FIRST AMENDMENT
A Daily Quotation
"The truth that makes men free is for the most part the truth which men prefer not to hear."
— Herbert Sebastian Agar, writer, 1942

10A

Editor: Paul Hurley, 735-3277

Kids with character are an inspiration

The Day of the Press Conference

■ *Review* your plan. Call those on the media list around 8:00 a.m. to confirm attendance. Again, ask to speak with the assignment editors. These are the people who will ultimately decide whether or not your story is covered.

■ *Meet members of the press* as they arrive. Take down their names and phone numbers and give each of them a press kit, including general information and a press release. Give them a rundown of what will be happening and where the speeches, statements and interviews will take place. Lead them to the key spokespersons who will be participating in the news conference. (Don't hover over them, but be ready to provide assistance if any is needed.)

■ *Start* the news conference no later than five minutes after the announced time. Have the speakers speak, then allow some time for questions and answers. Finally, ensure that the speakers are accessible to the press on a one-on-one basis.

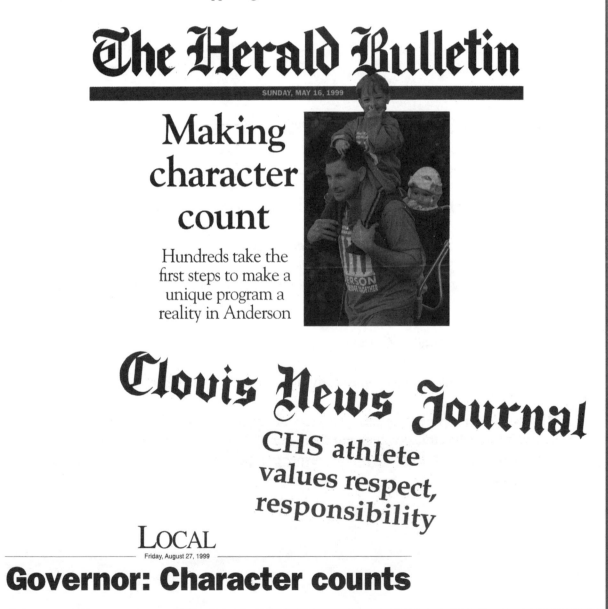

The Herald Bulletin

SUNDAY, MAY 16, 1999

Making character count

Hundreds take the first steps to make a unique program a reality in Anderson

Clovis News Journal

CHS athlete values respect, responsibility

LOCAL

Friday, August 27, 1999

Governor: Character counts

(Sample Media Advisory)

*** MEDIA ADVISORY ***

CONTACT: [your name]
[phone number, including area code]
[e-mail address]

DATE:

SPOKANE CELEBRATES GOOD CHARACTER
Press Conference
Monday, October 1_, 19__ — 10:00 a.m.

What: Spokane kicks off campaign on behalf of young people

Who: Actress Ashley Dunn, Mayor Doe, community activists, etc.

Where: Lewis and Clark High School, 500 West Fourth Street (parking available next to the field house)

When: 10 a.m., Monday, October 1_

Why: To recognize young people receiving Spokane's Youth Character Awards

Thousands of people across the country are joining in the nationwide effort to strengthen and reinforce the ethical values and character of the next generation, based on the Six Pillars of Character: <u>trustworthiness</u>, <u>respect</u>, <u>responsibility</u>, <u>fairness</u>, <u>caring</u> and good <u>citizenship</u>.

(Sample Press Release)

FOR IMMEDIATE RELEASE

CONTACT: [your name and name of organization]
[phone number, including area code]
[e-mail address]

DATE:

SPOKANE CELEBRATES GOOD CHARACTER!
Community Leaders on a Character-Building Crusade!

Spokane, Wash. — Spokane's own Ashley Dunn, the famous child actress, joined Mayor John Doe and hundreds of Spokanites today to kick off a campaign to improve the character of Spokane's young people.

"As a member of the next generation, I know how important it is that we learn about good character," Miss Dunn said. "I am proud that the character I play on television is a role model, and I am honored to be here today."

Nearly 30 different events have been underway over the past three months, including a community service project where the local Rotary Club has teamed up with the Boys and Girls Clubs and other youth organizations for a major cleanup in Riverside Park on Sunday.

"Citizenship is one of the Six Pillars of Character," Mayor Doe said. "Throughout National **CHARACTER COUNTS!** Week, we will see examples of all these Pillars in action. Spokane is a place of good character. As adults, we owe it to the next generation to teach these Pillars and make *character count* in our community."

Events taking place in Spokane are part of a nationwide movement sponsored by the **CHARACTER COUNTS!** Coalition, a nonpartisan and nonsectarian alliance comprised of hundreds of schools, youth-service organizations and communities across the country. Members of the Coalition, which together can reach millions of young people and their families, are working to put character development at the head of the American agenda.

As Mayor Doe noted, "No one will doubt Spokane's commitment to good character this week and every week."

Working With the News Media: Pitching a Story

A news conference may not be the best approach to get a story publicized. It may be just as effective to pitch your story to selected journalists or write an article (i.e., "op-ed" piece) about your event and its broader implications.

Pitching a story to a reporter, editor or producer is not difficult if you plan it wisely and follow some important guidelines. The key to opening the door is known as a *pitch letter*. Use these tips to write a good pitch letter:

1. Make it short — no more than one or two pages. Journalists want to get the gist of the idea with a quick scan of your letter.

2. Provide compelling reasons why your story warrants an article.

3. Make it interesting and unique. Grab the reader's attention in the first paragraph and find a creative angle to make your story stand out.

4. Cover all the bases. Journalists appreciate it when you lay out the story for them. Include background material (e.g., fliers, brochures, etc.) and a press release. Draw on the following sample pitch letter for ideas.

5. For television, emphasize the visual appeal of your event(s). This is the medium of pictures, not words.

(Sample Pitch Letter)

Dear [reporter's name]:

Spokane knows that CHARACTER COUNTS!. Hundreds of young people will celebrate this year's "National CHARACTER COUNTS! Week," set for the third week in October, with ceremonies, activities and programs promoting good character. Events will range from community-service projects to in-school programs, a "Character Fair," poster and essay contests and an overall commitment to bringing this important week to life in Spokane.

Last year's celebration brought together diverse members of our community: civic organizations joined with youth groups, parents joined with teachers, and the business community sponsored contests, awards and posters advocating the "Six Pillars of Character": trustworthiness, respect, responsibility, fairness, caring and citizenship.

Through our participation in National CHARACTER COUNTS! Week, we will join some 400 other members of the national CHARACTER COUNTS! Coalition who together can reach millions of young people and their parents.

Any and all of the Six Pillars of Character provide interesting hooks for stories focusing on the values of Spokane's youth. I will be calling you next week to discuss this further with you. Please feel free to call me if you have any questions.

Sincerely,

[your name]

Working With the News Media: Writing and Placing an "Op-Ed" Article

Another way to spread the word is to write an opinion piece in your local newspaper. Almost every newspaper accepts these essays for its "op-ed" page. As with everything else in the media, access to this page is competitive, so make your article compelling. Follow these seven suggestions for getting your piece in print:

1. Find out which newspapers in your area accept unsolicited op-ed articles.

2. Check with the newspaper beforehand to see if it has guidelines or suggestions regarding the length of the article. Make sure you follow these.

3. Propose to a prominent figure in the community that she/he co-author the article. The author's position can lend credibility to the article.

4. Make sure the author's name is included between the headline and the body of the article.

5. At the end of the article, there should be a one-sentence identification of the author.

6. Prepare a short cover letter to the contact person at the newspaper, explaining the nature of the article that you are submitting.

7. Follow-up with calls to the editor of the page.

Working With the News Media: Radio and TV Talk Shows

The radio and television talk-show circuit is another means of generating awareness of CHARACTER COUNTS!. Generally, radio is more accessible. Unfortunately, television talk shows — especially syndicated ones — can lean toward circus-act sensations and neglect the substantive issues. Local public affairs programs are good prospects. Small, noncommercial "public access" channels should definitely be contacted.

As with all your media relations, talk shows require a little research before you can get going. Check with local television stations to find out which shows are appropriate and how to contact the show's producer. Many libraries have media guides which may be useful.

Check with radio stations as well. Most talk radio stations have a number of programs from which to choose. Prepare a "pitch letter" to the contact person — usually the producer of the show — discussing the issue you would like to address. You should also include in the letter the name of the spokespersons who will speak on your behalf. In your letter, make sure to stress the timeliness of your story and invite them to call you. But don't wait by the phone — plan on having to make several follow-up calls.

If you get a placement, the spokesperson should be prepared with key points regarding the importance of character education, what your organization is doing in this area (for National CHARACTER COUNTS! Week, etc.), and what is happening at the national level. Include relevant statistics, such as those documented in the Josephson Institute's "Report Card on the Ethics of American Youth" survey reports. Make sure your spokesperson is prepared with answers to the kinds of questions that you think are likely.

Working With the News Media: Placing a Public Service Announcement (PSA)

A public service announcement (PSA) is essentially a commercial for a worthy cause that broadcasters air free of charge. PSAs are exclusively used for nonprofit organizations. Sample PSAs (30 and 60 seconds, respectively) are included below for placement on television and radio stations in your area. In general, radio PSAs are more accessible and less expensive because the announcer can read your PSA over the air. With television, you have to produce something similar to a commercial, which requires a budget and a production facility. You can reach a wide audience with a good radio PSA that is aired several times.

When placing a PSA, you will need to submit your request to the appropriate person — usually with a lead time of three or four weeks.

Call the station to find out the procedures for submitting PSAs; often recorded instructions explain this. When submitting a PSA, you generally will need to provide:

- proof of your organization's nonprofit status
- (for radio) a script of the PSA you want the announcer to read
- (for TV) a ¾-inch video tape of your PSA
- a letter about the importance of your cause

With hundreds of organizations vying for free air time, it is best if you cultivate and maintain strong relationships with the stations. If your PSA runs, don't forget to send a thank-you note to the station manager.

(Sample PSA — 30 seconds)

Honesty. Compassion. Respect. Responsibility . . . We all want our kids to develop these values, but it doesn't happen by accident. Parents, teachers, coaches and other role models have to provide a good example and do all they can to see that young people follow it.

That is why [your organization] is observing [exact dates of the third week in October] as "National CHARACTER COUNTS! Week" in [your city]. [Your organization] is planning various activities, including [specific event] to celebrate this important week. Call [your contact phone number] to find out how you can show that CHARACTER COUNTS! in [name of city] all year long.

(Sample PSA — 60 seconds)

Good character still counts in [your city], and we want to show it. During National CHARACTER COUNTS! Week, from [exact dates of the third week in October], events across [name of city] will take place that will help us shape the future: our young people. [Briefly describe your event.]

Events celebrating CHARACTER COUNTS! Week are centered on this national Coalition's "Six Pillars of Character": trustworthiness, respect, responsibility, fairness, caring and good citizenship. The values we all agree on. The values we all must teach.

Join with family, friends and neighbors in making National CHARACTER COUNTS! Week a year-round event. For information on programs, call [your contact number].

Kids are 27% of our population, but 100% of our future. Which way they go depends on us.

Good Ideas for Raising Awareness:
Speaking Engagements

Character development starts at home, but members of the community should understand that "it takes a whole village to raise a child." By drawing together parents, teachers, youth leaders and others of diverse backgrounds and professions, public speaking events can reinforce the message that everyone has a part to play in teaching young people to be responsible and live with integrity. Speakers provide a valuable service by affirming the importance of setting a good example and of working together with young people to strengthen the moral fiber of our society. And, of course, they introduce the concept of systematic character development to those who are unfamiliar with CHARACTER COUNTS!.

There are many community groups that host speaking events — and they want to hear from people like you about what is happening in the community. Assemble a group of speakers — including student leaders and other young adults.

Possible Speaking Venues

chambers of commerce
business & civic clubs (Rotary, Kiwanis, Lions, etc.)
PTA meetings
school events
religious functions
community events (festivals, town meetings)
groups that support youth causes

All towns have speaking opportunities. Remember, you want to reach the entire community, and successful and effective presentations are not limited to conventional venues. For starters, contact your local chamber of commerce and United Way for a list of local community organizations.

Many organizations designate someone to arrange for outside speakers. Begin by contacting local organizations. Introduce yourself and explain CHARACTER COUNTS!. You may be asked to write a letter describing your topic in greater detail.

When a speaking engagement is set, arrive early to meet the program chairperson and/or the group's president. Make arrangements to have props you need for your talk (i.e., an easel, overhead projector, slide projector, blackboard, etc.). Provide the organization with a biographical sketch so they may properly introduce you.

Ten Tips for Effective Speaking

1. Your audience is there to hear your message. Relax and deliver that message, instead of focusing on yourself.

2. Make sure that your speech is right for your audience. What was great for a youth group may not work at a Rotary function. Encourage adults to take responsibility and set good examples, and encourage young people to take responsibility for their future.

3. Take your time. Don't read your speech word-for-word and don't rush through it. Be conversational, as if you were talking with a group of friends.

4. Don't stand up there like a stick, clenching the podium at both sides. Be natural and animated. Use hand gestures, drink water, move around a little. But don't rock back and forth — that conveys nervousness.

5. Keep it simple. The appropriate length depends on the setting, but remember sometimes "less is more."

6. Make eye contact with the audience. Connect with them. Get them to nod their heads to acknowledge what you're saying. Make them pay attention to you.

7. Practice your speech ahead of time. Take time to pause in the right places to catch your breath. You may want to mark your speech where you want to pause. Let your commitment show.

8. Don't get into a debate if people interrupt with disagreements. Talk with them after your speech.

9. Field questions from the audience when you're finished.

10. Have fun with it! Share a relevant personal anecdote or two.

A Good Idea of What to Say

A sample speaking engagement request letter and a sample speech follow. This speech is probably too long for most occasions. But this allows you to omit or change parts of it to suit your audience. This speech, like most speeches, follows a simple format: Tell your audience what you are going to say; say it; then tell them what you've just said.

(Sample Speaking Engagement Request Letter)

Dear [name of organization chairperson]:

Across the country, the third week in October is recognized as "National CHARACTER COUNTS! Week" and [name of organization] will sponsor numerous events in [name of city] to celebrate the week. We would welcome the opportunity to speak before [name of organization] at one of your regular meetings to share with you our goals, and why we believe it is so important to fortify the moral character of future generations, not just during an annual observance, but all year long.

[Name of organization] is one of the members of the nonpartisan and nonsectarian CHARACTER COUNTS! Coalition. Nationally, hundreds of organizations that comprise this Coalition are working to reinforce the good character of young people today and thereby safeguard tomorrow for all of us. The movement's focus is on six core ethical values known as the "Six Pillars of Character": <u>trustworthiness</u>, <u>respect</u>, <u>responsibility</u>, <u>fairness</u>, <u>caring</u> and good <u>citizenship</u>. By rigorously teaching these consensus values, the Coalition works to combat violence, dishonesty and irresponsibility.

Across [name of city], we are building support for our efforts. Your organization's history of [insert something that personalizes the letter] demonstrates that you share our goals.

I will be calling you in a few days to see when we might be able to arrange a meeting. Thank you for your consideration.

Sincerely,

[your name and title]

(Sample Speech)

Thank you for that introduction, [name of person]. I'm particularly glad to be here today before the [name of organization].

Let me start by sharing with you some information about the ethics of young people in the United States. (Mention a local issue or news story which you can relate to the figures below.) According to a national survey (the "1999 Report Card on the Ethics of American Youth") released in 1999 by the nonpartisan Josephson Institute of Ethics:

- Forty-seven percent of middle and high school students said they had stolen something from a store within the past year.

- Seven of ten high school students admitted to cheating on an exam in the past year.

- More than one in three high schoolers said they would lie to get a good job.

What is going on here?

What do these statistics tell us? They tell us we've got some work to do. They tell us we haven't done the best job of teaching the fundamentals of good character to our children. We have an increasingly self-indulgent generation willing to do whatever it takes to win.

There are no simple answers to the problem. Except for one. Each of us must accept some responsibility and commit to do something. As adults, we cannot condemn this generation if we, too, are unwilling to model and commit to teaching ethical behavior.

For too long, we have been afraid to teach fundamental values. For too long, we have been avoiding explicit discussions of these values with our young people, discussing morality in such wishy-washy terms that young people are left adrift.

How do we improve the character of our young people? We must do it in a way that will make it easy for them to understand the message and to embrace it. We inevitably lead by example, whether we like it or not — but the direction we take our followers is another thing.

Now don't get me wrong — the solution is *not* to try to reclaim some mythical golden age where things were supposedly simpler and more honest.

Responsible adults acknowledge that we *can't* be old-fashioned. We must *refashion* — help refashion a generation that has great potential to make a difference — to make character count — but is lacking in role models.

We've got to help the younger generation fashion America's character. Provide them with role models. Help them understand and embrace the "Six Pillars of Character": <u>trustworthiness</u>, <u>respect</u>, <u>responsibility</u>, <u>fairness</u>, <u>caring</u>, <u>citizenship</u>.

(Sample Speech, cont.)

This concerted effort *must* be made. Fortunately, it is.

[Name of your organization] is teaming up with hundreds of other schools, communities and organizations comprising the **CHARACTER COUNTS!** Coalition to participate in activities related to character development. "National **CHARACTER COUNTS!** Week" has been declared the third week in October by about 40 states and over 500 cities, counties, school districts and chambers of commerce.

This week is a way to build awareness, and each year, thousands of schools, businesses and politicians are asked to sponsor or participate in programs — not so much to celebrate our best selves for a week, but to call the nation to action. This is action which must continue throughout the year.

These Coalition members range from the YMCA, 4-H and Little League to the National Education Association and La Raza. Together these groups can reach millions of young people and their families. Locally, [name of your organization] is representing the Coalition. We are pleased to have come upon the Six Pillars, a set of consensus ethical values that are the foundation of a free, democratic society. But we can't expect them to assume their rightful place without hard work; without being conscious of setting good examples; without consistent, systematic education; without teaching real compassion and purpose.

Let's get past the "Whose values?" debate and get to work making sure our young people know what's right and commit to doing it. I have yet to meet someone who objects to trustworthiness, respect, responsibility, fairness, caring and citizenship.

These words are not intended to remain on paper — or even on our lips. They must be words of action. We must teach them in our schools. We must develop and support activities and contests in our youth organizations. Community organizations should do their part by setting an example for young people to emulate. Business people should stress character development in the business sector. Governmental officials must do all they can to commend the development of good character.

It is a monumental task, but it has to start with each of us. U.S. clergyman and writer Edward Hale said, "It is true I am only one, but I *am* one. And the fact that I cannot do everything will not prevent me from doing what I can do."

I am ready to work with our young to build a better future. Won't you join me?

[uproarious applause]

Good Ideas on the Web

> **w w w . c h a r a c t e r c o u n t s . o r g**
> **w w w . j o s e p h s o n i n s t i t u t e . o r g**

The CHARACTER COUNTS! and Josephson Institute websites are loaded with information and resources. Currently, the site includes:

- **UPDATES AND INFORMATION** on the CHARACTER COUNTS! Coalition's approach, the structure of the organization, and on the Coalition's rapidly growing and evolving projects and programs: American Youth Character Awards, Character Development Seminars, CHARACTER COUNTS! Sports, CHARACTER COUNTS! Week, and more.

- **TIPS, GUIDES & DEFINITIONS** for parents, teachers and other character-builders.

- **DISCUSSION FORUM:** An electronic bulletin board that is continually refreshed with readers' postings on character, family, education, work life and current events.

- **ETHICSWATCH:** An ever-changing assortment of links to articles, surveys and other news reports, including sections on youth development/education and workplace issues.

- **QUOTEUNQUOTE:** A vast catalog of quotations organized by subject.

- **GOOD DEEDS:** A page with links and other contact information to help individuals help others. (Previous pages have focused on such issues as providing relief to victims of Central America's Hurricane Mitch and on helping refugees of the war in Kosovo.)

- **MAKING ETHICAL DECISIONS:** A multi-chapter guide (based on the Josephson Institute's popular booklet of the same name) that discusses differences between "ethics," "values" and "morals"; reviews decision-making models; and lists common rationalizations.

- **RADIO COMMENTARY:** Transcripts of Josephson Institute President Michael Josephson's daily radio spots on KNX 1070-AM in Southern California, with links to the discussion "Forum" for readers to share their reactions.

- **"THE POWER OF CHARACTER" ESSAYS:** A different essay each month from 41 of the country's most interesting and accomplished people — from Dan Rather and Marianne Williamson to Daniel Goleman and Stephen Covey. All the essays are from a book called *The Power of Character* by Jossey-Bass, available for purchase online, at booksellers or from the Josephson Institute.

- **WHAT PEOPLE ARE DOING:** Articles on character-building efforts that are changing lives in communities across the country — and around the world.

- **PHOTO ALBUM:** A pictorial narrative showing what's being done, state by state, to celebrate and advance character education.

- **CC! STORE** with various products and teaching resources available for sale.

- **ROSTER OF CC! COALITION MEMBERS** with links to their websites.

- **GOOD IDEAS** with lesson plans drawn from this book and from the first volume.

- **EVENTS CALENDARS:** One listing Coalition activities (e.g., training opportunities for teachers and youth-service workers), and another listing character-education conferences and events sponsored by other organizations.

- **YOUTH AND VIOLENCE:** Statistics, a guide on talking to kids about guns, plus information (with links) on innovative programs for "at-risk" young people.

- **REPORT CARD ON AMERICAN YOUTH:** What do young people think about ethics and values — and does their behavior correspond? Their answers are here, from the Josephson Institute's nationwide survey of over 20,000 middle- and high-school students.

Suggestions on the site are always appreciated. Send e-mail to webmaster@jiethics.org.

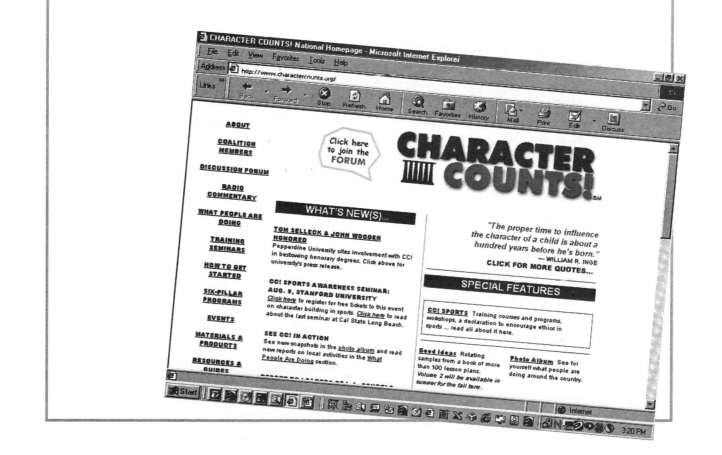

Good Ideas on the Web:
Help Young People Build a Website on Ethics and Character

The World Wide Web is a great place to find lesson plans and activity ideas. It is also a useful medium for young people to engage in character-building activities. If you have computers with Web connections, you might consider having students develop websites about CHARACTER COUNTS! or about other topics related to ethics and character.

The following companies are among the most popular providers of free web space:

- Xoom.com (**www.xoom.com/webspace**)
- Yahoo's GeoCities (**geocities.yahoo.com**)
- Freeservers.com (**www.freeservers.com**)

For more options, a searchable directory of hundreds of free Web hosts is available at **www.freewebspace.net**. (Because advertising revenue is what covers these companies' expenses, many of them require an advertising banner to be placed on some or all pages.)

The Lycos Free Homepage Builder (**pagebuilder.lycos.com**) offers a choice of fast and easy form-based templates that students can use to get started. Also, recent versions of Netscape's browser (4.0 and later) come packaged with a Web authoring tool called Composer that students can use to craft webpages. The browser can be downloaded for free at **home.netscape.com**. Webpage-building tools also are available at M&M Software's Shareware & Public Domain Library (**www.mm-soft.com**), which describes itself as "the best educational public domain and shareware library in the known universe." To see samples of student online publications go to **www.yahoo.com/News/Newspapers/K_12/**.

The national office of CHARACTER COUNTS! *would love to hear about anything you're doing on the Web that relates to character education. Please send e-mail to cc@jiethics.org. And don't forget to link to **www.josephsoninstitute.org** and **www.charactercounts.org**!*

Good Ideas on the Web:
Websites Related to CHARACTER COUNTS!

The following websites, all linked from the national office's site, are devoted to local CHARACTER COUNTS! *movements:*

- The Albuquerque CC! website (**www. abqcharactercounts.org**) includes an account of how this city adopted and expanded this values-education framework, along with an events calendar, the group's vision, mission and goals, and general information about CC! in New Mexico.

- The Humphreys County CC! website (**www.geocities.com/Athens/Thebes/9804**) describes local CC! activities, maintains a calendar, lists a "quote of the month," and showcases student essays on ethical values.

- CC! of Knoxville / Knox County (Tennessee) maintains a website (**www.korrnet.org/ ccknox**) with news and information on local events and training seminars for teachers, administrators, coaches and parents.

- The website of CC! in Martin County (Florida) (**www.charactercounts.net**) lists the group's mission statement and expectations of community members; provides general information about the CC! framework; and features an online form on which volunteers can choose among these options for lending a hand: "annual rally; children's opera; surveys; presentations; art and music projects; become a speaker, committee member or business sponsor; sponsor a classroom, set up booths, be a mascot."

- The Maryland 4-H "Character Counts in 4-H" website (**www.agnr.umd.edu/CES/4h/ update/february/ccounts.htm**) explains why 4-H is a member of the CC! Coalition and offers sample activities that teach core ethical values.

- The CC! in Michigan website (**www.msue.msu.edu/msue/cyf/youth/charcoun.html**) offers information about the group's character-education framework, and about local training and events for adults and teens, plus "Timely Tips for Families."

- The Minnesota Center for Corporate Responsibility, a CC! Coalition member, maintains a website (**http://tigger.stthomas.edu/mccr/CC_MN.htm**) "to promote CHARACTER COUNTS! throughout the state of Minnesota." The site presents an overview of the state's character-education movement, including pages tracking "CHARACTER COUNTS! in the News" and city and state proclamations declaring CC! Week.

- The CHARACTER COUNTS! in Nebraska website (**www.ianr.unl.edu/ianr/4h/character/ html/index.html**), hosted by the University of Nebraska in Lincoln and maintained by Nebraska 4-H, provides information about training opportunities, the group's plan to spread CC! throughout the state, and contacts in various parts of Nebraska for those who would like to become active in their community.

- The CC! in Northern Virginia website (**www.charactercountsnva.org**) provides information on local events and lists various character-education materials.

- The CC! in Roane County (Tennessee) website (**www.dagger.com/charactercounts**) discusses the Six Pillars of Character and provides a form for locals to fill out and submit online if they are interested in getting involved. This group also maintains an e-mail list to keep people apprised of local CC! activities; visitors to the site can subscribe online.

- SouthSound.Org, a Puget Sound youth organization that is a member of the CC! Coalition, has created a webpage (**www.southsound.org/character_counts.htm**) describing the Coalition and soliciting community members' involvement.

- The Tigerton (Wisconsin) CC! program, a member of the CC! Coalition, maintains a website (**www.uwex.edu/ces/cty/shawano/cctiger.html**) on its activities and history.

- Students at Horizon Community Middle School (Aurora, Colorado) maintain a webpage (**www.hcms.ccsd.k12.co.us/html/Activities/CharCounts.html**) with information about CC! and related student activities.

- National **CHARACTER COUNTS!** Week resolutions passed by the U.S. Congress as well as statements made about **CHARACTER COUNTS!** in the House of Representatives and Senate are available online at the Government Printing Office's searchable database (**www.gpo.ucop.edu/search/default.html**). Click on "Congressional Record" and type in "Character Counts" in the box below.

- An example of a Board of Education resolution supporting CC! Week is posted at **www.brightok.net/chickasaw/sch/sulphur/character.html** (from Sulphur Public Schools, Sulphur, OK).

- MidLink is an online magazine written by and for young people. One issue (**http://longwood.cs.ucf.edu/~MidLink/cc.home.html**) focusing on **CHARACTER COUNTS!** invites kids to post messages about character and people who show it.

- A graduate of the Josephson Institute of Ethics "Ethics Corps" training has set up a useful page on his site (**www.rt66.com/~epreble/usafa/ccount.htm**) about **CHARACTER COUNTS!** activities in Roswell, New Mexico.

- A student in Arp, Texas, has created an animated Shockwave file of the Six Pillars of Character at **www.arp.sprnet.org/Curric/cc!/media.htm**.

Good Ideas on the Web:
Websites of National Members of the CHARACTER COUNTS! Coalition

National Educational Organizations

- American Association of Community Colleges (**www.aacc.nche.edu**)
- American Association of School Administrators (**www.aasa.org**)
- American Federation of Teachers (**www.aft.org**)
- LeaderShape (**www.leadershape.org**)
- National Association of Secondary School Principals (**www.nassp.org**)
- National Education Association (**www.nea.org**)

National Youth Development and Service Organizations

- American Youth Soccer Organization (**www.soccer.org**)
- Babe Ruth League (**www.baberuthleague.org**)
- Big Brothers Big Sisters of America (**www.bbbsa.org**)
- Bobby Sox Softball (**www.bobbysoxsoftball.org**)
- Boys & Girls Clubs of America (**www.bgca.org**)
- Camp Fire Boys and Girls (**www.camp-fire.org**)
- Family, Career and Community Leaders of America (**www.fhahero.org**)
- Father Flanagan's Boys' Home (**www.boystown.org**)
- 4-H (**www.fourhcouncil.edu**)
- LeaderShape (**www.leadershape.org**)
- Little League Baseball (**www.littleleague.org**)
- National Abstinence Clearinghouse (**www.abstinence.net**)
- National Association of Police Athletic Leagues (**www.nationalpal.org**)
- Primary Focus (**www.primaryfocus.org**)
- United States Youth Soccer Association (**www.usysa.org**)
- USA Police Athletic League (**www.usapal.org**)
- YMCA of the USA (**www.ymca.net**)
- Youth Volunteer Corps of America (**www.yvca.org**)

National Community Service and Civic Organizations

- American Camping Association (**www.acacamps.org**)
- American Red Cross (**www.redcross.org**)
- International Association of Chiefs of Police (**www.theiacp.org**)
- National Council of La Raza (**www.nclr.org**)
- Points of Light Foundation (**www.pointsoflight.org**)
- United Way of America (**www.unitedway.org**)

Good Ideas on the Web:
Other Character-Education Groups and Websites

- The American Promise (**www.americanpromise.com**)
- America's Promise (**www.americaspromise.org**)
- Association for Moral Education (**www.wittenberg.edu/ame/index.html**)
- California University Character Education Institute (**www.cup.edu/character_ed/default.htm**)
- Character Education Center (**www.ethicsusa.com**)
- Campus Outreach Opportunity League (COOL) (**www.cool2serve.org**)
- Center for Civic Networking (**www.civic.net**)
- Center for Learning (**www.centerforlearning.org**)
- Center for Voting and Democracy (**www.igc.apc.org/cvd**)
- Center for Youth Citizenship (**www.clre.org**)
- Center for Youth as Resources (**www.yar.org/yar.htm**)
- Character Development Group (**www.charactereducation.com**)
- Character Education Partnership (**www.character.org**)
- Character Education Resources (**www.charactereducationinfo.org**)
- Character Matters (**www.geocities.com/~professorgough**)
- CHARACTER*plus* (**http://info.csd.org/staffdev/chared/characterplus.html**)
- Children Now (**www.childrennow.org**)
- Children's Defense Fund (**www.childrensdefense.org**)
- The Citizenship Education Fund (**www.rainbowpush.org/cef**)
- Close Up Foundation (**www.closeup.org**)
- Connect for Kids (**www.connectforkids.org**)
- The Content of Our Character: Voices of Generation X (**www.contentofourcharacter.org**)
- Do Something (**www.dosomething.org**)
- Eckerd Youth Alternatives (**www.eckerd.org**)
- Ethics Resource Center (**www.ethics.org**)
- Foundation for In (**www.ethics.org**)
- The Future of Children (**www.futureofchildren.org**)
- Giraffe Project (**www.giraffe.org**)

- Institute for Global Ethics (**www.globalethics.org**)
- Institute for the Study of Civic Values (**http://www.libertynet.org/edcivic/iscvhome.html**)
- Institute for Youth Development (**www.youthdevelopment.org**)
- International Center for Character Education (**www.teachvalues.org/icce**)
- International Education Foundation (**www.iefcharactered.org**)
- Kenan Ethics Program, Duke University (**http://kenan.ethics.duke.edu**)
- Learning for Life (**www.learning-for-life.org**)
- Live Wire Media (**www.livewiremedia.com/home.html**)
- National Campaign to Prevent Teen Pregnancy (**www.teenpregnancy.org**)
- National Mentoring Partnership (**www.mentoring.org**)
- National Network for Youth (**www.NN4Youth.org**)
- National Youth Network (**www.usdoj.gov/kidspage/getinvolved**)
- New Zealand Foundation for Values Education (**www.es.co.nz/~cstone/home.html**)
- Olivet College Character Education Resource Center (**www.olivetnet.edu/ccrc**)
- Paul Tracey's "Your Character Counts" Assemblies (**http://members.aol.com/scambig/tracey.htm**)
- Pro Kids Show (**www.schoolshow.com**)
- Project Wisdom (**www.projectwisdom.com**)
- Prudential Spirit of Community Initiative (**www.prudential.com/community/spirit**)
- Quest International (**www.quest.edu**)
- Readers NDex (random acts of kindness info) (**www.readersndex.com/randomacts**)
- The Responsive Classroom (**www.responsiveclassroom.org**)
- Safe Schools Coalition, Inc. (**www.ed.mtu.edu/safe**)
- School for Ethical Education (**www.ethicsed.org**)
- Search Institute (**www.search-institute.org**)
- Stand for Children (**www.stand.org**)
- The Virtues Project (**www.virtuesproject.com**)
- Washington Ethical Society (**ethicalsociety.org**)
- WiseSkills (**www.wiseskills.com**)
- YouthLink (**www.youthlink.org**)

Character-Building Sites for Kids

> Find links to these and other websites at
> www.charactercounts.org/links.htm

- Aesop's Fables (**www.pacificnet.net/~johnr/aesop/**) is a collection of over 600 fables, some of which are available as RealAudio files.

- Making Hearts Sing (**www.wildgear.com/stories**) is a collection of fables that teach universal moral lessons. The stories are from China, Japan, Korea, Russia and France.

- "Whootie Owl's Fairytales & Values Class Plan" is an online resource for teachers, parents and other caregivers available at "Absolutely Whootie: Stories to Grow By" (**www.storiestogrowby.com**).

- Adventures from the Book of Virtues (**www.pbs.org/adventures**), from the PBS series based on William Bennett's popular book, includes numerous stories, a "virtual" essay contest and a "treasure box" of puzzles and games.

- The Kidz Care! Story Center (**http://members.aol.com/kidz4peace/stories/index.htm**) uses online picture books to teach young children compassion, appreciation of cultural diversity and good citizenship. Also includes posters to print out and color.

- "KIND (Kids in Nature's Defense) News" (**www.kindnews.org**) is produced by the National Association for Humane and Environmental Education "to help elementary-school students develop values of kindness toward people, animals, and the Earth." It features contributions from young readers, celebrity profiles, articles (with questions to test reading comprehension), puzzles and other activities.

- Young people can find practical ways to make their communities better at **www.mightymedia.com**. Click on the "Youth in Action Network" icon and you will be prompted to enter a username and password ("guest" will work for both). The site offers lessons about citizenship and altruism and provides channels for kids to talk with each other about these issues on-line. Then they are encouraged to go out and make a difference using the Youth in Action "Power Tools."

- Young people can read about the importance of serving others and find practical information and opportunities to do so at Servenet (**www.servenet.org**). The Presidents' Summit for America's Future (**www.americaspromise.org**) also helps match volunteers to community needs.

- The mission of Kids Helping Kids (**www.gopbi.com/community/groups/KidsHelpKids**) is "to educate, engage, and encourage our nation's youth about the importance of charitable giving and provide opportunities for charitable services that directly benefit children who are at risk or have life threatening illnesses." Children ages 6 to 18 audition to become part of performances that benefit other children in need.

- Craig Kielburger, a 13-year-old Canadian, is working hard to combat child labor. His work was inspired by Iqbal Masih, a 12-year-old Pakistani who spoke out against this practice in his own country until he was murdered for his efforts. Young people (and adults) can visit Free the Children at **www.freethechildren.org** to find out how they can contribute to this cause.

- It's never too early to learn about participating in a democracy. The White House for Kids (**www.whitehouse.gov/WH/kids/html/home.html**) offers a guided tour, historical information and an opportunity to send mail to the president.

- *Time* magazine's "Heroes for the Planet" section (**www.time.com/time/reports/environment/heroes**) examines environmental crises and profiles "heroes" who are working for solutions.

Users can submit forms online to nominate ecological crusaders for inclusion in this series. The website also features an "eco challenge" that tests users' abilities to save Earth from such environmental time bombs as air pollution, global warming and rain forest destruction.

- The Environmental Protection Agency's "Recycle City" (**www.epa.gov/recyclecity**) uses games, activities and fun facts to teach kids about recycling.

- Rainforest Action Network's "Kid's Action" page (**www.ran.org/ran/kids_action/ index.html**) contains tips on what kids can do to help preserve natural resources, stories, contests and an art gallery of work done by kids in previous contests.

- Kindness Coupons (**www.fleetkids.com/fleet/ kc/kc.b.html**) includes printable coupons for home (e.g., "Do Someone Else's Chores," "Serve Someone Breakfast in Bed") and school (e.g., "Clean up the Blackboards" and "Pick up School Yard Litter"). An online form enables the user to personalize coupons with his or her name printed on them.

- The KidsCom page (**www.kidscom.com**) helps young people learn to appreciate cultural diversity. With a posting "wall" for kids 11 and younger and another for 12- to 15-year-olds, their site allows young people to chat live with other kids from all over the globe. Both "walls" have a built-in "filter" to keep them clean.

- The Giraffe Project's (**www.giraffe.org**) "Giraffe Program" curriculum helps teachers and youth leaders build courage, caring and responsibility in kids from 6 to 18, then guides the kids in designing and implementing their own service projects. The organization seeks to inspire young people by telling the stories of unsung heroes ("giraffes") who are sticking their necks out for the common good. The site profiles a new "giraffe" each month.

- America's Heroes and You (**www.webcom. com/~webspin/heroes**) examines specific virtues and historical figures who have exhibited them. Designed for elementary and junior high school students, sample lessons with discussion questions and related activity ideas are included. Also check out the My Hero home page at **www.myhero.com** where kids are encouraged to read and write (in the site's guest book) about what it means to be a hero.

Useful Sites for Adults Who Work With Kids

Find links to these websites at www.charactercounts.org/links.htm

(Many of the sites maintained by members of the **CHARACTER COUNTS!** Coalition include helpful information for educators and other adults who work with young people. See the list at the end of this section.)

- Produced by the U.S. Department of Education, Creating Safe and Drug-Free Schools (**www.ed.gov/offices/OESE/ACTGUID/ index.html**) includes tips on lowering dropout rates, keeping weapons off campus and establishing mentoring programs. Packages of "action steps" for schools, parents, local businesses and students help you generate community support.

- Match underprivileged youngsters with mentors — or arrange for mature and responsible teens to become mentors — with Big Brothers Big Sisters of America (**www.bbbsa.org**), a member of the **CHARACTER COUNTS!** Coalition. More mentor-mentee matchmakers:

  □ America's Promise: Alliance for Youth (**www.americaspromise.org**)

  □ Impact Online (**www.impactonline.org**)

  □ One to One/National Mentoring Partnership (**www.mentoring.org**)

  □ Project America (**www.project.org**)

- Connect for Kids: Guidance for Grown-ups (**www.connectforkids.org**) is a vast resource of useful articles, "ideas for action" and volunteer opportunities — all geared to helping adults improve communities, schools, families and other institutions that protect and enrich young people's lives.

- Talking With Kids About Tough Issues (**www.talkingwithkids.org**) is a national initiative by Children Now and the Kaiser Family Foundation to encourage parents to talk with their children earlier and more often about tough issues like sex, HIV/AIDS, violence, alcohol, and drug abuse.

- For a worldwide directory of programs, research, references and resources dedicated to the prevention of youth problems, visit the Prevention Yellow Pages (**www.tyc.state.tx.us/prevention/40001ref.html**).

- The New Century School House (**www.landmark-project.com**) provides a forum for teachers to exchange ideas about how schools can produce a generation of citizens "ready for the 21st Century."

- I-SAFE Character Education (**www.legalpadjr.com/school/lessons/character/**) suggests discussion prompts and vocabulary words to teach these lessons: Be Responsible, Be Prepared, Be a Tough Worker, Be a Good Listener, Be Friendly, Be Honest and Be Polite.

- A to Z Character Building Through the Arts! (**www.character4kids.net**) includes information about products and workshops, plus a sample activity "to instill in children positive behavior and attitude traits through the expression of their creativity."

- Stage Kids The Edu-Tainment Company (**www.stagekids.com**) develops and produces original musicals, many of which are described on the website as ideal CHARACTER COUNTS! Week presentations. "Musical theatre performance kits" — including scripts, lead sheets and cassettes with music — are available for purchase from the website. Also posted are excerpts from scripts, summaries of plays and RealAudio samples of songs used in the productions.

- Baby Think It Over (**www.btio.com**) seeks to prevent unplanned pregnancies by helping teens understand consequences and parental obligations before they are faced with the responsibility of caring for kids.

- Help your students learn how to settle classroom and school yard differences peacefully with Conflict Resolution the Peaceful Way (**www.stark.k12.oh.us/Docs/units/conflict**). This site, developed by some innovative teachers in Ohio, offers conflict resolution lesson plans and activities.

- St. Olaf College has set up a free service to help teachers and groups of students link with partners in other countries for classroom pen-pal and project exchanges (via e-mail). Currently over 2,200 university and K-12 teachers from 30 countries participate in The Intercultural E-Mail Classroom Connections (**www.stolaf.edu/network/iecc/**), a project which seeks to foster greater understanding and respect among people of different cultures.

- All One Heart (**www.alloneheart.com**), a website promoting tolerance of diversity, offers a pledge for parents and teachers to discuss and sign with students, plus tips on how to help young people guard against racism and prejudicial behavior.

- Sympatico (**http://kidshelp.sympatico.ca/help/divrsity/index.htm**), a Canadian youth-service organization, provides tips on talking to young people about the following issues: "What Is Prejudice?" "What Are Its Effects?" and "What Can Be Done?"

- "Thought, Word & Deed" (**www.statefarm.com/educate/twdpage.htm**), a State Farm Insurance-sponsored character-development program for young children, teaches lessons about decision making and personal responsibility. Includes lesson plans, handouts and a poster.

- Character Education Resources (**www.charactereducationinfo.org**) is a clearinghouse with links to recommended sites and a list of various character education books available for sale on their site.

- The Future of Children (**www.futureofchildren.org**) is a journal focusing on various issues related to children's well-being.

- CharacterMatters (**www.charactermatters.com**) lists various character-education materials in addition to a character quote of the week and archives of "Character Matters," a newspaper column written by Professor Russell Gough, the website's developer.

- Project Wisdom's (**www. projectwisdom.com**) "action ideas" and sample announcements (to be read over a school's intercom) use inspirational quotes to teach ethical values.

- "Teaching Kids Responsibility" (**www.nes.org/tkr/tkr.html**) is a newsletter from the National Educational Service.

Sites Related to Sportsmanship

Find links to these and other websites at
www.charactercounts.org/links.htm

- The Athlete Network (**www.athletenetwork.com**) includes information about *The Real Athletes Guide: How to Succeed in Sports, School, & Life*, plus links to articles on sports and sportsmanship.

- Citizenship Through Sports Alliance (**www.sportsmanship.org**) includes links to pages of professional sports leagues, plus articles on sportsmanship.

- CoachWooden.com (**www.coachwooden.com**) includes ideas from and interviews with former UCLA basketball coach John Wooden.

- Eteamz (**www.eteamz.com**) serves as an online meeting place for amateur sports leagues. The site also offers webspace for teams and leagues to build their own websites.

- MyTeam.com (**www.myteam.com**) describes itself as the "official online community" of the Amateur Athletic Union (**www.aausports.org**), Little League Baseball (**www.littleleague.org**) Police Athletic League (**www.nationalpal.org**), Amateur Softball Association (**www.softball.org**), Youth Basketball of America (**www.yboa.org**) and Reviving Baseball in Inner Cities.

- National Alliance for Youth Sports (**nays.org**) provides lots of general information and links for parents, coaches and kids.

- National Sportsmanship Day (**www.internationalsport.com/nsd/nsd.cfm**): Coordinated by the Institute for International Sport (**www.internationalsport.com**), this day is celebrated annually on the first Tuesday in March.

- NCAA Sportsmanship & Ethics (**www.ncaa.org/sportsmanship**) includes information on the NCAA's National Youth Sports program and Youth Education through Sports program (YES), plus links to dozens of related articles from *NCAA News*.

- Play With Safety!: The *Boston Globe* Safety in Youth Sports Campaign (**www. boston.com/extranet/pubrelation/safesport.stm**) offers an online pamphlet to help parents, teachers and coaches prevent injuries and promote players' well-being.

- Sport Safety Training (**www.redcross.org/hss/sst2.html**), a 6½-hour course created by the Red Cross and the United States Olympic Committee, helps coaches prevent, prepare for and respond to sports-related injuries.

GOOD IDEAS

SECTION TWO: LESSON PLANS AND ACTIVITIES

THE SIX PILLARS OF CHARACTER

TRUSTWORTHINESS
- Be honest.
- Don't deceive, cheat or steal.
- Be reliable — do what you say you'll do.
- Have the courage to do the right thing.
- Build a good reputation.
- Be loyal — stand by your family, friends and country.

RESPECT
- Treat others with respect; follow the Golden Rule.
- Be tolerant of differences.
- Use good manners, not bad language.
- Be considerate of the feelings of others.
- Don't threaten, hit or hurt anyone.
- Deal peacefully with anger, insults and disagreements.

RESPONSIBILITY
- Do what you are supposed to do.
- Persevere: keep on trying!
- Always do your best.
- Use self-control.
- Be self-disciplined.
- Think before you act — consider the consequences.
- Be accountable for your choices.

FAIRNESS
- Play by the rules.
- Take turns and share.
- Be open-minded; listen to others.
- Don't take advantage of others.
- Don't blame others carelessly.

CARING
- Be kind.
- Be compassionate; show you care.
- Express gratitude.
- Forgive others.
- Help people in need.

CITIZENSHIP
- Do your share to make your school and community better.
- Cooperate.
- Stay informed; vote.
- Be a good neighbor.
- Obey laws and rules.
- Respect authority.
- Protect the environment

GOOD IDEAS

to Help 4- to 6-Year-Olds Develop Good Character

IDEA #1

A Walk in the Dark

> **OVERVIEW:** Children appreciate how it feels to be trusted when they help a blindfolded friend navigate through a circle of toys.
>
> **PREPARATION / MATERIALS:**
> - toys or objects to toss into a circle (one for each child)
> - tape or string to make the circle
> - blindfolds

PROCEDURE:

Ask the children: *If all the lights went off in this room, how would you find your way around?* Wait for responses. When the children say they would talk to one another, ask: *How could your friends help you? How could you help your friends?* Field responses and then emphasize the importance of providing honest information. Compare what would happen if they offered dishonest directions instead. Then explain: *When others know you speak honestly, they can trust you and believe you. If people believe you, how do they treat you?* Discuss some examples that illustrate the benefits of being honest. Next ask: *Why is it sometimes difficult to be truthful?* Discuss their answers and tell them: *Learning to be honest takes practice just like everything else.* Point to the circle and say: *We will use this circle to practice being trustworthy.*

Divide the children into pairs. Distribute to each child a small toy or object. Then instruct each child to set his/her item in the circle and to state one benefit of telling or being told the truth. Then blindfold one member of each pair. Instruct the non-blindfolded children to verbally guide their blindfolded partners through the trust circle without stepping on the objects. When all the blindfolded children have gone through the circle, have them switch places with their partners until everyone has walked through the circle.

Conclude the lesson with a discussion, asking: *What did your guide do to help you trust him/her? Why was it easy or hard to trust your partner? Did you want to peek? Why? What can you do to be trusted by others? How do you feel when people believe you? How do you think people feel when they can trust you?*

*E*very man has three characters: that which he shows, that which he has, and that which he thinks he has.

— Alphonse Karr

Adapted from an idea submitted by Mary Jo Williams, 4-H youth development specialist (4-H Youth Program, University Extension, University of Missouri System, Lincoln University) based on a lesson in "Show-Me Character All Star" (Missouri 4-H Youth Development's character education program).

IDEA #2

Living Truth

Security is a

false god.

Begin making

sacrifices to it

and you

are lost.

— Paul Bowles
20th-century
American
novelist

OVERVIEW: Children associate positive images with honesty and are encouraged to be trustworthy.

PREPARATION / MATERIALS:
- copy of *A Big Fat Enormous Lie*, by Marjorie Weinman Sharmat (E.P. Dutton, 1993)
- plain paper folded in half
- crayons

PROCEDURE:

Discuss the meaning of trustworthiness. Ask: *Who can you trust? What does trust mean to you?*

Read aloud *A Big Fat Enormous Lie*. Discuss how what starts as a small fib grows to become a giant web of lies.

Next, tell the children to think of a lie as a living creature. Ask what it would look like and have them explain their answers. Then have them describe what the truth would look like as a living creature.

Distribute the folded paper and crayons and instruct the children to draw on one half what they imagine the truth would look like and on the other half what they envision a lie to look like.

Have the children share and explain their pictures to the rest of the group. Display the drawings under a banner entitled "What You See Is What You Get."

Adapted from an idea submitted by Katherine Boyer, a librarian at Conewago Township Elementary School in Pennsylvania. Her idea is based on a lesson in <u>Building Character and Community in the Classroom, K-3</u> by Rhonda Howely, et al. (Cypress, CA: Creative Teaching Press, 1997).

IDEA #3

Meet a Character: Shinrai

OVERVIEW: Children are introduced to the notion of good character, discuss and define it and then learn about Shinrai, the "Character Carousel" animal that represents trustworthiness. They conclude with a coloring activity.

PREPARATION/MATERIALS:
Refer to the description of the "Character Carousel" on page 9.
- copies of the "Shinrai the Camel" handout (one for each child)
- crayons

Our lives teach us who we are.

— **Salman Rushdie**
20th-century
Anglo-Indian
novelist

PROCEDURE:

Before discussing the Pillar of trustworthiness, introduce the children to the concept of character. Say: *When you watch cartoons on TV, you see many different kinds of characters. Can any of you tell me who some of the characters are that you see?* Field answers and compliment them on their choices. Next, say: *The word "character" also has another meaning; it's what we are inside. It shows itself when we behave certain ways. If we behave well, we show good character. What are some examples of behavior that shows good character?* List and help explain their answers. Suggest others (e.g., telling the truth, helping others at home and in school, following instructions, sharing, etc.).

After you feel that they have an understanding of the concept, explain trustworthiness to them. Say: *One way to show your good character is to act trustworthy.* Hold up the handout of Shinrai for them. *This is Shinrai the Camel. She has the courage to do the right thing even when it is difficult. She also keeps her promises, does what she says she will do and is always on time.*

Go through the descriptions of Shinrai's behavior and help the children define how the cartoon characters that they mentioned earlier show the trait of trustworthiness. Then ask them how they can show trustworthiness in their own lives.

Conclude the discussion with a coloring activity using the Shinrai the Camel handout. Invite them to take her home and explain her good character to others.

---

*The coloring handout is reproduced from the "Character Carousel" posters printed by Frank Schaffer Publications (Torrance, CA). Materials featuring the Carousel animals are available through the **CHARACTER COUNTS!** national office, (800) 711-2670.*

TRUSTWORTHINESS

Are you trustworthy?

- Are you honest in your words and actions?
- Do you keep your promises?
- Do you stand up for your beliefs and do what is right?
- Are you a good friend?

Character Counts!℠

IDEA #4

"Respect-acle" Vision

OVERVIEW: Children are introduced to the concept of respect; they discuss the feelings that accompany receiving and giving it.

PREPARATION / MATERIALS:
Twist the pipe cleaners to form a pair of eyeglasses, or "respect-acles." (See instructions below.)
- 12-inch pipe cleaners (one for each child)
- 6-inch pipe cleaners (two for each child)

PROCEDURE:

Ask: *What does it mean to be respectful? How do we show respect?* Ask for and offer examples (listening to the teacher or to your parents, saying "please" and "thank you"). Suggest: *We have to show respect to others if we expect them to respect us.* Ask: *How can we show respect in the classroom?* Again, field answers and offer examples (not talking when the teacher is speaking). Next, say: *Sometimes we can forget to be respectful. We all need a little help to remind us.*

Ask the children if any of them know what "spectacles" are. Tell them that this is another word for glasses. Put on your "respect-acles." Say: *These are my "respect-acles." Why do some people wear glasses?* Field answers. *People wear glasses to help them see better. My "respect-acles" help me see respectful behavior. Today we are going to make "respect-acles" to remind us to watch for and show respect.*

Pass out pipe cleaners and demonstrate construction:

1. Twist ends of 12-inch pipe cleaner together to form circle.
2. Twist the circle to make a figure 8.
3. Give the figure 8 an added twist to make the nose bridge.
4. Attach two 6-inch pipe cleaners to each side.

After the task is complete say: *Now we are going to test them. Put on your glasses and let's see how well you can spot respect.* Ask several questions about respect, such as: *If the teacher is reading aloud to the class, how should we act to show respect? If the class is lining up for recess and people are shoving each other, how should they act to show more respect? If there is only one toy that everyone wants to play with, how can we show respect?* Field answers.

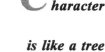

Character

is like a tree

and reputation

like its shadow.

The shadow is

what we think

of it; the tree is

the real thing.

— **Abraham Lincoln**
16th U.S. president

Before the lesson ends, discuss the following: *We respect others even if we don't think or look the same way. We respect others even if they like to do different things than we do. We respect others even if they are not our friends.*

Conclude with these questions: *How does it feel when you see others being respectful? How does it feel to show respect?*

_____

Adapted from an idea submitted by Mary Jo Williams, 4-H youth development specialist (4-H Youth Program, University Extension, University of Missouri System, Lincoln University). Her idea is based on a lesson from the "Thought, Word and Deed Program" by State Farm Insurance Company. See www.statefarm.com/educate/twdpage.htm.

E very man is to be respected as an absolute end in himself; it is a crime against the dignity that belongs to him as a human being to use him as a means for some external purpose.

— Immanuel Kant
18th-century Prussian geographer and philosopher

IDEA #5

Imagined Respect

OVERVIEW: Children associate the concept of respect to positive experiences and images.

PREPARATION / MATERIALS:
- drawing paper
- crayons or markers

What a man's mind can create, man's character can control.

— Thomas Edison
19th/20th-century American inventor

PROCEDURE:

Distribute paper and crayons.

Demonstrate polite behavior: Invite a student to come up to the front of the room. Ask him or her: *May I borrow one of your crayons, please?* When the child hands it to you, reply: *Thank you very much.* Next ask: *How was respect demonstrated here?* Field answers. Remind the children that you said "please" and "thank you." *When we show good manners and ask to share things politely, we are showing respect. How else do we show respect when we are sharing?* Field answers and cite examples, emphasizing that respectful behavior makes others feel good. Remind them of the Golden Rule: we respect others by treating them how we would like them to treat us.

Ask metaphorical questions such as: *What color is respect? What kind of weather is respect? What animals are respect?* Ask them to explain their answers.

Instruct them to draw respect as a color, a type of weather, an animal or a holiday on the paper in front of them. Afterward, invite them to share their creations and to comment (respectfully, of course!) on others' work.

Inspired by an activity idea posted on the website of the Kids' Conscious Acts of Peace Project. This project was developed by the Resolving Conflict Creatively Program, an initiative of Educators for Social Responsibility and Ben & Jerry's. For more information and activity ideas, visit www.euphoria.benjerry.com/esr/cap.

IDEA #6

Meet a Character: Austus

A kind word is like a spring day.

— **Russian Proverb**

OVERVIEW: Children are introduced to the notion of good character, discuss and define it and then learn about Austus, the "Character Carousel" animal that represents respect. They conclude with a coloring activity.

PREPARATION/MATERIALS:
Refer to the description of the "Character Carousel" on page 9.
● Austus the Lion handout (one for each child)
● crayons

PROCEDURE:

Before discussing respect, introduce the children to the concept of character. Say: *When you watch cartoons on TV, you see many different kinds of characters. Can any of you tell me who some of the characters are that you see?* Field answers and compliment them on their choices. Next, say: *The word "character" also has another meaning; it's what we are inside. It shows itself when we behave certain ways. If we behave well, we show good character. What are some examples of behavior that show good character?* List and help to explain their answers. Suggest other examples (e.g., treating others as you would like to be treated, helping others at home and in school, following instructions, sharing, etc.).

Prejudice is the child of ignorance.

— **William Hazlitt**
18th-century English essayist and literary critic

After you feel that they understand the concept, introduce them to the Pillar of respect. Say: *One way we show good character is by being respectful.* Hold up the handout of Austus for them and say: *This is Austus the Lion. He uses good manners and is considerate of the feelings of others. He also deals peacefully with disagreements and accepts people's differences.*

Go through the descriptions of Austus's behavior and ask the children to share examples of how the cartoon characters that they mentioned earlier show respect for others. Then have them suggest how they could show respect.

Conclude the discussion with a coloring activity using the "Austus the Lion" handout. Invite them to take him home and explain his good character to others.

The coloring handout is reproduced from the "Character Carousel" posters printed by Frank Schaffer Publications (Torrance, CA). Materials featuring the Carousel animals are available through the **CHARACTER COUNTS!** *national office, (800) 711-2670.*

IDEA #7

Counting on King Alfred

> **OVERVIEW:** Children discuss what it means to count on someone and then hear a story illustrating this. Cupcakes or cookies remind them of the lesson in the story.
>
> **PREPARATION / MATERIALS:**
> - burned cupcakes or cookies, properly-baked cupcakes or cookies (enough good ones for entire class)

PROCEDURE:

Say: *Today, I am going to read a story about being responsible. What does a responsible person do?* Field answers. Offer examples, such as: *If our parents count on us to brush our teeth or clean our rooms, we do it.* Next, ask the children what it means to count on someone. Say: *Doing what we are supposed to do when people count on us shows them that we are responsible.*

Read aloud "King Alfred and the Cakes" (next page). Afterward, ask the children to explain why King Alfred was not responsible. Remind them that the woman counted on him to do something, and he didn't do it. Point out that other people were affected. Show them a couple burned cupcakes or cookies to remind them what happened in the story. Say: *If King Alfred had been responsible, everyone would have had cakes to eat.* Pass out the properly-baked cupcakes or cookies for the children to eat. Equate the good taste of the cookie with responsible behavior. Suggest that King Alfred and the couple would have been able to enjoy tasty treats if the king had been responsible.

Ask if the king did anything to try to make up for failing to do what he was supposed to do (he stacked the wood). Discuss the importance of being accountable for one's mistakes and resolving to do better.

To conclude, go around the room and invite the children to share an example of how others count on them.

*W*e are

shaped and

fashioned by

what we love.

— **Johann Wolfgang von Goethe**
18th/19th-century German statesman, poet and dramatist

Inspired by "Elementary Lesson Plan Ideas" from Betty Chamberlin (Granite School District) suggested on the Utah State Office of Education's Character Education website (www.usoe.k12.ut.us/curr/char_ed).

IDEA #7 Story: King Alfred and the Cakes

After being defeated by warriors from another land, King Alfred and his soldiers were forced to leave their homes. To avoid being captured by these warriors, the king disguised himself as a poor shepherd and went into the woods to hide. But the king was not familiar with the woods and soon became lost. Unable to find his way out of the forest, he wandered alone for several days. Finally, he came upon a cottage. He knocked on the door and told the man and woman who lived there that he hadn't had a meal or a warm place to sleep for many nights. The woman, not noticing that this ragged fellow was actually the king, asked him for something in return.

"We must go chop and gather wood for the stove," she said, "so when I'm gone if you will watch the cakes baking on the stove and prevent them from burning, I will give you supper when I return."

Alfred thanked the couple and agreed to watch the cakes. But he was tired from wandering in the woods and shortly after they left, Alfred fell asleep. He awoke to the smell of smoke. The cakes now looked like small, black lumps and it was too late to save them.

The couple returned to the cottage and the woman scolded Alfred for not keeping his promise. "You lazy man! You told me you would watch the cakes, but you slept while they burned."

She turned to look at him more closely and suddenly realized that the man she was scolding was actually the king of the land! Both the man and woman dropped to their knees, apologizing for speaking to the king so harshly.

"Please, my friends, you owe me no apologies," said King Alfred. "It is I who must beg for your forgiveness. I accepted responsibility for watching the cakes and I have no one to blame but myself for letting them burn. I apologize to you, for anyone who agrees to a task, big or small, should do what is promised."

All was forgiven and the couple fed the king and prepared a bed for him to sleep in that night. The next morning when the man and wife awoke they found that King Alfred had chopped and neatly stacked their gathered wood by the door before going on his way.

A version of this classic tale appears in The Book of Virtues: A Treasury of Great Moral Stories, *by William J. Bennett (New York: Simon & Schuster, 1993) and on the "Adventures From the Book of Virtues" website (www.pbs.org/adventures).*

IDEA #8

Charting Responsible Behavior

OVERVIEW: Children identify rules and learn to be responsible for their own behavior.

PREPARATION / MATERIALS:
- a large chart listing the name of each child
- a photo of each child (instruct them ahead of time to bring photos from home)
- reward markers (e.g., stars, smiley stickers, etc.)

PROCEDURE:

Discuss with the children the components associated with responsibility. (See the "Six Pillars" listing at the beginning of this section.) Clarify vocabulary words they may not understand.

Remind them: *Part of being responsible is doing what we are supposed to do — even when it is difficult.* Ask them for examples of something they had to do that was difficult. Then have the children sit in a given number of rows with a given number of kids in each row (determine this based on how many are in your group). Ask them what rules they had to follow to sit in this arrangement. Have them explain why rules are important. Suggest: *Rules help us to act responsibly.* Ask each student to name a classroom or school rule. After each student shares an answer, have them state how this rule helps them behave responsibly.

Point out the *rewards* for responsible behavior (e.g., it helps everyone get along, it makes things easier for the group, we avoid punishment, etc.).

Introduce the chart and display it in a place where everyone can see it. Attach a photo of each student alongside his/her name. Other students can then recognize whom each name identifies. Explain that whenever you notice someone going out of his or her way to act responsibly and obey rules, a sticker will be posted next to that person's name. Draw attention to the chart periodically and praise the children for being responsible.

Y ou can tell

the size of

the man by

the size of

the thing

that makes

him mad.

**— Adlai
Stevenson II**
20th-century
American
politician

IDEA #9

Positive Mistakes

> OVERVIEW: To reinforce perseverance, children are encouraged to look at a mistake as a learning opportunity.
>
> PREPARATION / MATERIALS:
> - copies of the handout (one for each child)
> - crayons
> - *A Big Mistake*, by Lenore Rinder and Susan Horn (optional)

PROCEDURE:

Ask: *How can we show that we are responsible?* Explain and review examples of responsible behavior. (See the "Six Pillars" listing at the beginning of this section.)

Say: *Responsible people are not afraid to admit when they are wrong. They understand that everyone makes mistakes, but they try to learn from their mistakes. What are some mistakes we might make?* Field answers. Lead a discussion about the examples they suggest. (You might also mention such mistakes as breaking rules and failing to follow instructions.) Emphasize that these are mistakes everyone makes.

Discuss with the children how they feel when they make mistakes and compare this to their feelings after the mistakes are corrected.

Distribute the mistake handout and crayons. Say: *Pretend you made this line accidentally — it was a mistake you made. But you are responsible students, which means you keep on trying. So see if you can turn the line into something nice.* Turn the paper various ways to model the many perspectives from which the children can view the "mistake" line. Once the task is complete, encourage the children to share their "beautiful mistakes" with the class.

(Optional: You may want to introduce and read aloud the book *A Big Mistake* to further enhance this lesson.)

Adapted from an idea submitted by Katherine Boyer, a librarian at Conewago Township Elementary School in New Oxford, Pennsylvania. Her idea is based on an activity in <u>Building Character and Community in the Classroom, K-3</u>, by Rhonda Howely, et al. (Cypress, CA: Creative Teaching Press, 1997).

Character cannot be developed in ease and quiet. Only through experience of trial and suffering can the soul be strengthened, vision cleared, ambition inspired and success achieved.

— **Helen Keller**
20th-century
American activist,
public speaker
and author

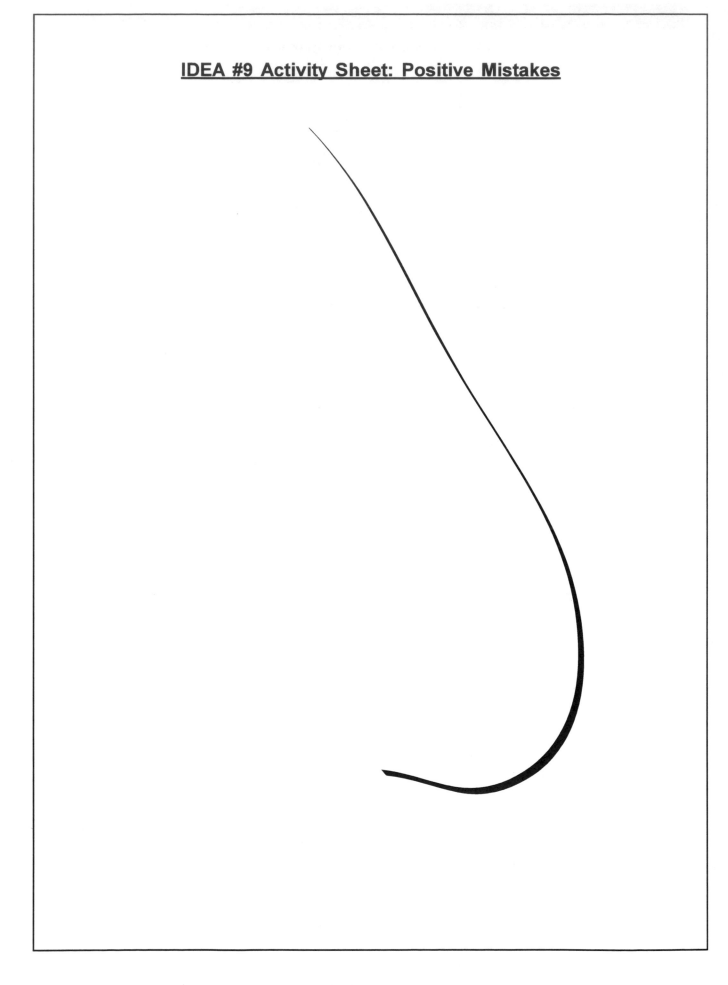

IDEA #10

Meet a Character: Ansvar

OVERVIEW: Children are introduced to the notion of good character, discuss and define it, and then learn about Ansvar, the "Character Carousel" animal that represents responsibility. They conclude with a coloring activity.

PREPARATION / MATERIALS:
Refer to the description of the "Character Carousel" on page 9.
- Ansvar the Elephant handout (one for each child)
- crayons

O ur life

is what

our thoughts

make it.

— Marcus Aurelius
Roman leader

PROCEDURE:

Before discussing responsibility, introduce the children to the concept of character. Say: *When you watch cartoons on TV, you see many different kinds of characters. Can any of you tell me who some of the characters are that you see?* Field answers and compliment them on their choices. Then say: *The word "character" also has another meaning; it's what we are inside. It shows itself when we behave certain ways. If we behave well, we show good character. What are some examples of behavior that show good character?* List and help to explain their answers. Suggest other examples (e.g., helping others at home and in school, following instructions, sharing, etc.).

After you feel that they understand the concept, introduce the Pillar of responsibility. Say: *One way to show your good character is to act responsibly.* Hold up the handout of Ansvar for them. *This is Ansvar the Elephant. He thinks before he acts and is accountable for his choices. He works hard and tries to fulfill his promises.*

Go through the descriptions of Ansvar's behavior and help the children define how the cartoon characters that they mentioned earlier show the trait of responsibility. Then ask them to suggest how they can show responsibility in their own lives.

Conclude the discussion with a coloring activity using the Ansvar the Elephant handout. Invite them to take him home and explain his good character to others.

The coloring handout is reproduced from the "Character Carousel" posters printed by Frank Schaffer Publications (Torrance, CA). Materials featuring the Carousel animals are available through the **CHARACTER COUNTS!** *national office, (800) 711-2670.*

IDEA #11

Standing in Another's Shoes

> **OVERVIEW:** To learn about seeing others' perspectives, they stand in the traced outlines of their classmates' feet.
>
> **PREPARATION / MATERIALS:**
> - paper; pencils and/or crayons
> - scissors

PROCEDURE:

Say: *Today we are going to talk about being fair. How do fair people act?* Solicit answers. Offer examples: following rules, sharing, letting others play with the same toy for the same amount of time, etc. *Another way people act fairly is when they try to see things the way others see them.*

Divide children into pairs. Place two pieces of drawing paper side-by-side on the floor for each pair. Instruct them to stand on the paper and face each other, and have one of the students trace his/her partner's feet. Then have the child whose feet were traced do the same for his/her partner.

Next, tell them to take turns standing in the outlines of their partner's feet looking straight ahead. Instruct them to describe to their partner all the things they see. Ask them about the differences between the two points of view.

Once everyone has done this, say: *Part of being fair is trying to see things as others see them. When we stepped in our friends' shoes, we noticed that they may not see things the same way we do. Fair people know that different people see things differently, and it affects the way they feel.*

Have the children color the outlines of their shoes and cut them out. Write their names on them and display them on a section of the floor or on the wall.

Activity submitted by Nat Cooper, director of Lubbock Christian University's Center for Character Development in Lubbock, Texas.

*M**en are**

not punished

for their sins,

but by them.

— **Elbert Hubbard**
19th/20th-century American entrepreneur and publisher

IDEA #12

Listening: A Step to Fairness

> **OVERVIEW:** Children learn that being a good listener takes practice and is important to being fair.
>
> **PREPARATION / MATERIALS:** none

PROCEDURE:

*T**here is no way to peace. Peace is the way.*

— A.J. Muste

Ask students: *What does it mean when we say we are listening?* Field answers. Distinguish between "hearing" someone and "listening" to someone. Ask: *When do we need to listen to other people?* List answers. Say: *We must listen when we need to make a fair decision. We often need to get lots of information in order to be fair.* Give an example such as: *A student doesn't have his or her homework. What should the teacher do?* Field answers. Then explain: *Before the teacher can decide whether to give the student a zero, he or she must listen to the student's explanation. The teacher needs all the facts to the story. If the teacher were to punish the student before hearing the whole story, he or she would be unfair.* Have the students help you define fairness. (See the "Six Pillars" listing at the beginning of this section.)

Tell the children that they are going to practice listening to help them learn about fairness. Divide children into pairs (preferably, pairs would consist of two children who do not know each other well) and have them stand back-to-back. Instruct one partner in each pair to say two things about something he or she did over the weekend. Then ask the other student to repeat what was just stated. Once he or she has done this, go around the class and see who can repeat what the first person said. Then reverse roles, having the listener of the pair mention two things that he or she did over the weekend. Repeat the process until every pair has had the opportunity.

Afterward, ask the children why it was sometimes hard to repeat exactly what their partner said. Have the children reiterate what they can do to listen to people better and why it is an important element of fairness.

Inspired by an activity in <u>Lesson Plans for Character Education</u>, elementary edition, by Sharon Fincham, et al. (Manhattan, KS: The MASTER Teacher, Inc., 1998).

IDEA #13

Meet a Character: Guisto

OVERVIEW: Children are introduced to the notion of good character, discuss and define it, and then learn about Guisto, the "Character Carousel" animal that represents fairness. They conclude with a coloring activity.

PREPARATION/MATERIALS:
Refer to the description of the "Character Carousel" on page 9.
● Guisto the Giraffe handout (one for each child)
● crayons

PROCEDURE:

Before discussing fairness, introduce the children to the concept of character. Say: *When you watch cartoons on TV, you see many different kinds of characters. Can any of you tell me who some of the characters are that you see?* Field answers and compliment them on their choices. Then say: *The word "character" also has another meaning; it's what we are inside. It shows itself when we behave certain ways. If we behave well, we show good character. What are some examples of behavior that show good character?* List and help to explain their answers. Suggest other examples (e.g., helping others at home and in school, following instructions, sharing, etc.).

After you feel that they understand the concept, introduce them to the pillar of fairness. Say: *One way to show your good character is to be fair.* Hold up the handout of Guisto for them. *This is Guisto the Giraffe. He plays by the rules, takes turns and shares.*

Go through the descriptions of Guisto's behavior and help the children list examples of how the cartoon characters that they mentioned earlier show fairness. Then ask them to suggest how they can show fairness in their own lives.

Conclude the discussion with a coloring activity using the Guisto handout. Invite them to take him home and explain his good character to others.

The coloring handout is reproduced from the "Character Carousel" posters printed by Frank Schaffer Publications (Torrance, CA). Materials featuring the Carousel animals are available through the **CHARACTER COUNTS!** *national office, (800) 711-2670.*

*T*he

jealous are

troublesome

to others, but

torment to

themselves.

— **William Penn**
17th-century
American
colonial leader

FAIRNESS

Are you fair?

- Do you play by the rules?
- Do you take turns and share?
- When you disagree, do you try to see the other person's side?
- Do you speak up if you know something is unfair?

Character Counts!℠

IDEA #14

Taking Care of Each Other

OVERVIEW: Children role play with stuffed animals and dolls (or cut-out figures) and share ways people and pets can take care of each other.

PREPARATION / MATERIALS:
- dolls and stuffed animals (as an alternative, children can draw and cut out figures on paper)

PROCEDURE:

Ask the children: *What do people do when they want to show they care about someone or something?* Field answers. Cite examples and encourage the kids to offer their own, such as: telling family members you love them, helping friends when they need it, not teasing others, being kind to animals, etc. Explain that a caring person is nice and thinks about the feelings of others.

Pair the children up and distribute the stuffed animals and dolls. Have one child in each pair play the animal and have the other play the doll. (If you are not using toys, have the kids draw or trace figures, color, and cut them out.)

Say: *Now, I want you to pretend that the animal and the person in your group are friends and have to take care of each other.* Let the children role-play with these figures. Make sure they have the figures tell the other how they would care for them. Encourage them to have the characters demonstrate caring behavior.

Afterward, invite each pair to share how the "animal" and "person" took care of each other.

In conclusion, ask: *How did these caring actions make the figures feel?* Suggest that when a pet or person is treated well they feel better and are more willing to be kind in return.

What wisdom can you find that is greater than kindness?

— Jean-Jacques
Rousseau
18th-century
French
philosopher

IDEA #15

Caring for Needy Children

We should give as we would receive — cheerfully, quickly and without hesitation; for there is no grace in a benefit that sticks to the fingers.

— Seneca
Roman
statesman

OVERVIEW: Children discuss ways to help needy children and then make sock puppets and bring in new socks to donate to them.

PREPARATION / MATERIALS:
A few days before this activity, ask children to bring in old — but clean! — pairs of socks, or single socks that are missing their mates.
● art supplies: glue, yarn, ribbon, markers, buttons, felt, colored paper, etc.

PROCEDURE:

Hold up one of the old socks that you've collected. Ask the children to describe it. Then ask them to explain what a sock is used for. After fielding answers, ask: *Why are you lucky to have socks to keep your feet warm when it's cold?* Field answers. Suggest that some children are not as fortunate. Have them help you explain why (e.g., the children are poor, orphans, homeless, etc.). Next, ask: *How could we show that we care for these children who need the help of others to stay healthy?* Invite the children to offer caring solutions. Suggest that they can bring in pairs of socks for children at a nearby shelter. (You should probably notify and explain your plan to the students' parents beforehand. Encourage the parents to take their children out to help pick out the socks that they will purchase and donate.)

Once you have discussed why such a donation shows that they are caring, inform them that they are also going to make toys to donate to the needy children. Explain that they are going to use the old socks to make sock puppets. (Have one already made to display as a model.)

Have the children work together in pairs designing puppets. Tell them to take turns placing a sock over a hand while their partners mark where the eyes, nose and mouth should be. Then let the children use the art supplies to create eyes, noses, mouths, hair and clothes for their puppets.

When everyone has completed the project, invite them to sit in a circle with their puppets, introduce them, and then have their puppet explain how he or she is going to help a needy child.

Adapted from an idea in <u>A Parent's Guide to Developing Character in Your Preschooler</u>, by Q.L. Pearce (Don Mills, Ontario, Canada: Brighter Vision Publication, 2000).

IDEA #16

Meet a Character: Karina

OVERVIEW: Children are introduced to the notion of good character, discuss and define it, and then learn about Karina, the "Character Carousel" animal that represents caring. They conclude with a coloring activity.

PREPARATION/MATERIALS:
Refer to the description of the "Character Carousel" on page 9.
- Karina the Kangaroo handout (one for each child)
- crayons

PROCEDURE:

Before discussing caring, introduce the children to the concept of character. Say: *When you watch cartoons on TV, you see all different kinds of characters. Can any of you tell me who some of the characters are that you see?* Field answers and compliment them on their choices. Then say: *The word "character" also has another meaning; it's what we are inside. It shows itself when we behave certain ways. If we behave well, we show good character. What are some examples of behavior that show good character?* List and help to explain their answers. Suggest other examples (e.g., helping others at home and in school, following instructions, sharing, etc.).

After you feel that they understand the concept, introduce them to the Pillar of caring. Say: *One way to show your good character is to show you care about others.* Hold up the handout of Karina for them. *This is Karina the Kangaroo. Her name comes from the Spanish word for caring. She is kind, thankful, forgiving and helps those in need. She thinks about how her actions will affect others.*

Go through the descriptions of Karina's behavior and help the children define how the cartoon characters that they mentioned earlier show caring behavior. Then ask them to suggest how they can show caring in their own lives.

Conclude the discussion with a coloring activity using the Karina the Kangaroo handout. Invite them to take her home and explain her good character to others.

No act of kindness, no matter how small, is ever wasted.

— Aesop
Greek moralist

The coloring handout is reproduced from the "Character Carousel" posters printed by Frank Schaffer Publications (Torrance, CA). Materials featuring the Carousel animals are available through the **CHARACTER COUNTS!** *national office, (800) 711-2670.*

IDEA #17

Appreciating Nature

OVERVIEW: Children take a "field trip" to study and observe a tree, appreciating its unique qualities and structure.

PREPARATION / MATERIALS:
- bags for picking up litter

SETTING: area with a large tree

PROCEDURE:

Take the children to a large tree and direct them to sit under it. Begin by asking the children to name things they care about. Say: *Just like people and pets, nature needs us to care for it. How can we care for nature?* Solicit answers and cite examples. *What can happen if we don't take care of nature?* Discuss how the area around the tree and the tree could become "unhealthy" (e.g., litter makes the area look bad, animals that live in the tree could become sick after eating the trash, the tree and the grass could die if we don't water them).

Next, study the tree. Ask the children about the height of the tree. Have them compare its size to buildings and houses. Ask them to describe the shape of the tree and invite them to mimic the shape with their bodies. Have the children feel and smell the leaves and ask them to compare these leaves to other items. Lastly, have the children put their arms around the trunk of the tree to measure the width of its trunk.

Afterward, ask: *What can we do to say thank you to the tree for giving us so many ways to have fun today?* Share answers and model some of the suggestions (e.g., pick up any litter near the tree before you leave).

Invite the children to observe the area over time and to notice how people treat nature there.

Inspired by an activity in Pollution, Recycling, Trash, and Litter, by Doris Roettger (Carthage, IL: Fearon Teacher Aids, Simon & Schuster Supplementary Education Group, 1991).

One can acquire everything in solitude — except character.

— Henri Beyle (a.k.a. Stendahl)
19th-century
French novelist

IDEA #18

Envisioning a Safer World

OVERVIEW: Students are shown a globe and then draw their own after discussing what kinds of things make up the world and how they can improve them to make the world safer.

PREPARATION / MATERIALS:
- globe (optional)
- drawing paper cut in the shape of a globe (one for each student)
- crayons or markers

A free society is one where it is safe to be unpopular.

— Adlai Stevenson II
20th-century American politician

PROCEDURE:

Show the students a globe. Ask them to help you explain what it is. Invite them to describe all the different things that make up the world. Discuss various examples from their own communities and environments (e.g., forests, stores, parks, homes, etc.). Next ask: *How can these things in our world be hurt?* Field answers. Say: *As good citizens, you can protect these things from being harmed. First, let's refresh our memories about what a good citizen does.* Go over the Pillar of citizenship definitions (see page with descriptions of the Six Pillars). *OK, now let's give examples of how we can protect these things.* Prompt and solicit answers.

Once everyone has shared an answer, invite the children to imagine what a safer world of good citizens would look like. Pass out a blank piece of drawing paper shaped like a globe. Instruct the students to draw their version of a safer world of good citizens. Lastly, display their "safer " worlds all over the room.

Inspired by an idea from "In the Palm of Your Hand" by the YMCA Earth Service Corps (Y Care International, CreActivity, 1998). The original idea is posted on www.mightymedia.com.

IDEA #19

Pulling-Together Web

OVERVIEW: Through demonstration children see how one person's actions can affect others.

PREPARATION / MATERIALS:
- ball of string

PROCEDURE:

Have children sit in a circle. Hand a ball of string to one child. Instruct him/her to hold onto the end of it. Then have him/her roll the ball of string to a classmate on the other side of the circle. Instruct the recipient of the ball to hold onto a piece of the string and then roll it to someone else. Have each child repeat these actions until everyone in the group holds a piece of string.

When everyone has the string, a "web" will have formed in the center of the circle. Step into the center of the circle and tug on the string. Ask which student felt the pull. Repeat this several more times.

Afterward, ask the children what citizenship means. Emphasize that being a good citizen means doing one's share to help the whole group. Then say: *We must all work together as a team because one person's actions are felt by others. If one of us didn't hold onto the string the web wouldn't be complete.* Demonstrate how they are connected by pulling on part of the "web" again. Ask them to share other examples of how they are "connected" to others and how their actions affect people around them.

Adapted from an activity submitted and developed by Debbie Gilbert Taylor, executive director of the Trumbull Chamber of Commerce in Connecticut.

Life is the sum of your choices.

— Albert Camus
20th-century Nobel Prize-winning French novelist

IDEA #20

Meet a Character: Kupa

OVERVIEW: Children are introduced to the notion of good character, discuss and define it, and then learn about Kupa, the "Character Carousel" animal that represents citizenship. They conclude with a coloring activity.

PREPARATION / MATERIALS:
Refer to the description of the "Character Carousel" on page 9.
- Kupa the Bear handout (one for each child)
- crayons

Character, in the long run, is the decisive factor in the life of an individual and of nations alike.

— Theodore Roosevelt
20th-century American president

PROCEDURE:

Before discussing citizenship, introduce the children to the concept of character. Say: *When you watch cartoons on TV, you see many different kinds of characters. Can any of you tell me who some of the characters are that you see?* Field answers and compliment them on their choices. Then say: *The word "character" also has another meaning; it's what we are inside. It shows itself when we behave certain ways. If we behave good, we show good character. What are some examples of behavior that show good character?* List and help to explain their answers. Suggest and discuss other examples (e.g., helping others at home and in school, following instructions, sharing, doing your chores, etc.).

After you feel they understand the concept, introduce them to the Pillar of citizenship. Say: *One way to show your good character is to be a good citizen.* Hold up the handout of Kupa for them. *This is Kupa the Bear. She obeys laws and rules and works hard to make her community a better place.*

Go through descriptions of Kupa's behavior and help the children define how the cartoon characters that they mentioned earlier show the trait of citizenship. Then ask them to suggest ways they can show citizenship in their own lives.

Conclude the discussion with a coloring activity using the Kupa the Bear handout. Invite them to take her home and explain her good character to others.

The coloring handout is reproduced from the "Character Carousel" posters printed by Frank Schaffer Publications (Torrance, CA). Materials featuring the Carousel animals are available through the **CHARACTER COUNTS!** *national office, (800) 711-2670.*

CITIZENSHIP

Character Counts!℠

Are you a good citizen?

- Do you cooperate with others?
- Do you obey rules and laws?
- Do you do your share to make your school and neighborhood better?
- Do you help protect the Earth?

IDEA #21

Good Sports

OVERVIEW: Children practice good sportsmanship while improving their motor skills.

PREPARATION/MATERIALS:
- one small ball per two students
- five paper cups per two students

SETTING: large open area

PROCEDURE:

Introduce the concept of good sportsmanship. Start by discussing proper behavior in the classroom. Afterward, say: *Just as we have to be polite and respectful of others in the classroom, we also have to show good manners to others when we are playing a game or sport, especially when we lose.* Ask the students to share examples of disrespectful behavior after losing a game. Then contrast them with examples of good behavior.

Divide the children into pairs. Say: *Now we are going to practice the good behavior we've talked about.* Emphasize that the more we practice good behavior, the more naturally it comes to us.

Have each pair stand behind a designated line. Hand out five paper cups to each pair of students and instruct them to line them up in a row at a designated area (about fifteen feet away from where they will roll the ball). Next hand out a small ball to each pair of students. Inform them that they will each take *one* turn rolling the ball at the cups that they set up. The partner who is not rolling the ball is to display *courteous* behavior and reset the knocked-down cups. He/she then takes his/her turn rolling the ball. Inform them that the individual from each pair who knocks down more cups is the winner and must be congratulated by his/her partner with kind words and a handshake. Demonstrate the activity with a student before they begin. Model how they should act and practice things they could say.

Mix up the pairs so that each child has an opportunity to interact and experience a different end result. Afterward, ask the children how they felt when the other person congratulated them for winning.

Inspired by an idea in <u>Lesson Plans for Character Education</u>, by Sharon Fincham, et al. (Manhattan, KS: The MASTER Teacher, Inc., 1998).

> *What lies behind us and what lies before us are small matters compared to what lies within us.*
>
> — **Ralph Waldo Emerson**
> 19th-century American essayist

IDEA #22

Character Countdown Bulletin Board Project

OVERVIEW: Students create paper rocket ships to track on a bulletin board their progress in practicing the Six Pillars of Character.

PREPARATION / MATERIALS:
Create a bulletin board (see below) and a few cardboard stencils of rocket ships before the activity.
● scissors
● construction paper

PROCEDURE:

Create a bulletin board titled "Character Countdown." (Draw land at the bottom and, toward the top, a scene of stars, a "Six-Pillar planet" and a moon. Also, draw faint, evenly-spaced horizontal lines on the board to indicate levels.)

You may want to read a book about astronauts to introduce this topic. Then discuss the meaning of "character" and the Six Pillars. Ask the children why astronauts must have good character to fly the space shuttle or a rocket. (Examples might include: self-discipline in order to learn many complicated tasks and to get their bodies ready for the long trip; courage in order to face challenges they may not know about, trustworthiness in order to conduct truthful experiments in space, respect for others in order to work out problems during the trip, etc.).

Pass out rocket ship stencils (have them share these) and instruct the children to trace the rocket ships onto pieces of construction paper. Have them cut out the rocket and color it, writing their name somewhere on it to identify it as their own.

Next, explain that all the rocket ships will be placed at the bottom of the bulletin board. For every action of good character that they display, they will be able to move their rocket up one notch on the board toward the "Six-Pillar planet." Every week or day (it's up to you), name a type of behavior that exemplifies one of the Six-Pillar traits. If children demonstrate this during the course of the day or week, let them move their rocket ships up one notch on the board. Recognize and reward students when their rocket ships make it to the top.

T o sensible

men, every day

is a day of

reckoning.

— **John Gardner**
20th-century
American
nonprofit leader
(founder of
Common Cause)

*Adapted from an activity in Spotlight on Character: Plays That Show **CHARACTER COUNTS!** by Sara Freeman (Torrance, CA: Frank Schaffer Publications, 1999). This publication is available from the **CHARACTER COUNTS!** national office, (800) 711-2670.*

IDEA #23

Making Decisions

T he way of

the sage is to

act but not

to compete.

— Lao-Tzu
Chinese sage
(from the *Tao Te
Ching*)

OVERVIEW: Children identify stakeholders in their decisions and the effects that their choices have on these people.

PREPARATION/MATERIALS:
● paper lunch bag (one for each student)
● crayons or markers
● variety of snacks

PROCEDURE:

Offer a selection of snacks, making children choose which to take.

Say: *Today we're going to talk about choices. Another word for "choices" is "decisions." When you picked a snack, you made a choice, or a decision.* Ask them what made them pick the snacks. Summarize their responses. Say: *The decision about which snack to take didn't really matter to anyone else, unless you took the last piece of something someone else wanted. Most decisions we make can affect other people — and the choices that they have. We always want to make choices that are good for as many people as possible. We want to make decisions that don't make good people sad. Pretend your mom asked you to stay out of her closet, but you want to try on her new boots. Who will care about what you decide?* Solicit answers, then tell them: *Your mom will care. If you do something to these new boots, it affects her because the boots belong to her.*

Distribute lunch bags to make hand puppets. Have them color in and design the puppets' faces, adding hair, eyes, ears, noses and mouths. Demonstrate how to make the puppet. Then say: *When you are finished, use your puppet to talk to the puppet made by the person next to you. Talk about how good decisions are made.*

Instruct the children to take their puppets home and have the puppets tell a family member why it is important to think about other people before making a decision.

Reprinted from "Exercising Character: Ages 4-6," by Peggy Adkins (Marina del Rey, CA: Josephson Institute, 1995-1998). These lesson plans and activity ideas are available from the CHARACTER COUNTS! national office, (800) 711-2670.

THE SIX PILLARS OF CHARACTER

TRUSTWORTHINESS

- Be honest.
- Don't deceive, cheat or steal.
- Be reliable — do what you say you'll do.
- Have the courage to do the right thing.
- Build a good reputation.
- Be loyal — stand by your family, friends and country.

RESPECT

- Treat others with respect; follow the Golden Rule.
- Be tolerant of differences.
- Use good manners, not bad language.
- Be considerate of the feelings of others.
- Don't threaten, hit or hurt anyone.
- Deal peacefully with anger, insults and disagreements.

RESPONSIBILITY

- Do what you are supposed to do.
- Persevere: keep on trying!
- Always do your best.
- Use self-control.
- Be self-disciplined.
- Think before you act — consider the consequences.
- Be accountable for your choices.

FAIRNESS

- Play by the rules.
- Take turns and share.
- Be open-minded; listen to others.
- Don't take advantage of others.
- Don't blame others carelessly.

CARING

- Be kind.
- Be compassionate; show you care.
- Express gratitude.
- Forgive others.
- Help people in need.

CITIZENSHIP

- Do your share to make your school and community better.
- Cooperate.
- Stay informed; vote.
- Be a good neighbor.
- Obey laws and rules.
- Respect authority.
- Protect the environment

GOOD IDEAS

to Help 6- to 9-Year-Olds Develop Good Character

IDEA #24

Building Trust

OVERVIEW: Children learn about the need for trust in working together.

PREPARATION / MATERIALS:
- an object made from Legos or other building-block materials
- Legos or blocks to make a replica of the object (enough for each group)

PROCEDURE:

Ask: *When do we need to trust other people?* Field answers. Then ask: *When do people need to trust you?* Define and discuss cooperation and teamwork. Emphasize the importance of being able to trust the accuracy of information when people work together. Say: *When we work together to achieve a goal, we must be able to trust each other. Can anyone tell me why?* Discuss some examples of what may go wrong when people work together but don't trust one another. Ask: *How can we get people to trust us?* List answers.

Divide the children into groups and distribute building blocks. Make sure the model object is hidden from view. Next, introduce the activity. Say: *We are going to practice teamwork and show our trustworthiness by constructing an exact copy of an object made out of blocks* (or Legos, etc.). *The problem: the object is hidden, and only one person from each group can come up and see it. This person then must go back and tell the rest of his/her group how to build it based on what he/she saw.* Instruct them to take turns adding a piece to build a replica. Be sure they understand that the person who saw the object is not allowed to touch the replica his/her group is building.

When all groups have finished discuss the process. Ask the children to explain what skills were needed, how they showed trustworthiness and the effect it had on the outcome of their construction.

Adapted from an idea submitted by Herb Gould, a CHARACTER COUNTS! Character Development Seminars trainer and police officer in Waverly, Tennessee.

The great enemy of truth is very often not the lie — deliberate, contrived and dishonest — but the myth — persistent, persuasive and realistic.

— **John F. Kennedy**
20th-century U.S. president

IDEA #25

Be a Good Egg

> **OVERVIEW:** Students watch an eggshell decay over time to understand what happens when a person loses someone's trust.
>
> **PREPARATION / MATERIALS:**
> - jar or container, eggshell and cup of vinegar (for each child)
> - graph paper; pencils; markers (for each child)

The foundation of morality is to have done, once and for all, with lying.

— Thomas Henry Huxley
20th-century English writer

PROCEDURE:

As a class, discuss what *decay* means. Then list examples, such as tooth decay, a building's decay, food that has rotted, etc. Next, introduce the activity, saying: *We are now going to take an eggshell and demonstrate over the course of the next week what happens when something decays.* Distribute a jar labeled with the student's name, an eggshell, and a cup of vinegar to each student.

Instruct them to place the eggshells in the jar, pour the vinegar on it, and cap the jars. Inform them that they will have to monitor their eggshells over the course of the week. Pass out graph paper. Have them draw the shape of the eggshell on the paper. Instruct them to blacken graph blocks with a marker in the same areas where the actual eggshell decays.

After they have witnessed several days of decay, and the eggshells have noticeable holes, ask them to think about how their graphed pictures of decay might represent *lying*. Field answers. Explain: *Think of the black spots as lies. When we tell a lie, we are not taking care of ourselves or others. Our character is decaying. And just as the eggshells or our teeth decay, the amount of trust people have in us decays. What happens to the eggshell as it decays over time? Less of it is there.* Have them explain why less of it is there. Mention that the eggshell weakens as it decays. *If we don't brush our teeth regularly, they can become like the eggshell. And in a similar way, the trust people have in us disappears if we tell lies. Why is it important to tell the truth?* Field answers.

Sum up the lesson: *If we tell the truth, people will trust us more and more. They won't see our honesty decaying and disappearing like the eggshell. Truth keeps us strong.*

Inspired by an activity about tooth decay posted on the Organization for Community Networks Academy Curricular Exchange website (www.ofcn.org/cyber.serv/academy/ace), by Melodie Hill, a staff member at Lewis Arriola Elementary School in Cortez, Colorado.

● **read up and reach out at www.charactercounts.org** ●

IDEA #26

Everyone Can Be a Hero

OVERVIEW: The essence of heroic behavior is courage, a key element of trustworthiness. Children read about heroes, research heroes and then create a plan to act like a hero.

PREPARATION / MATERIALS:
- access to a library or the Web (for research purposes)
- handout (for each student)
- pencils

PROCEDURE:

List the Six Pillars on the board. Have the students help you define them. Invite them to describe behaviors that display these traits. Ask them what kind of people might show them. Say: *People who exhibit these Six Pillars could be defined as heroes.* Ask them to help you explain what a hero is. Suggest that they act in courageous and compassionate ways that inspire others to do the same. List their responses and then introduce an age-appropriate resource chronicling the story of someone (preferably a real person) who showed integrity and courage and did the right thing.

After reading the story to them, discuss why the person in the story was heroic. List ways his or her actions inspired others and what resulted. Suggest ways this hero's community benefited. Instruct them to find a similar story about someone whom they would consider heroic and to write something describing the heroic actions. If possible, have them discuss the topic at home so their parents can suggest heroic figures to profile. Help them at a library to find information that they can read and share with the rest of the class. They might also decorate their papers with artwork related to the hero they profiled.

Once everyone has completed this part of the project, pass out the handout. Read it over with them. Explain that they will now create their own plan to become people who display courage and integrity. (Of course, you should explain the meaning of the word *integrity*.)

Invite the children to share their responses with the rest of the class. You may want to follow up with them in several weeks or months and have them chronicle their progress with these goals.

*M*ost of our

faults are more

pardonable

than the means

we use to

conceal them.

— **Francois
duc de la
Rochefoucauld**
17th-century
French
memoirist

IDEA #26 Worksheet: Everyone Can Be a Hero

Answer the following questions (in complete sentences) to help set up a practical plan to act with the *courage* and *integrity* of a hero.

1. How are you going to be a hero by showing trustworthy behavior?

2. List several ways someone displaying this behavior would act.

3. How are you going to act this way?

4. When and where is it especially important to act this way?

5. What do you hope others will do if you act this way?

6. I, _____, pledge to make a difference and earn the trust of others by following these plans and by encouraging others to act heroically.

IDEA #27

Good Character in Conversation

OVERVIEW: Children discuss the purpose of conversation and list the key ingredients needed for it to be successful. They apply these lessons to conversation in the lunchroom.

PREPARATION / MATERIALS:
- index cards
- shoebox
- paper; pencils or pens
- bulletin board

PROCEDURE:

Discuss the purpose of lunchtime and what the children hope to achieve at lunch. Suggest that certain behaviors and character traits are required to meet their goals for having an enjoyable lunch (e.g., staying in your seats, table manners, listening, etc.).

Have students role-play scenes from the lunchroom to model the behavior you discussed. Afterward, have the students point out the positive and negative results. Make sure they offer solutions to improve the conversation.

Ask why people talk with friends and what makes a conversation interesting. Create a list of possible elements that would make a conversation successful.

Next, brainstorm a list of topics that would be fun and interesting to talk about at lunchtime (e.g., favorite foods, traits of a hero, best ways to do your homework, etc.). Pass out index cards. Instruct students to write a topic on them. Then place them in a shoebox labeled "Quality Conversation Topics." Draw a topic from the box periodically. During lunch, assign topics to the children and tell them to discuss their topics with friends.

Discuss their efforts the next time you meet. Talk about what made the conversation better and what made it more difficult. Have the students compliment each other on their respectful behavior. Then have the students write down what they learned about their friends. Display the results of their positive conversations at lunchtime on a bulletin board in the room.

There is a secret pride in every human heart that revolts at tyranny. You may order and drive an individual, but you cannot make him respect you.

— William Hazlitt
18th-century
English essayist
and literary critic

Adapted from the article "Let's Do Lunch!" by Marlynn K. Clayton in The Responsive Classroom. This idea is also posted on www.responsiveclassroom.org.

IDEA #28

We Are All Different; We Are All the Same

> OVERVIEW: Students share examples of things they like and learn how much they have in common as well as how to accept differences.
>
> PREPARATION / MATERIALS:
> - scissors
> - paper bags
> - pencils or pens
> - strips of paper (one for each student)
> - magazines for students to cut out pictures

The highest result of education is tolerance.

— **Helen Keller**
20th-century Nobel Prize-winning American social activist and author

PROCEDURE:

Explain that part of respect is taking the time to learn about other people and listening to what they have to say. Field questions and comments about this. Then divide the students into groups of three or four. Tell them to take turns telling their group what they like (e.g., kinds of food, activities, places, movies, TV shows). Instruct them to look through the pile of magazines designated for their group and cut out pictures of all the things that they like. Have them place these in a paper bag designated for their group.

Once the groups have completed this task (you may want to set a time limit), collect the bags. Have the groups reunite as one class. Pull some of the pictures from each bag. As you pull out each picture, explain what it is, and have the students raise their hands if they like the item shown. The students will be able to see how many interests they have in common.

Afterward, have them share other ways they are similar and different. Reiterate that respectful people may come from different types of families, or appear different, but there are still many things they have in common. Emphasize that one of those common traits is the ability to accept others' differences. Ask the students to help you describe ways that they can show respect for others' differences. Have them write at least one example down on a slip of paper that you can post on a bulletin board about respectful tolerance.

Adapted from an idea in A Parent's Guide to Developing Character in Your Preschooler, *by Q.L. Pearce (Don Mills, Ontario, Canada: Brighter Vision Publications, 2000).*

IDEA #29

Tell Me; I'll Listen

OVERVIEW: Children learn the importance of listening, a hallmark of respect.

PREPARATION / MATERIALS:

- *Angel Child, Dragon Child* by Michele Maria Surat (or any story that points out the role listening plays in understanding)
- drawing paper
- crayons

PROCEDURE:

Read or summarize *Angel Child, Dragon Child* by Michele Maria Surat.

In this story a little Vietnamese girl named Hoa is teased and ridiculed at her new American school because of her language and dress. In one instance she is taunted by a classmate and she fights back. To settle the dispute, and to teach the children a lesson, the principal orders the two angry children to complete an unusual assignment. The girl must tell her tormentor about Vietnam, and the boy who teased her must listen carefully and write down her story. This leads to a friendship between the two children — and ultimately to the involvement of the whole school in a fundraiser to help reunite Hoa's family.

Discuss how this story illustrates the importance of listening and how our viewpoints about other people change if we take the time to understand them better.

Inform the students that they will practice the art of listening. Divide students into pairs. Instruct them to tell each other about their own families and what they like to do together. Have each child draw a picture of an activity that their listening partner shared about his or her family.

Have the children share with the class what they learned about their partners from listening to them. If possible, have the children share pictures of their partner's family with the class.

Adapted from Developing Character When It Counts, by Barbara Allman (Torrance, CA: Frank Schaffer Publications, 1999).

Anger is never without a reason, but seldom a good one.

— Benjamin Franklin
18th-century American Founding Father, inventor and statesman

IDEA #30

Persevering Poetry

> **OVERVIEW:** Children discuss and focus on perseverance. Taking a few minutes each day to memorize lines to a poem, they eventually see their efforts pay off as they learn to recite the entire poem.
>
> **PREPARATION / MATERIALS:**
> ● a poem appropriate to the children's developmental level

PROCEDURE:

The first and the best victory is to conquer self. To be conquered by self is, of all things, the most shameful and vile.

— Plato
Greek philosopher

Define *perseverance*. Say: *Perseverance is sticking to a task even when it is difficult. It is pushing to reach the finish when it would be much easier to give up. When you try to be the best person you can be, especially when it is difficult, you are showing perseverance.*

Ask students to share examples of perseverance. Discuss these and why perseverance is important.

Introduce the task. Explain that to model perseverance, they are going to memorize one line of a poem each day until they have memorized the whole poem.

Read the title and first line of the poem. Have them repeat the line back to you. If necessary, explain to them what each line means. Then read the line again and have them commit it to memory. Before they leave, ask them to recite the line one last time.

Each day have them learn a new line. Once they have memorized the whole poem, have the children recite it together in front of another class.

Inspired by an idea in Lesson Plans for Character Education, *by Sharon Fincham, et al. (Manhattan, KS: The MASTER Teacher, Inc, 1998).*

IDEA #31

"The Finger of Blame" Play

OVERVIEW: Students read aloud and perform a play about fairness and then discuss it.

PREPARATION / MATERIALS:
- copies of play (for students to read)
- paper; pencils or pens

People fail many times, but they only become failures when they blame someone else.

— Anonymous

PROCEDURE:

Define *accountability.* Explain that responsible people are accountable for their actions — they accept responsibility for what they've done rather than blaming others for mistakes.

When you are confident they understand these terms, write these questions on the board: *Why did Andrew try to blame Chloe for something that he did? What happened to Andrew? Who showed accountability? Who didn't show accountability?*

Instruct the students to copy these questions on a piece of paper and keep them in mind as they read the play. Explain that they are going to read a play about being accountable.

Assign character roles to students and have them read the "The Finger of Blame" play aloud.

IDEA #31 Play: "The Finger of Blame"

Cast of Characters:

Andrew: A third-grade boy
Mark: Andrew's friend
Jack: Andrew's friend
Tanya: Andrew's older sister
Mom: Andrew's mother

Scene One: Kitchen of Andrew's home.
There is a birthday cake on the counter.

Enter Mom and Tanya
Tanya:　Wow, Mom! The cake is so beautiful! I'm going to have a great birthday party tomorrow.
Enter Andrew, Jack and Mark. They are running and bumping into each other. Andrew is holding a baseball bat. Mark has a glove.
Andrew: Hi, Mom. What do we have to drink?
Mom:　Slow down. I told you that there is no rough-housing allowed inside.
Mark:　Wow, cake!
Tanya:　Don't even think about it! That's for my party.
Jack:　Good, 'cause I wouldn't want to come anyway.
Andrew and Mark laugh.
Tanya:　*(whining)* Mom!
Mom:　OK, settle down. Andrew, there are plenty of cold sodas in the refrigerator. You boys can help yourselves and then go back outside. Tanya, let's go put up the decorations in the living room.
Tanya:　OK, but don't you guys touch anything.
Tanya and Mom leave the kitchen.
Mark:　That icing really does look good. She wouldn't miss just a little bit down here at the edge. (*He sticks his finger in the icing and takes a taste.*)
Andrew: Come on. Don't do that. I'll get in trouble.
Jack:　They won't even notice. I want to try some. (*He reaches out his hand to take a taste. Andrew tries to stop him and the cake topples to the floor.*)
Mark:　Oh, man!
Andrew: My mom is going to kill me!
Jack:　What are we going to do? (*A dog barks outside the kitchen door.*)
Andrew: We can go back outside to play ball and one of us can "accidentally" let my dog Chloe in.
Mark:　OK, let's go!

Scene Two: The backyard.

Enter Andrew, Jack and Mark.
Jack:　Maybe Chloe will eat all the evidence.

Mark: What a waste. That was a really good cake. What's the matter, Andrew?

Andrew: I was just thinking that Tanya's really excited about her birthday. I don't think my mom has time to bake another cake. This will ruin it for them.

Jack: Yeah, but if your mom finds out that we knocked the cake over, you'll get grounded for a month. And she'll probably call my mom.

Mark: Let's not worry about it. Tanya can have a special cake next year. Let's play ball.

Andrew: I don't feel like playing right now.

Mom: *(from off stage)* Oh, no! Chloe, what have you done?

Jack: Uh, maybe we'd better be going.

Mark: See you later.

Mark and Jack run off. Andrew waits for a moment, listening.

Tanya: *(off stage)* Oh, Mom, look at my cake! Chloe, you bad, bad dog!

Andrew exits.

Scene Three: Andrew's kitchen.

What's left of the cake is on the floor.

Andrew enters from stage right. Mom and Tanya enter from stage left.

Mom: Be careful, Andrew. There's cake all over. Chloe got into the kitchen somehow and must have knocked it down. Your dad took her to the vet.

Andrew: The vet? Why?

Tanya: It was a chocolate cake, Andy. Chocolate is very bad for dogs. She ate a lot of it and might get sick.

Mom: I can't believe Chloe would do such a thing. She's usually so good.

Andrew: *(softly)* She didn't do it.

Mom: What?

Andrew: She didn't knock it over, Mom. I did. I was goofing around with Jack.

Tanya: You did this?

Andrew: I tried to blame it on Chloe. Now she's sick and Tanya's party is ruined. I'm sorry, Mom. What can I do?

Mom: I'm glad you told me the truth and you're being accountable for your actions. I'm sure Chloe will be alright. Her tummy might feel a little upset for a day or two. I think I can get another cake at the bakery. But for you to take responsibility for your mistake, I think you should pay for it with your allowance.

Andrew: I will. And I think I'll have to buy something else.

Tanya: What's that?

Andrew: A dog treat for Chloe.

Fade.

Give the students time to write answers to the questions you wrote on the board. Then invite them to share their thoughts and opinions.

Adapted from Spotlight on Character: Plays That Show CHARACTER COUNTS!, Grades 2-3, by Q.L. Pearce (Torrance, CA: Frank Schaffer Publications, 1999). This booklet is available from the CHARACTER COUNTS! national office, (800) 711-2670.

IDEA #32

Responsibly Running a Candy Store

> *T*he way
>
> to succeed is
>
> never quit.
>
> That's it.
>
> But really
>
> be humble
>
> about it.
>
> — **Alex Haley**
> 20th-century
> American
> journalist and
> author

OVERVIEW: To model responsibility, as well as math, reading and writing skills, students make geometric shapes out of gum drops and pretzel sticks and then create a "store" to sell them in at school.

PREPARATION / MATERIALS:
- gum drops, pretzel sticks
- paper; pencils or pens

PROCEDURE:

Invite students to think about when they go into a store. Prompt them to describe the kinds of jobs that the people they see in these stores might have. Ask them to guess what their responsibilities might be. List their answers. Discuss the different types of daily tasks performed to run a store and the responsibilities involved with them. Inform them that they will be running a candy store eventually and should start thinking about what tasks they would like to perform responsibly.

Distribute the gum drops and pretzel sticks. Have the students make various shapes. (You may want to assign particular ones to particular students). Discuss the names of the shapes and what defines them (number of sides, edges, etc.). Explain pricing. Decide what prices to charge.

After the shapes have been priced, have students name them. Discuss creative names that will encourage people to want to purchase them. Instruct them to create posters (advertisements) to sell them. Then, name the store and create a sign for it. Next, set up the shop and open it (in an area of the cafeteria to actually sell the candy). Use the profits to benefit the class or school.

Afterward, have the students write out what they learned. Instruct them to explain how they demonstrated responsible behavior and what skills they learned to help them be more responsible.

Adapted from "The Delicious Shape Shop" by Bob Krech in <u>Scholastic Instructor</u> (Nov. 1999).

IDEA #33

Taking Turns

OVERVIEW: Children reinforce lessons about fairness by playing a cooperative game that involves taking turns.

PREPARATION / MATERIALS:
- empty milk carton
- various-sized playground balls

PROCEDURE:

On the board, draw a chart with two columns: one labeled *Cooperation* and the other *Competition*. Ask the children to help you define both. Then have them help you list activities that involve cooperation (e.g., singing in a group, working together on something as a team, etc.). Next, compare those to activities involving competition. Again, list examples. Suggest that both require following rules. Discuss how following rules is part fairness.

Introduce another trait of fairness: taking turns. Ask: *How does taking turns show we are fair?* Field answers. Suggest that taking turns is part of cooperation. Then say: *Now we are going to play a game that will test your cooperation skills and show how well you can follow the rule of taking turns.*

Set up an the empty milk carton. Distribute the playground balls to the children. Designate the place from which the children will roll their balls. Explain the game: *After the first ball is rolled, each of you will work together to help it hit the milk carton without knocking it over. You will each take a turn rolling your balls to try and gently bump the first ball rolled so it can lightly touch the carton. Remember, we don't want to knock the carton over.* You may want to demonstrate for the children.

Each child takes a turn rolling a ball until the first ball touches the carton. If the carton is knocked over, the child who rolled the last ball begins the next game.

Afterward, ask the children to summarize how they cooperated and why taking turns was important to their success with this game.

Adapted from Developing Character When It Counts: Grade 2-3, by Barbara Allman (Torrance, CA: Frank Schaffer Publications, 1999). This booklet is available from the CC! national office.

All seems infected that the infected spy / As all looks yellow to the jaundiced eye

— Alexander Pope
17th-century English poet

IDEA #34

Equality for Everyone

OVERVIEW: Students study the women's rights movement to develop an awareness of equality for men and women. (This lesson can be incorporated into a whole unit on Civil Rights.)

PREPARATION / MATERIALS:

● biography of Susan B. Anthony (possible sources: *Great Americans* by John and Patty Carratello; encyclopedias, including www.britannica.com)

PROCEDURE:

Ask the students to define *equality*. List their responses on the board. Clarify the definition for them. Emphasize fairness for *all* people. When you feel they understand the concept, discuss the women's suffrage and civil rights movements. Then introduce Susan B. Anthony. Read selections from her biography aloud.

Discuss unfair judgements that people might make about boys and girls. Discuss what causes people to make unfair judgments and to treat people unfairly (e.g., making assumptions about people without knowing anything about their background or experience, not listening to people, going along with popular perceptions rather than thinking independently, not following rules, "playing favorites," etc.).

Have them write a letter to Susan B. Anthony, acknowledging her contributions to creating more fairness in the world. When they are finished, have them share their letters and display them.

You might explore this topic in greater depth by comparing the roles of men and women in other cultures or by investigating the current state of women's rights (in the U.S. and in other countries. Also, invite a women's activist or leader to your class to discuss the issue of gender inequality.

You can't have everything. Where would you put it?

— Steven Wright
20th-century American humorist

Inspired by "Civil Rights," a lesson plan by Sue Hamilton and Staci Matthews (City Heights Elementary School, Van Buren) posted on www.ericir.syr.edu.

IDEA #35

Teams Playing Fair

OVERVIEW: Students discuss the teamwork displayed by athletes, are divided into teams with designated tasks to model the appropriate behaviors discussed and then create logos and posters promoting their team's fair behavior.

PREPARATION/MATERIALS:
- pencils; markers
- magazines (to cut up)
- scissors

PROCEDURE:

Review with students what it means to be fair. List their interpretations. Invite them to explain why it is important to be fair. Again, note their answers. Ask them to define why acting fair is important in the classroom. Suggest: *When we are in here together, we are like a team, all working together to help each other learn things. Each of us must behave in ways that makes learning possible for everyone.* Ask why it is important for team players to understand how to act fair. Discuss whether or not they think athletes on various sports teams behave fairly with their own teammates. Have them cite examples of their claims such as: "Professional basketball players from a particular team do not pass the ball to their open teammates. Instead, they try to shoot so that their stats look the best, and they can earn more money the following year." Follow up with the question: *How could these players or teams behave more fairly and promote fairness?*

Next, divide them into teams (groups) of at least three or four.

Explain that they are going to be a team that promotes fair behavior in their class and school. They are to come up with a team name that suggests fairness and then design a logo for it. Once that is completed, they are to put the logo on a sheet of drawing paper and create a poster that promotes fair behavior through words and pictures. After completing the task, each team will share their posters and explain the meaning of their logos. Display them around the room for reminders.

Inspired by ideas from social study lessons posted on www.stark.k12.oh.us/Docs/units/conflict/lessons/soc/lesson1.txt.

There are two kinds of people: those who do the work and those who take the credit. Try to be in the first group; there is less competition there.

— **Indira Gandhi**
20th-century Indian prime minister

IDEA #36

Kings and Queens of Caring

OVERVIEW: Children discuss the rewards and riches that come with caring for others through their actions.

PREPARATION / MATERIALS:
- pipe cleaners
- colored beads

PROCEDURE:

*L*ight

tomorrow

with today.

— Elizabeth
Barrett
Browning
19th-century
English poet

Ask the children to define *reward* and to give examples. Field and list answers. Then discuss why people receive rewards and how that makes them feel. Explain the expression "A good deed is its own reward."

Next, list examples of caring and compassionate behavior. Ask who receives rewards when people show that they care about others. Emphasize that caring is contagious and that both the caring person and the one cared-for receive rewards.

Bring out the beads and pipe cleaner. Hang the pipe cleaner in a permanent spot that is visible to everyone. Then say: *Every time I spot one of you performing a caring deed for someone, we will add a bead to the pipe cleaner. Once we have 20 beads on the pipe, we will take a vote and decide who has been the most caring person in the class. If you are chosen, you will be given the caring bracelet to wear for a day.* You might designate this person the "King/Queen of Caring" and give him/her a special reward on his/her special day.

Continue the activity with a new pipe cleaner and new beads — and a new "king" or "queen" once the pipe cleaner has collected another 20 beads on it.

Adapted from an idea submitted by Cynthia D. Casselman, fourth grade teacher at Knox County Schools in Tennessee.

● read up and reach out at www.charactercounts.org ●

IDEA #37

Tale of the Four Wishes

OVERVIEW: Students listen to a Native American tale about selfishness and then make a wishing pouch like the main character's, to place a wish in *for someone else*.

PREPARATION / MATERIALS:
- a wishing pouch stencil (for students to trace) (optional)
- scissors, 2 sheets of construction paper, yarn, crayons
- paper; pencils or pens
- bulletin board

PROCEDURE:

Share this "Tale of the Four Wishes":

Four Indian men travel very far to meet a great magical leader who grants wishes. Three of the men wish for selfish things. The first man wishes to have a lot of money; the second wants to be more handsome, and the third wishes to be taller. Only the fourth man wishes for something that will benefit others. He asks to be a great hunter so that he can provide food for the villagers. The magical leader gives each of the men their wishes in pouches but instructs them not to look in the pouches until they get home. But the three selfish men cannot wait; they are too eager. Halfway home, they open the pouches. The first man finds that his pouch is full of money, but he is immediately attacked and robbed by a crowd of other greedy men like himself. The second man finds a mirror in his pouch and looks in it. His reflection proves that he has become very handsome, and he is instantly surrounded by a crowd of women who never leave him alone. When the third man opens his pouch he instantly grows taller, but everywhere he goes his head gets tangled in tree branches. However, the fourth man waits until he returns home to open his pouch. And just as he had hoped, he becomes a great hunter loved by many because he was able to feed them.

Ask the children to explain what this tale teaches about caring. Have them explain how the fourth man showed he was caring. After discussing the story say: *The fourth man was thoughtful. What does that mean?* Field answers. Then say: *Thinking of others before ourselves shows that we care. How else can we show that we care?* Again, field answers. Ask: *If you could make a wish to help someone else, what would it be?* Have students share some of their answers. Then distribute strips of paper on which each of them write a caring wish.

N o man

is more

cheated than

a selfish man.

— Henry Ward Beecher
19th-century American preacher

Distribute art materials. Instruct them to make a pouch to put the wish in:

1. Trace (if using stencil) and cut two identical pouch shapes.
2. Punch holes around edges of pouch shapes.
3. Decorate both pouch shapes with crayons. (Have the children try to depict caring with their artwork.)
4. With yarn, match up the holes on each pouch shape and lace them together.
5. Once all the holes have been threaded, tie off yarn close to pouch.
6. Put wish in bag.

Have the students share their wishes with the class and then take the pouches home and share them with their parents. Tell them that you will be checking to see if they did anything to help make their caring wishes come true.

Inspired by the article "Instructor Theme Unit: Legends of Native Americans," by Ann Flagg in Scholastic Instructor *(Nov. 1999). Story adapted from the retelling of a traditional tale from the Wabanaki people of New England by Joseph Bruchac in* Scholastic Instructor (Nov. 1999).

Do good with what thou hast, or it will do thee no good.

— William Penn
17th-century
American
colonial leader

IDEA #38

Beams of Appreciation

OVERVIEW: Children demonstrate respect by expressing appreciation for each other.

PREPARATION/MATERIALS:
- copy of worksheet with a student's name written on it (one for each child)
- photo or illustration of a flower
- pencil or pen (one for each child)

PROCEDURE:

Show the students a picture of a flower. Ask them how it grows. Discuss their answers. Once someone offers an answer involving sunlight, say: *The sunlight helps make the flower healthy and helps it grow. We too can be like the sunlight and help others feel good. When we show respect for others, we are sharing our light.* Give an example, such as: *What if Beth offers Joey a piece of candy and Joey says "thank you?" Who is sharing their light?* Point out that both are showing respect. Ask how this respectful behavior makes each person feel. After fielding answers, say: *Both their actions made the other person smile. They were happier. An important way to show respect is through appreciation — by saying "thank you." That's what we are going to do today.*

Pass out a copy of the flower worksheet to each child. Tell them that their assignment for the week is to "share their light" with the person whose name is written on their flower. At the end of the week, make time for the children to write words of appreciation in the space provided on the flower.

Invite the children to read aloud what they wrote before giving it to the person named on the worksheet.

Finally, ask the children how they felt hearing the respectful words of appreciation.

Adapted from <u>Developing Character When It Counts: Grades 2-3</u>, by Barbara Allman (Torrance, CA: Frank Schaffer Publications, 1998).

*D*o not sound a trumpet before thee as the hypocrites do...that they may have glory from men...but when thou doest alms let not thy left hand know what thy right hand doeth.

— Christian New Testament
(Matthew 6:1-4)

IDEA #38 Worksheet: Beams of Appreciation

Dear: _____

You are a ray of sunshine.
I appreciate you because:

_____
_____
_____
_____
_____

Good Ideas to Help Young People Develop Good Character — Vol. 2

IDEA #39

Recycling Responsibly

OVERVIEW: To become more responsible about waste management, students discuss which objects to recycle and reuse and then make a chart reinforcing this awareness.

PREPARATION / MATERIALS:

- magazines (to cut up)
- glue
- scissors
- paper; pencils or pens
- bulletin board

PROCEDURE:

In front of the class, crumple up a piece of newspaper and throw it in the wastebasket. Ask: *Why was my action not responsible?* After soliciting answers, say: *While it was good that I was throwing my trash away — I was not littering — it was not responsible because my trash was a piece of paper. Paper can be recycled.* Explain what recycling is and what kinds of products can be recycled. (You may want to display actual objects that are recyclable.) Ask the students to name examples of trash that can be recycled. Next, discuss why recycling shows responsibility. Offer examples of how it helps the environment. Discuss ways to recycle and reuse items (e.g., a glass jelly jar can be used to hold marbles, etc.).

Distribute scissors, magazines and glue to students. Demonstrate on the board what you would like them to do on the paper. Have them cut out of magazines objects that can be found in the trash and are reusable or recyclable. Next, have them glue each item to the paper and label it "reusable" or "recyclable."

Display the items somewhere in the room and designate areas for recyclable items.

You may want to take the children on a field trip to a recycling plant or have them bring in items from home that can be reused in the classroom.

Inspired by an activity in Pollution, Recycling, Trash, and Litter, *by Doris Roettger (Carthage, IL: Fearon Teacher Aids, Simon & Schuster Supplementary Education Group, 1991).*

Ah, but a man's reach should exceed his grasp / Or what's a heaven for?

— Robert Browning
19th-century
English poet

IDEA #40

A Gifted Community

OVERVIEW: Children write out responsible acts and chores they will perform to improve the community and then work together to wrap them in a package, symbolizing the gift of their commitment.

PREPARATION / MATERIALS:

- notecards
- pencils or pens
- magazines (for cutting)
- art supplies, including: scissors, glue, large box, ribbon

PROCEDURE:

Words without actions are the assassins of idealism.

— **Herbert Hoover**
20th-century U.S. president

Ask the students to explain why people give gifts. List answers (e.g., to show they care). Next, ask: *What kind of gifts do we give to show we care?* Again, list answers, reminding them that gifts don't have to be objects; they can be favors or acts of kindness.

Discuss the meaning of "citizenship" and say: *Part of being a good citizen involves gift giving. The best gift you can give the community is the gift of yourself. What do I mean by that?* Field answers and cite examples (e.g., throwing away trash, helping others, participating in community-service activities, etc.). Clarify how these actions help the community.

Introduce the task: *We are going to offer our school community gifts of ourselves.* Pair students up. Pass out notecards and pencils to each one. Say: *First, think of something you can do to help the community. Write it down on the notecard. Once everyone has done that, we are going to decorate this large box and give it to our principal.*

When the notecards have been completed, distribute magazines to the pairs. Instruct students to look through the magazines and cut out examples of good citizenship. Afterward have the children take turns pasting their cutouts onto the box. Once it is completely decorated, have the children come up in pairs, read their notecards and place them in the box. When everyone has shared their "gifts," tie the bow around the box. Present the box to the principal and explain its significance. Then arrange for the students to give their time to the community in the ways they suggested.

Inspired by an idea posted on www.ed.gov/pubs/parents/Behavior/pt4.html.

IDEA #41

Picture (More) Perfect

OVERVIEW: Children become more aware of global issues and imagine ways to make the world better.

PREPARATION / MATERIALS:
- photos depicting global problems
- paper; pencils or pens
- paste

PROCEDURE:

Show the children photos of global problems from magazines or newspapers (e.g., famine-striken regions, polluted beaches, property damage from floods, earthquakes, hurricanes, etc.). Ask them to describe what they see. Field answers and then say: *These are pictures from different parts of the world — different parts of our global community.* Ask the children to help you define "community." Explain that a community is a larger extension of a family. Ask: *What do we learn about our community from these photos?* Field answers, then ask: *Can you think of things we could do to make these pictures look better?* Suggest some answers (e.g., give money to groups working to end hunger, support disaster-relief efforts, take better care of our environment). Ask: *What are some problems in our local community? Can you think of things we could do to solve them?*

Encourage the children to be aware of their surroundings when they go home during the week. Instruct each of them to take a picture of something that can be improved to make the world a better place. Alternately, they might take (or draw) pictures of people who are doing something to improve the community. If children don't have access to a camera, instruct them to draw pictures. Have them bring their pictures to class and paste them onto pieces of paper. Instruct them to write "What people could do to make the community better" underneath their pictures. Invite the students to share their pictures with the class.

Display the photos/drawings on a bulletin board with the heading: "Picture a More Perfect Community."

Inspired by a contest idea sponsored by the public forum for youth "To Make the World a Better Place" in Hope *magazine (September/October 1998). To view images or participate in the forum at "To Make the World a Better Place" visit www.liska.com/betterplace.*

*A*ll who would win joy, must share it; happiness was born a twin.

— Lord Byron
19th-century English adventurer and poet

IDEA #42

"Time Warp" Party

If we were logical the future would be bleak indeed. But we are more than logical. We are human beings, and we have faith and we have hope, and we can work.

— Jacques Cousteau
20th-century French environmental pioneer

> **OVERVIEW:** Students dress up as outstanding global, national or local civic figures and explain what they have done to make a difference.
>
> **PREPARATION / MATERIALS:**
> - access to resource materials (library, Internet, etc.)

PROCEDURE:

Reiterate how a good citizen acts as a member of different communities: family, town, state, nation and world. Suggest that citizens of these groups have certain rights as well as duties. Have them help you define the term *duty*. Next say: *Good citizenship means that we have to do whatever we can to help make life better for people. That requires knowledge about other members of our communities and about what others have done in the past to contribute to what we have today.* Ask them to explain why this is an important step before actually *doing* something to make a difference. Suggest that if we know what problems someone else faced when trying to make a difference, we might be able to avoid the same mistakes and overcome the same obstacles more effectively. Also, it is important to appreciate what others have done on our behalf.

Inform the students that the class is going to have a "time warp" party. Explain what a time warp is. Make it clear that they are going back in time to learn about people who helped to improve their communities and world. Instruct them to pick an outstanding citizen from the history of their community, state or nation — or even from another part of the world — and find out information about them. (You might want to compile a list of examples beforehand from which students can choose.) Instruct students to state clearly how and why this person made a difference in others' lives. Explain that once they have researched their figure, they will dress up like him or her on a specific day and play the role of that person for the party.

During the party have each figure formally describe to the rest of the class what "they" have done to make a difference in a community.

Adapted from "Exercising Character," by Peggy Adkins (Marina del Rey, CA: Josephson Institute, 1995-1998).

IDEA #43

The Six-Pillar Wheel

> **OVERVIEW:** Students use a wheel of Six Pillars to randomly pick a core value that they will have to demonstrate in their daily life.
>
> **PREPARATION / MATERIALS:**
> - paper; pens or pencils
> - crayons or colored pencils or pens
> - copies of the "Six-Pillar Wheel" handout (one for each pair of students)

PROCEDURE:

Pair up the students. Pass out one "Six-Pillar Wheel" handout to each pair. Explain that the class is going to review the Six Pillars of Character. Invite students to help you read and define them. Have them offer examples of behavior and tasks that exemplify each value. After you discuss each Pillar, let the students color in the portion of the wheel that represents that trait with its corresponding color (trustworthiness is blue; respect is yellow; responsibility is green; fairness is orange; caring is red; and citizenship is purple).

Next, have members of the pair take turns closing their eyes and randomly placing an index finger on the wheel. Whichever Pillar it lands closest to is the Pillar that they will have to work on, emphasizing that value in their behavior over the next week. The student of each pair whose eyes are not closed is to write down the Pillar his/her partner chose.

Afterward, have all students write down or share with the group what task they will perform in school or at home to show this core value to others.

To follow up, inform the students that they will have to orally share the results and effects of their actions in one week. (If the students are able, you might have them write a one-page summary of their actions and how things changed as a result of emphasizing the Pillar).

Ideals are like stars; you will not succeed in touching them with your hands. But like the seafaring man, you choose them as your guides and following them, you will reach your destiny.

— **Carl Schurz**
19th-century
German
American
politician

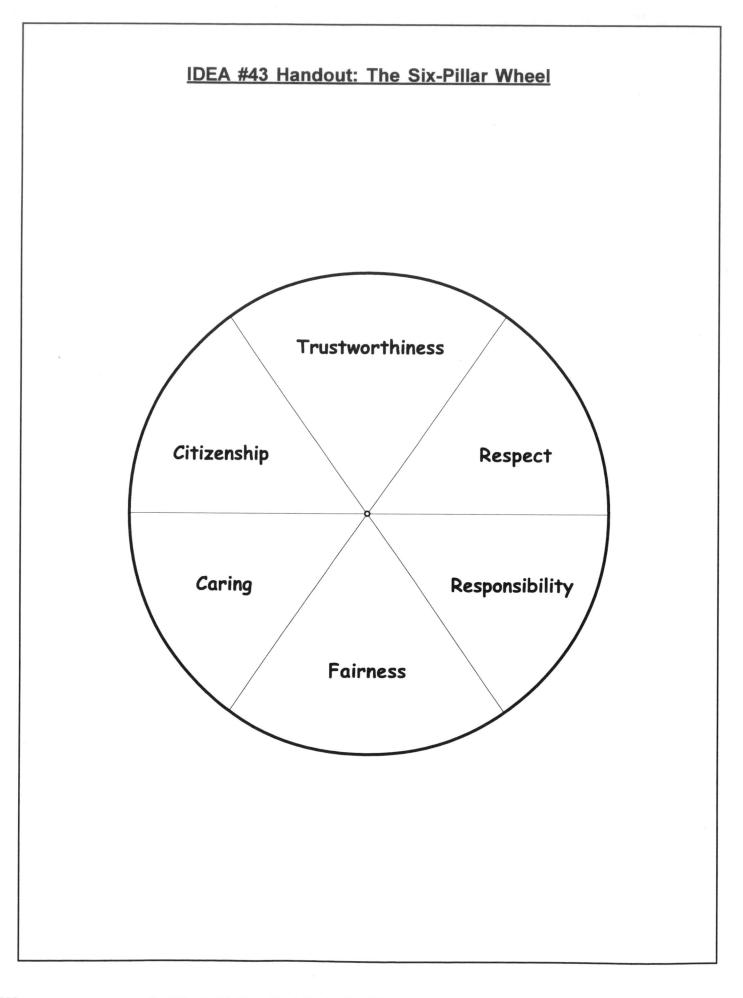

IDEA #44

Pedaling to Character

OVERVIEW: Children perform a skit reinforcing core ethical values.

PREPARATION/MATERIALS:
- copy of skit for each student

PROCEDURE:

Introduce the Six Pillars of Character to students. Discuss these values, then instruct the students to look for instances when these values are and are not apparent in a play that they are going to read.

Select students to read the lines and act out parts in the following play. Assign the following roles:

- Narrator
- Michael
- Judge
- Mother
- Father

- Henry
- Juror I
- Juror II
- Juror III
- Juror IV

The essence of greatness is the perception that virtue is enough.

— **Ralph Waldo Emerson**
19th-century American essayist, public speaker and poet

IDEA #44 Play: Pedaling to Character

(A courtroom)

Narrator: Hear Ye! Hear Ye! Hear Ye! Hear Ye!

Judge: Michael and Henry, please approach the bench. (Michael and Henry step forward.) Michael, Henry is accusing you of stealing his bike from the front porch. How do you plead?

Michael: Not guilty, your honor! Not guilty!

Judge: (to Henry) What evidence do you have that Michael stole your bike?

Henry: My bike was on my porch. When I looked out the window at 8:00 that night, Michael was standing on the porch next to my bike.

Judge: Why didn't you lock your bike and bring it into the house?

Henry: I didn't think anyone would take it since it was on my porch, and everyone knew it was my bike, and the brakes were bad.

Judge: Henry, what color is your bike?

Henry: Blue with white stripes, and my seat is torn on the side.

Judge: Michael did you steal Henry's bike?

Michael: No, your honor, I have a bike. It is blue with white stripes. The brakes are fine.

Judge: Michael, would you mind if we take a look at your bike? (Michael brings in a bike). Henry, is this your bike? It looks like the seat has been torn.

Henry: It is my bike. Look, here is my name right here.

Michael: Judge, I tore my seat, too.

Judge: (Judge looks at seat.) Michael, I need to speak to your parents, please.

(Parents approach the bench.)

Mother: Yes, Your Honor?

Judge: Michael has been accused of stealing Henry's bike.

Father: Michael told me his friend traded the bike for a baseball bat and glove.

Judge: Michael, what do you have to say about this?

Michael: Uh...Uh... I didn't mean to steal it or lie about not stealing it, but once I had lied it became hard to stop. I had to continue to cover up for the first lie. I am sorry.

Judge: We will see what the jury says.

(Jury leaves room, but soon returns to jury box.)

Juror I: He needs to show *citizenship* by obeying laws and rules.

Juror II: I feel he should learn the meaning of being *trustworthy*.

Juror III: He needs to know what it means to *respect* others and their property.

Juror IV: Whatever happened to *honesty*?

Judge: Michael and Henry, please approach the bench. (To the jurors) You have heard the case. What is your verdict?

Jury: We, the Jury, find the defendant, Michael, guilty as charged.

Judge: Please return the bike to its rightful owner. Michael, I hope you have learned a lesson. Everyone is dismissed.

Afterward, ask: *What lessons could Michael and Henry have learned? Why? What character traits could have been used to avoid this consequence? How? What kinds of good character will Michael and Henry have to practice now? Why?*

Skit written and submitted by Johnnie Wheeler, a **CHARACTER COUNTS!** *coordinator at the Upper Cumberland Human Resource Agency in Cooksville, Tennessee.*

IDEA #45

Six Pillar Puzzle

> **OVERVIEW:** Children learn new vocabulary words as they complete a puzzle.
>
> **PREPARATION / MATERIALS:**
> - copies of the puzzle (one for each student)

PROCEDURE:

If we only wanted to be happy it would be easy, but we want to be happier than other people, which is almost always difficult.

— Charles-Louis de Secondat Baron de Montesquieu 17th/18th-century French jurist and philosopher

Introduce the Six Pillars of Character to the students. Discuss these values and some of their aspects, listed below. Instruct the students to look for these words in the puzzle you will hand out to them. You may also want to hand out a sheet with the answers or simply go over the answers together as a class.

These are the words hidden in the letters:

• **Honesty**	• **Citizenship**	• **Kindness**
• **Integrity**	• **Truth**	• **Sharing**
• **Loyalty**	• **Courage**	• **Compassion**
• **Respect**	• **Courtesy**	• **Vote**
• **Responsibility**	• **Tolerance**	• **Charity**
• **Accountability**	• **Stakeholders**	• **Volunteer**
• **Excellence**	• **Reliability**	• **Recycle**
• **Fairness**	• **Diligence**	• **Conserve**
• **Caring**	• **Disciplined**	

Puzzle submitted by Debbie Gilbert Taylor, executive director of the Trumbull Chamber of Commerce in Connecticut.

IDEA #45 Worksheet 1: Six Pillar Puzzle

```
W  I  A  P  C  C  D  F  H  R  E  S  P  E  C  T  G  E
D  S  E  F  M  O  I  D  I  S  C  I  P  L  I  N  E  D
B  C  A  A  F  D  M  T  T  F  S  T  E  E  H  R  M  E
N  A  C  H  I  A  I  P  I  O  S  L  O  Y  A  L  T  Y
O  R  A  E  N  E  S  L  A  Z  L  H  O  T  R  E  O  T
V  I  C  C  T  S  T  E  I  S  E  E  A  I  E  E  Q  O
O  N  C  O  E  T  A  C  X  G  S  N  R  R  E  O  T  C
L  G  O  N  G  R  K  R  O  C  E  I  S  A  I  P  E  F
U  E  U  S  R  U  E  E  E  U  E  N  O  H  N  N  E  A
N  S  N  E  I  T  H  C  N  L  R  L  C  N  I  C  G  I
T  C  T  R  T  H  O  Y  A  O  I  A  L  E  R  P  E  R
E  O  A  V  Y  A  L  C  A  A  T  A  G  E  A  L  R  N
E  U  B  E  Z  V  D  L  T  E  E  D  B  E  N  T  I  E
R  R  I  N  E  O  E  E  N  A  E  N  E  I  F  C  S  S
O  T  L  F  S  T  R  H  O  N  E  S  T  Y  L  O  E  S
W  E  I  M  E  E  S  C  H  A  R  I  T  Y  I  I  B  E
I  S  T  V  R  E  S  P  O  N  S  I  B  I  L  I  T  Y
W  Y  Y  O  E  E  K  I  N  D  N  E  S  S  R  E  G  Y
```

Honesty	Citizenship	Kindness
Integrity	Truth	Sharing
Loyalty	Courage	Compassion
Respect	Courtesy	Vote
Responsibility	Tolerance	Charity
Accountability	Stakeholders	Volunteer
Excellence	Reliability	Recycle
Fairness	Diligence	Conserve
Caring	Disciplined	

THE SIX PILLARS OF CHARACTER

TRUSTWORTHINESS

- Be honest.
- Don't deceive, cheat or steal.
- Be reliable — do what you say you'll do.
- Have the courage to do the right thing.
- Build a good reputation.
- Be loyal — stand by your family, friends and country.

RESPECT

- Treat others with respect; follow the Golden Rule.
- Be tolerant of differences.
- Use good manners, not bad language.
- Be considerate of the feelings of others.
- Don't threaten, hit or hurt anyone.
- Deal peacefully with anger, insults and disagreements.

RESPONSIBILITY

- Do what you are supposed to do.
- Persevere: keep on trying!
- Always do your best.
- Use self-control.
- Be self-disciplined.
- Think before you act — consider the consequences.
- Be accountable for your choices.

FAIRNESS

- Play by the rules.
- Take turns and share.
- Be open-minded; listen to others.
- Don't take advantage of others.
- Don't blame others carelessly.

CARING

- Be kind.
- Be compassionate; show you care.
- Express gratitude.
- Forgive others.
- Help people in need.

CITIZENSHIP

- Do your share to make your school and community better.
- Cooperate.
- Stay informed; vote.
- Be a good neighbor.
- Obey laws and rules.
- Respect authority.
- Protect the environment

GOOD IDEAS

to Help 9- to 11-Year-Olds Develop Good Character

IDEA #46

A Monument to Value

OVERVIEW: Students discuss traits related to trustworthiness and then suggest images that represent this value. They build a "monument" to trustworthiness to reinforce the lesson.

PREPARATION / MATERIALS:
- photo of at least one famous monument
- paper; pencils or pens
- drawing paper, markers, crayons
- building materials: scissors, glue, clay, straws, Popsicle sticks, etc. (optional)

PROCEDURE:

Present a picture of a famous monument (e.g., the Washington Monument, the Lincoln Memorial, the Thomas Jefferson Memorial and the Vietnam Veterans Memorial). Discuss with the students what it represents. Offer information and explain the history of the monument. Discuss why it was built and why monuments in general are constructed.

Then discuss trustworthiness. Be sure to explain these four components of the value: *honesty, promise-keeping, integrity* and *loyalty.* List these on the board. Then ask: *What kind of people, animals or images could represent trustworthiness? Why?* List their ideas on the board.

Divide students into groups. Say: *Now that we have discussed trustworthiness, you are going to build a monument to celebrate and honor this value.*

Encourage them to be creative in coming up with a representation of trustworthiness. You might help them along by reminding them of the four components that you discussed earlier and suggesting that their monument could be an animal, a person or an object.

Distribute building materials (or drawing paper and crayons). Instruct them to design and construct (or draw) an image that represents trustworthiness. Inform them that they will have to present their monument of trustworthiness to the class and explain what aspect of trustworthiness their image represents.

The house

of delusions

is cheap to

build but drafty

to live in.

— **A.E. Housman**
20th-century
English poet

IDEA #47

Sweet Honesty

OVERVIEW: Students read and discuss a story about a dishonest merchant, then write their own moral tale about trust.

PREPARATION / MATERIALS:

- copy of "Ali Coglia and the Merchant of Baghdad" (for each student)
- jar of sweet olives, jar of bitter olives (optional)

PROCEDURE:

Display two jars of olives. Invite a student who likes olives to taste one of the sweet olives. Have the student share his or her reaction with the class. Next, invite a student to try a bitter olive. Again, solicit the student's reaction. Ask the student to describe the difference in taste between the two olives. Point out to the class that the first olive was sweet and the second bitter.

Assure the students that the bitter olive you offered wasn't old or rotten, but that food items that have gone "bad" often taste sour or bitter. Discuss why this happens. Use the following explanation, tailored to the developmental level of your students: Food decomposes as microorganisms such as bacteria attack it. This changes its chemical makeup and produces various acids and alkalis. Acids are substances that taste sour; in fact, the word acid comes directly from the Latin word *acidus*, meaning "sour." The process of decomposition also can produce alkalis, which are characterized by a bitter taste and are slippery to the touch.

Draw a comparison between the decomposition of food to the decomposition of a person's trustworthiness as a consequence of lying. Note how a bad spot on an apple, for instance, will eventually cause the whole fruit to rot. Also explain how certain measures can be taken to protect one's character (e.g., being honest and keeping promises), just as we must take certain safeguards to keep food fresh. Ask: *How can trust turn "sour"? What kind of behavior attacks our trustworthiness?* Discuss their answers and list them on the board.

Introduce "Ali Coglia and the Merchant of Baghdad." Suggest that the story shows the effects of dishonesty. Before reading the story, explain where the story originated. Point out where Iraq is located and that Baghdad is the country's capital. (You may want to give an overview of Iraq's history and provide some general information on the Arab world.) Also, you may want to discuss these vocabulary

T ruth is like the sun. You can shut it out for a time, but it ain't goin' away.

— Elvis Presley
20th-century American entertainer

words, which are used in the story: *obliging, caravan, summon, meddled, unfounded, caliph, vizier, rogue* and *monarch*.

Read the story aloud. Stop before the merchant makes his decision to steal the money and ask them what they would do in the same situation. After he steals the money, stop again, and ask the students to explain what they would do if the merchant were their friend, and they knew what he had done. Encourage them to be specific. Then finish reading the story.

Discuss the consequences of the merchant's behavior. Then have them write their own tale focusing on trustworthiness and honesty.

_____

Inspired by an idea posted on "Absolutely Whootie: Stories to Grow By" (www.storiestogrowby.com).

*W*hoso

diggeth a pit

shall fall

therein.

— **Bible**
(Proverbs)

*G*od looks

at the clean

hands, not the

full ones.

— **Publilius**
Syrus
Roman leader

IDEA #47 Folk-Tale:
"Ali Coglia and the Merchant of Baghdad"

Over a thousand years ago, in the reign of the famous Caliph Harun al-Raschid, there lived in Baghdad a merchant who needed to travel on an extended journey. He sold nearly all of his household goods and sold his home. The only thing left for him to do was to find a safe place to leave his private treasure — one thousand pieces of gold. Finally, he decided to put the thousand pieces of gold into a large jar and cover the gold with olives. When he had closed the mouth of the jar, he carried it to a friend of his, who was also a merchant, and said to him, "You know, my friend, that in a few days I plan to depart on my journey. I beg you to take charge of a jar of olives, and keep it for me until I return."

The merchant promised that he would, and in an obliging manner said, "Here, take the key of my warehouse and set your jar where you please. I promise you shall find it there when you return."

Ali Coglia's journey was extended much longer than he had expected. In fact, he was seven years absent from Baghdad, when he finally decided to return. All this time his friend, with whom he had left his jar of olives, neither thought of him nor of the jar. One evening this merchant was eating dinner with his family and the conversation happened to fall upon olives. The merchant's wife mentioned that she had not tasted any for a long while.

"Now that you speak of olives," said the merchant, "you remind me of a jar that Ali Coglia left with me seven years ago. He put it in my warehouse to be kept for him until he returned. What has become of him I know not, though when the caravan came back, they told me he had gone to Egypt. Certainly he must be dead by now, since he has not returned in all this time, and we may go ahead and eat the olives, if they are still good. Give me a plate and a candle. I will fetch some of them and we'll taste them."

"Please, husband," said the wife, "do not commit so base an action; you know that nothing is more sacred than what is committed to one's care and trust. Besides, do you think the olives can be good, after they've been kept so long? They must be all moldy and spoiled. Besides, if Ali Coglia should return and find that they had been opened, what would he think of your honor? I beg of you to let them alone."

Nevertheless, after supper, the merchant entered the warehouse, found the jar, opened it and found the olives moldy. But to see if they were all in the same condition to the bottom, he shook the jar. This caused some of the gold pieces to tumble out. The merchant noticed at once that the top only was laid with olives, and what remained was gold coins. He immediately put the olives into the jar again, covered it up, and returned to his wife. "Indeed, wife," said he, "you were in the right to say that the olives were all moldy for I found them so, and have made up the jar just as Ali Coglia left it. He will not notice that they had been touched, if he should ever return."

In the days ahead the merchant thought often about how he might use Ali Coglia's gold for his own purposes, and yet escape detection in case his old friend should return and ask for the jar. The next morning the merchant went and bought some olives of that year, and then secretly went and emptied the jar both of the old moldy olives and of the gold. Then, filling the jar entirely with new olives, he covered it up and put it in the place where Ali Coglia had left it.

About a month later, Ali Coglia arrived in Baghdad. The next morning he went to pay a visit to his friend, the merchant, who expressed great joy at his return after so many years away. After having chatted a while, Ali Coglia asked the merchant to return him the jar of olives which he had left with him, and thanked him for having kept the jar safely for all this time. "My dear friend," replied the merchant, "your jar has been no inconvenience. Here is the key to my warehouse. Go and fetch your jar; you will find it where you left it."

Ali Coglia went into the merchant's warehouse, took his jar, and after having returned the key, and thanking his friend once again for the favor, he returned with the jar to the room where he was temporarily staying. But on opening the jar, and putting his hand down as low as the pieces of gold had lain, he was greatly surprised to find no gold pieces in the jar. At first he thought he might perhaps be mistaken, and to discover the truth, he poured out all the olives, but without so much as finding one single piece of gold. For some time, he stood motionless. Then he cried out, "Is it possible?"

Ali Coglia immediately returned to the merchant. "My good friend," said he, "be not surprised to see me come back so soon. I know that the jar of olives is the same one I placed in your warehouse, but with the olives I put into the jar a thousand pieces of gold, which I do not find. Perhaps you might have used them in your business; if so, they are at your service till it may be convenient for you to return them. Only give me an acknowledgment of my loan to you, after which you may repay me at your own convenience."

The merchant, who had expected that Ali Coglia would come with such a complaint, was prepared with an answer. "Friend Ali Coglia," said he, "when you brought your jar to me, did I touch it? Did I not give you the key of my warehouse? Did you not carry it there yourself? And did you not find it in the same place, covered in the same manner as when you left it? And now that you have come back, you demand one thousand pieces of gold. Did you ever tell me such a sum was in the jar? I wonder you do not demand diamonds or pearls! It is easy enough for you to storm into my house, make a crazy accusation, insult me, and tarnish my good name. Be gone!"

These words were pronounced in such passion that those in the warehouse started to gather around. Neighboring merchants came out of their shops to learn what the dispute was about. Ali Coglia shared with one and all the injustice done to him by the merchant, and the merchant continued to hotly deny any wrongdoing.

Ali Coglia speedily summoned the merchant to court. To the judge, Ali Coglia accused the merchant of having stolen his thousand pieces of gold, which he had left with him. The judge asked him if he had any witnesses, to which he replied that he had not taken that precaution because he had believed the person he entrusted his money with to be his friend, and always took him for an honest man. Then the merchant made the same defense he had before, saying that though it's true that he had kept Ali Coglia's jar in his warehouse, he had never once meddled with it. The merchant swore that as far as he knew, the jar contained only olives. Once again, he strongly objected that he should be brought to court on the basis of such unfounded accusations. He proposed to make an oath that he never had the money he was accused of taking, and to swear that he did not know such a sum ever existed. The judge agreed to take his oath. After the merchant swore his ignorance of the entire matter, the judge dismissed the case for lack of evidence.

Ali Coglia, extremely upset to find that he must accept the loss of so large a sum of money, returned to his room and drew up a petition to seek justice from the Caliph Harun al-Raschid himself. He forwarded his petition to the officer of the palace, who presented it to the caliph. The caliph told the officer to notify Ali Coglia that an hour would be scheduled for the next day for the complaint to be heard at the palace. The officer was also told to summon the merchant.

That same evening the caliph, accompanied by the grand vizier, went disguised through the town as it was his custom occasionally to do. On passing through a street, the caliph heard a noise. He came to a gateway through which he saw ten or twelve children playing by moonlight. The caliph heard one of the children say, "Let's play courtroom."

As the affair of Ali Coglia and the merchant was widely discussed in Baghdad, the children were familiar with the case and quickly agreed on the part each one would assume.

The child who played the judge asked the make-believe Ali Coglia to speak. The child playing Ali Coglia, after bowing low, related every particular and begged that he might not lose so considerable a sum of money. The pretend judge turned to the merchant and asked him why he did not return the money. The child playing the part of the merchant gave the same reasons as the real merchant had done. Then he also offered to give an oath that what he had said was the absolute truth.

"Not so fast," said the pretend judge, "before you give your oath, I should like to see the jar of olives." The child playing the part of Ali Coglia bowed low, walked away and in a few moments returned. He pretended to set a jar before the judge, telling him that it was the same jar he had left with the merchant. The supposed judge turned to the child playing the merchant and asked him to confirm that it was in fact the same jar. He confirmed this. Then the judge ordered Ali Coglia to take off the cover, and the pretend judge made as if he looked into it. "They are fine olives," said he, "let me taste them." Pretending to eat some, he added, "They are excellent, but I cannot think that olives will keep seven years and be so good. Therefore we must call before this court some olive merchants, and let me hear what is their opinion."

Two boys, posing as olive merchants, presented themselves. "Tell me," said the supposed judge, "how long will olives keep fit to eat?"

"Sir," replied the two merchants, "no matter how great the care taken of them, olives will hardly be worth anything the third year, for then they have neither taste nor color."

"If that is so," answered the judge, "look into that jar and tell me how long it has been since those olives were put into it." The two merchants pretended to examine and to taste the olives, and told the judge that they were new and good. "But," said the judge, "Ali Coglia himself said he put them into the jar seven years ago."

"Sir," replied the merchants, "we can assure you they are of this year's growth, and we will maintain that any olive merchant of repute in Baghdad will say the same."

The pretend judge pointed an accusing finger at the merchant. "You are a rogue," he cried, "and deserve to be punished!" The children then concluded their play, clapping their hands and seizing the actor playing the criminal, they pretended to carry him off to prison.

Words cannot express how much the caliph admired the boy who had passed so just a sentence in an affair which was to be pleaded before himself the very next day. "Take notice of this house," said the caliph to the vizier, "and bring the boy to me tomorrow, that he may appear in court with me to try this case himself. Take care also to remind the real Ali Coglia to bring his jar of olives with him. And bring two olive experts as well."

The next day Ali Coglia and the merchant pleaded one after the other at the palace before the boy, whom the caliph had seated on the throne beside him. When the merchant proposed his oath to the court as before, the child said, "It is too soon. It is proper that we should see the jar of olives."

At these words Ali Coglia presented the jar and placed it at the caliph's feet. The boy asked the merchant whether this was in fact the jar that had been left in his warehouse for seven years, and the merchant agreed that it was so. Then the boy opened the jar. The caliph looked at the olives, took one and tasted it, giving another to the boy. Afterwards the merchants were called, who examined the olives and reported that they were good, and of that year. The boy told them that Ali Coglia had said that it was seven years since he had put the olives in the jar. Therefore, the boy concluded, the jar must have been tampered with since that time.

The accused saw plainly that the opinions of the olive merchants would convict him. He confessed to his crime, and revealed where the thousand pieces of gold were hidden. The fortune was quickly located and returned to Ali Coglia. The caliph sternly told the merchant that it was good for him that he decided to confess and to return the gold; that otherwise he would have received one hundred floggings in addition to his sentence of ten years in prison. The caliph turned to the judge who had tried the case before and advised him to take a lesson from the child so that he would perform his duty more exactly in the future. Embracing the boy, the monarch sent him home with a small pouch full of gold pieces as a token of his admiration.

Reprinted with permission from "Absolutely Whootie: Stories to Grow By" at www.storiestogrowby.com. Adapted by Elaine Lindy from "The Story of Ali Coglia, a Merchant of Baghdad," a story from <u>The Arabian Nights' Entertainments</u> *by Reverend George Flyer Townsend (New York: Frederick A. Stoke, 1891, pp. 158-170).*

IDEA #48

Role Playing with Papier-Mâché Puppets

OVERVIEW: Students write a scene involving a character who displays trustworthy behavior, create papier-mâché puppets, and use the puppets to role-play the scene.

PREPARATION / MATERIALS:

- wheat paste
- newspaper
- scissors
- dishpan
- balloons
- paints
- paintbrushes
- petroleum jelly

PROCEDURE:

Tell the students you are going to have a discussion about trustworthiness. Ask them what makes a person worthy of trust. List their answers on the board, making sure to include these fundamental components of trustworthiness: *honesty, integrity, promise-keeping, reliability* and *loyalty.*

Invite the students to name people in their lives who are trustworthy. Ask them to explain how others know these people are worthy of trust. If they cite scenarios that proved someone was trustworthy, list these examples on the board. Then ask them to think of other examples (hypothetical scenarios) that would serve to demonstrate someone's trustworthiness. Add these to your list.

Divide the students into groups of at least three. Instruct them to write a skit for one of the situations on the board.

After they have written their skit, have them make papier-mâché puppets to represent the characters in it. Supply each group with balloons, petroleum jelly, dishpan, wheat paste mixture, scissors and newspaper strips.

Have them follow these steps to create the puppets:

1. Blow up a balloon and tie the end.
2. Cover the balloon with petroleum jelly.
3. Dip newspaper strips into wheat paste and put strips on the balloon until it is covered.
4. Add four or five layers of strips leaving the tied end uncovered.
5. Let balloons dry overnight.

One man with courage makes a majority.

— **Andrew Jackson**
19th-century American military hero and fifth U.S. president

6. Cut hole at tied end as big as second finger after the balloons are dried.
7. Supply each group with paints and brushes.
8. Paint puppet head to look like characters in skits.
9. Add materials to represent the puppets' clothing.

Set up an area where the students can perform the skits in front of the class. If possible, arrange for the students to perform their skits for younger children.

Procedure to make puppets from "Newsworthy Papier-Mâché Puppet Heads" lesson plan by Mary Beth Lewison, posted on the "AskEric Lesson Plans" website (www.ericir.syr.edu/Virtual/Lessons/Interdisciplinary/INT0049.html).

*N*o man

chooses evil

because it is

evil; he only

mistakes it for

happiness, the

good he seeks.

— Mary Wollstonecraft
19th-century
English novelist
("Frankenstein")

IDEA #49

Pointing Out Difficult Information Respectfully

> **OVERVIEW:** Students examine ways to respect someone even though they have an opinion or habit (smoking is the example here) with which they don't agree. (Note: Be clear with students that smoking is not only harmful to their health, but illegal at their age as well.)
>
> **PREPARATION / MATERIALS:**
> - resources to learn about the effects smoking has on the body
> - paper; pens or pencils

*M*orality,

when formal,

devours.

— Albert Camus
20th-century
Nobel Prize-
winning French
novelist

PROCEDURE:

Write "respect" on the board. Tell the students that this is one of the Six Pillars of Character, and ask them to share examples of how we show respect to others (following the Golden Rule, being tolerant of differences, using good manners, being considerate of the others' feelings, and dealing peacefully with anger, insults and disagreements). Encourage students to offer examples of specific actions that show respect.

Explain to the children that modeling these traits may be easy when we agree with the way a person acts and thinks, but that it becomes more difficult when others are behaving in a way we don't agree with. Discuss the difference between liking someone and respecting someone. Mention that sometimes respectful behavior means "agreeing to disagree" with others. Discuss what this means and list possible examples when this might be true. You might suggest: *When actions are clearly harmful or wrong — like vandalism or cheating on a test — we should have the courage to tell others that their behavior is wrong. However, in some situations someone may be doing something we don't agree with, but they may have a right to make that choice — even if we know it isn't good for them.*

Introduce the dilemma of dealing with an adult who smokes. Discuss the following:

- If we know about the harmful effects of smoking, do we have a responsibility to give this information to friends and family members who smoke? How do we do this while still showing respect for these people?
- Why do people smoke and how can this help us determine how we should respond to it?

Next, explain how we might respond respectfully to people who act in a way that we don't agree with.

1. Put yourself in the other person's shoes and think about how you would want someone to treat you if you were the one acting questionably.
2. Express your concern and show that you care about the person even if you don't agree with him or her.
3. Be as informed as you can about a topic or situation.
4. Offer constructive alternatives to the person.

To emphasize the importance that understanding an issue has in being respectful and in helping others whose behavior might be destructive, instruct students to research the effects of smoking and present their findings to the class.

For more information on discussing tobacco with young people, contact the Cooperative Extension of the University of Nebraska-Lincoln (Institute of Agriculture and Natural Resources), which has developed a "Doing What Counts!" anti-tobacco curriculum for the Nebraska state 4-H office:

4-H Youth Development
114 Agricultural Hall, P.O. Box 830700
Lincoln, NE 68583-0700
(402) 472-2805

My son, these maxims make a rule / An lump them ay thegither: / The Rigid Righteous is a fool, / The Rigid Wise anither.

— Robert Burns
18th-century
Scottish poet

IDEA #50

Respectful Listening

OVERVIEW: Students watch the instructor model good and bad listening skills and then attempt to emulate the positive ones.

PREPARATION / MATERIALS:
- paper; pencils or pens

PROCEDURE:

Ask students to explain why it is important to listen to other people. List answers. Suggest that listening promotes respect, tolerance, and helps to resolve problems between people. Ask the students to help you explain how listening accomplishes these things. Have them help you cite examples to back up your claims.

Tell them that you are going to demonstrate bad and good listening skills. Invite a student to join you in front of the class. Instruct the student to talk to you about a particular topic that he or she is interested in (and one that is appropriate for a class forum). Before he or she starts, instruct the students to pay attention to your behavior while the conversation is taking place.

As the student talks to you, display negative listening skills: let your eyes wander; show signs of being distracted and impatient (look at your watch if you are wearing one); interrupt frequently; reply to the student's comments with irrelevant responses; look fidgety; etc. Afterward ask the students to share what they observed about your example of disrespectful listening. List observations. Then ask the students to describe how your behavior affected the speaker and how it made him or her feel. Invite them to offer suggestions of how you could have been a better listener.

Next, have another student come up and talk to you. This time display positive listening skills: make direct eye contact; stand still; acknowledge comments; lean closer to the speaker at times; let the student finish speaking before asking a question; be sure your questions are relevant and follow the issue that the student addresses before you start speaking.

Have the students share their observations about how you were a respectful listener. Ask them how your good listening affected the speaker this time. Suggest that a good listener makes the speaker feel comfortable and confident and encourages him or her to share information.

More people are flattered into virtue than bullied out of vice.

— Robert Smith Surtees

Divide the students into groups of three. Assign one person the role of speaker, one the role of listener, and one the observer role. Tell them that the observer's job is to note examples of respectful and disrespectful listening. The observer should also coach the listener. Walk around the room and try to facilitate the process for each group.

After a specified amount of time, have the members of each group rotate positions and do it again. Continue this until each group member has had a turn being the speaker, observer and listener.

Once the activity is completed, instruct each group to write down what was hardest and what was easiest about being a respectful listener, and have them share these with the class.

Adapted from "Conflict and the Story of Our Lives," by Barbara Stanford. This activity is posted in the "Lesson Plans" section of the University of Arkansas at Little Rock College of Education website (www.ualr.edu/~coedept).

It is the characteristic of the magnanimous man to ask no favor but to be ready to do kindness to others.

— Aristotle
Greek
philosopher

IDEA #51

The Art of Peacemaking

> **OVERVIEW**: Students discuss how negotiation can solve conflict and then come up with solutions to problems in real life.
>
> **PREPARATION / MATERIALS:**
> ● paper; pencils or pens

PROCEDURE:

A man cannot be comfortable without his own approval.

— Samuel Clemens (a.k.a. Mark Twain) 19th-century American humorist and novelist

Ask the students to share examples of when they had a disagreement with a family member or friend and acted in respectful ways to solve the problem. Offer examples like sitting and talking, not yelling, not fighting, looking at things from the other person's point of view, etc.

Suggest that resolving disagreements often involves compromise. As a class, define what *compromise* means. Then explain that these are all examples of respectful *peacemaking*.

Discuss when we need to be peacemakers. Cite and list examples. Emphasize that respectful peacemaking involves "talking things out with each other" to create a peaceful solution. List and discuss these types of solutions:

- *Win-Win Solution* — both people talk things out so that each gets something they want. There is no "loser." It is peaceful.
- *Win-Lose Solution* — one person gains something at the expense of the other person. It reflects competition instead of compromise.
- *Lose-Lose Solution* — no one gets what they want. This isn't really a "solution," but sometimes this outcome is inevitable. As long as the conflict is settled peacefully and respectfully, then something has been achieved.

Pair the students up. Invite them to discuss conflicts that may occur at school or that they've heard about in the news. Instruct each pair to imagine one of these situations was peacefully resolved. Have them write how a solution was reached, who helped, and if it was a "win-win" outcome. Afterward, have them share their solutions. Suggest that we must act respectfully if we want to gain self-respect and earn the respect of others.

Inspired by an idea posted on the Ben & Jerry's "Kids' Conscious Acts of Peace" website (www.euphoria.benjerry.com/esr/cap).

IDEA #52

Responsible Pet Owners

OVERVIEW: Students identify responsible behavior and create rules to model it when caring for a pet.

PREPARATION/MATERIALS:
- paper; pencils or pens
- activity worksheet

SETTING: classroom, animal shelter or humane society (optional)

PROCEDURE:

Ask which students own pets, then ask: *Why do people own pets?* Discuss and list answers. Say: *For people to receive love and loyalty from their pets, they also have to give it. Having a pet, like having a family, takes a lot of responsibility.*

Discuss the different stages in the life of a dog or cat (e.g., puppy, full-grown dog, old dog). Discuss the different needs the pet has in each stage. Invite the students to list how the pet owner can meet those needs responsibly. Ask: *Why does caring for a pet take a lot of responsibility?* Discuss how being a responsible pet owner involves reliability, dependability and self-control (not losing one's temper when the pet misbehaves).

Say: *We have to follow certain rules to take good care of our pets.* Divide students into pairs. Pass out one activity worksheet to each pair and instruct them to write down rules that responsible pet owners should follow.

When the students have finished, have them share their answers with the class.

Plan a field trip to a humane society or animal shelter to reinforce the lesson.

Inspired by information on the website of the National Association for Human and Environmental Education (www.nahee.org).

*K*now the true value of time ... never put off till tomorrow what you can do today.

— **Lord Chesterfield**
18th-century English man of letters

IDEA #52 Worksheet: Responsible Pet Owners

Rules for Responsible Pet Ownership

Complete each statement with a different "Rule of Responsibility."

1. *Every good pet owner should:*

   Why?

2. *Every good pet owner should:*

   Why?

3. *Every good pet owner should:*

   Why?

4. *Every good pet owner should:*

   Why?

5. *Every good pet owner should:*

   Why?

6. *Every good pet owner should:*

   Why?

IDEA #53

Preparation, Perseverance, Patience ... and Butterflies

OVERVIEW: Students discuss the metamorphosis of a caterpillar into a butterfly and create a butterfly garden as an exercise in preparation, perseverance and patience.

PREPARATION/MATERIALS:
Consult books on the life cycle and habitats of butterflies, or visit these useful online resources: The Butterfly Website (www. butterflywebsite.com), Ask Jeeves for Kids (www.ajkids.com), The Butterfly Pavilion and Insect Center (www.butterflies.org) and Insect Lore (www.insectlore.com).

- flowers to plant
- planting trowels
- empty milk jug
- scissors
- (optional) drawing paper and markers for students to makes charts, diagrams, etc.

SETTING: Outdoor area protected from the wind, with moist soil and plenty of sunlight.

If you want

the rainbow,

you gotta put

up with the

rain.

— **Dolly Parton**
20th century
American
entertainer

PROCEDURE:

Begin by discussing how responsible people approach a task. Write these words on the board: *preparation*, *perseverance* and *patience*. Explain these terms and discuss the importance of taking a long-term look at a project — preparing an area to make it easy for things to fall into place, persevering to get the job done, and being patient about reaping the rewards of your labor.

Offer the example of how teachers teach a lessons: they first must prepare by doing research, by organizing the material, making handouts, etc. Then they must teach it, persevering even when they find it difficult to reach some students. If their first attempt at explaining something doesn't work, they have to come up with a second, and maybe even third or fourth lesson, incorporating new ways to present and share the information. They may have to add certain details to help students understand the subject.

Next, use the caterpillar-to-butterfly metamorphosis as an example. Explain how the caterpillar must prepare by finding the right environment for the metamorphosis to take place. (Most caterpillars are specific about the plants they feed on, so female butterflies must find a suitable caterpillar food plant on which to lay their eggs. Also, there must be enough sun, not too much wind, etc.) Photos and diagrams may help you illustrate this. Once the caterpillar hatches from an egg, it must prepare for the metamorphosis by consuming enough nutrients and finding a safe environment for the process to take place. Explain that the caterpillar has only a limited time to do this, so it must work hard and persevere if resources are not immediately available. Finally, encased in its cocoon, it must be patient for the process to reach completion.

You might provide reading and writing assignments to familiarize students with the butterfly, then present the task of preparing a garden for butterflies. Find a sunny, moist area that is protected from the wind. Have students plant different types of flowers and plants that provide food, shelter, and can act as a host for an adult female butterfly to lay eggs. To provide a drinking-water source for butterflies, cut the tops off a few milk jugs and fill them each with one to two inches of water.

After you've created the garden, tell the students that it is time for them to demonstrate patience, as they wait for butterflies to come. If the garden succeeds in attracting caterpillars and butterflies, offer the students time to observe the behavior and growth of the creatures. If no caterpillars or butterflies are found, discuss the need to accept circumstances that are not ideal. Assess why the butterflies did not come and offer students the chance to display their perseverance by taking measures to improve, or even replant, the garden.

T hings

work out best

for those who

make the

best of the

way things

work out.

— Anonymous

IDEA #54

Responsibility in Sports

OVERVIEW: Students discuss responsibility in team sport activities and then demonstrate it in a class relay-race.

PREPARATION / MATERIALS:

- slips of paper from activity sheet (one copy of all slips for each group)
- 4 baseball caps
- pencils or pens

PROCEDURE:

Prompt a discussion about responsibility in team sports. Ask: *What does it mean when people say we are good "team players"?* Field answers, then ask: *What responsibilities does a player have to the team he or she is playing for?* List answers. Then ask them what responsibilities a player has to the team he or she is playing against, and list answers. Be sure to include these components of responsibility in your discussion: *pursuit of excellence, accountability* and *self-restraint.* Ask students to offer examples displaying these qualities.

Next, introduce the relay race. Say: *Now, it's your turn to demonstrate some of the examples we've suggested. We're going to have a relay race.*

Divide them into two teams. Place two caps on each side of the room. Fill one cap with the slips of paper from the activity sheet. Instruct each team to stand next to the cap with the slips of paper in it.

Explain the rules: *When I say "responsibility," someone from each team will draw a slip of paper out of the cap, read it to his or her team and write the team's answer on the slip. Then this person will run to the opposite cap, drop it in, run back and tags another teammate to pick a new slip of paper from the cap. The first team to go through all the slips of paper is the winner.*

When the race is over discuss the process. Possible questions to ask include: *How did you show responsibility in the relay race? Why is being responsible important when playing sports? Why can you feel good even if you don't win?*

Adapted from an idea submitted by Mary Jo Williams, 4-H youth development specialist (4-H Youth Programs, University Extension, University of Missouri), based on an activity in the CHARACTER COUNTS! "Exercising Character" lesson plans.

*B*e happy.

Talk happiness. Happiness calls out responsive gladness in others. There is enough sadness in the world without yours.

— **Helen Keller**
20th-century Nobel Prize-winning American social activist and author

IDEA #54 Responsibility in Sports Activity Sheet

Responsibility in Sports: Pursuing excellence — doing your best

Example:

Responsibility in Sports: Persevering — finishing what you start

Example:

Responsibility in Sports: Being informed

Example:

Responsibility in Sports: Being on time

Example:

Responsibility in Sports: Being careful and safe

Example:

Responsibility in Sports: Modeling good habits

Example:

Responsibility in Sports: Working to do better

Example:

Responsibility in Sports: Doing what is right

Example:

IDEA #54: Responsibility in Sports Activity Sheet

Responsibility in Sports: Being accountable — taking the blame when it's due

Example:

Responsibility in Sports: Controlling your words

Example:

Responsibility in Sports: Controlling your temper

Example:

Responsibility in Sports: Waiting for rewards

Example:

Responsibility in Sports: Thinking long-term

Example:

● read up and reach out at www.charactercounts.org ●

IDEA #55

Fairness Discussion Points and Survey

> **OVERVIEW:** Students learn to examine aspects of fairness as they discuss real life situations.
>
> **PREPARATION:** none

*M*an's

capacity for

justice makes

democracy

possible, but

man's

inclination to

injustice

makes

democracy

necessary.

— **Reinhold Niebuhr**
20th-century German theologian and philosopher

PROCEDURE:

Review with students the "do's and don'ts" of fairness (listed at the front of this section). Ask students some or all of the following questions:

■ *Does fairness mean everyone gets the same amount, like an equal piece of pie? Does fairness mean enforcing the rules for everyone, even if it means losing a game? Is it possible to treat everyone fairly?*

■ *What does it mean to treat people equally? Give examples of equal and unequal treatment.*

■ *What does it mean to be open-minded? What does it mean to be impartial? What do these things have to do with fairness?*

■ *Is it possible to be fair without considering everyone who will be affected by your decision? Give an example.*

■ *Think of yourself as a coach. What would be the benefits of having athletes who played fair and treated others fairly?*

■ *Can you think of a situation in which it might be right to give someone a special advantage? Are there ever good reasons why there should be different consequences for the same offense?*

■ *How should you treat people who are not fair with you?*

■ *What are the benefits of people treating each other fairly?*

Direct students to conduct a survey in your school or community, asking questions such as: Do you think people are fair enough? What are some unfair acts that annoy you? What are some fair acts that you appreciate? Compile the results into a report and discuss.

Adapted from the discussion points and group activity ideas in the discussion guide for "In Search of Character," a video series produced by Elkind + Sweet Communications in association with **CHARACTER COUNTS!** *. See www.goodcharacter.com for more ideas from "In Search of Character."*

IDEA #56

A Tall Order of Fairness

OVERVIEW: Working as a team to complete a competitive task with limiting rules, the children learn what skills are necessary to play fair.

PREPARATION/MATERIALS:

- 40 straws (for each group)
- 20 paper clips (for each group)
- adhesive tape (for each group)
- scissors (one pair for each group)

PROCEDURE:

Explain that the lesson will focus on fairness. Reiterate key qualities of fairness. Then ask: *How do rules affect fairness?* Offer the students examples and have them come up with more. Next ask: *What types of situations make sets of rules hard to follow? Why?* Lead the discussion to the importance of teamwork and the influence of competition on fairness. Ask them to explain why people cheat. Then solicit examples of consequences for such behavior.

Introduce the task. Say: *We are going to complete a competitive task today to see who can build the tallest tower out of certain materials. However, there are certain rules and limitations.* Distribute materials and divide the students into four or five groups. Say: *Your group will have five minutes to design a tower and five minutes to build it. Every person in the group must be involved in the planning and building of the tower. Finally, you can only talk while you are designing the tower. Once you start building it, you cannot talk to one another. If you talk during the building stage, your group will have to start over and will lose any materials that have been used up to that point.*

Finally, ask: *What is the most important thing to remember?* After fielding answers say: *The most important thing is not to win but to play fair.*

Once the game is over, discuss the role of fairness in their tasks and what this taught them about solving problems fairly.

Adapted from an idea submitted by Mary Jo Williams, 4-H youth development specialist (4-H Youth Program, University Extension, University of Missouri System), based on an activity in "Boomerang! Character Education Program" (4-H Youth Development, Iowa State University, University Extension). Used with permission.

*I**deology is just an escape from thought.***

— John Kenneth Galbraith
20th-century North American economist, author and public servant

IDEA #57

Unfair Feelings

> **OVERVIEW:** Students experience unfair treatment and then react, leading to a discussion about the feelings of unjust actions and the process of arriving at fair solutions.
>
> **PREPARATION / MATERIALS:** none

Welcome

everything

that comes to

you but do

not long for

anything else.

— Andre Gide
20th-century
French novelist

PROCEDURE:

Before discussing fairness, implement several <u>unfair</u> activities or rules over the course of the day, such as:

1. Divide the class into two teams for a question-and-answer contest in a particular subject, but rig the contest so that one team gets all the easy questions and handily beats the other.
2. Allow one set of students to participate in an independent study period while requiring the other set of students to complete a laboriously specific worksheet or activity for a class period.
3. Pass out stickers or some other form of reward for good behavior, but purposely have less than the number needed for all students in the class.

Once students begin to notice and object to the unfair treatment, explain that these activities were designed to be unfair. Have the students express why they feel they were treated unfairly, and how it made them feel. Discuss the importance of fairness in school, and how this lesson might be applicable in other contexts (e.g., a workplace, a professional sports activity, a political matter, etc.).

Then discuss what kinds of problems result from unjust treatment. List them. Next, put the students into groups and have each group write a step-by-step solution to redress one of the resulting problems you listed. Have the groups share these with the class.

Ask the students to name specific types of behavior that are necessary for the solutions to be effective — and for the problems to be avoided altogether. Finally, invite them to offer one way they can help ensure a fairer environment in their school.

Inspired by "Justice, Is It Fair?" by Phyllis Muranaka, posted on the Organization For Community Networks Academy Curricular Exchange website (www.ofcn.org/cyber.serv/academy/ace).

IDEA #58

Caring for All in the Family

OVERVIEW: Students interview a family member and draw parallels between the growth and change of a family and the way we care for ourselves.

PREPARATION/MATERIALS:
- paper; pencils or pens
- markers
- glue (optional)

PROCEDURE:

Display a green tree leaf and a brown or multi-colored tree leaf. Ask: *How are these two leaves different?* Field answers. *Why do the leaves of certain trees change in different seasons?* Summarize their responses: *The leaves change because the conditions, including the weather, change. In order for the tree to keep growing, it has to adjust to the different conditions. It has to take care of itself in different ways.* Cite examples (e.g., when it is dry, the tree must store more water).

Next, say: *Families also work this way. As they grow and change — or the people in them grow and change — the way they care for themselves and others changes. What are some ways families grow and change?* Ask the students to cite examples (e.g., a child is born, a sibling leaves home, families move).

Ask: *When you were younger, what did your parents have to do to care for you? How did you care for yourself?* List answers. *These days, how do your parents care for you? How do you care for yourself?* Again, list answers. Reiterate that over time families change and grow along with the way we care for each other.

Instruct the students to interview a parent or guardian. Make sure they have their interview subject answer the following questions: *What main event — or events — have helped the family grow? How did you care for the family before the event? After the event? Why?* Instruct them to write a summary of the interview and to supplement it with photos, letters or artwork related to the event(s).

When they have completed the assignment, invite them to share their answers orally. (Of course, some of the information may be sensitive, so don't insist on this.)

Seek to do good and you will find that happiness will run after you.

— James Freeman Clarke

IDEA #59

Smile, You're on Caring Camera

OVERVIEW: Students focus on their actions and learn to model respectful behavior. To reinforce the lessons, their actions are documented.

PREPARATION/MATERIALS:
- camera (a polaroid or disposable camera may be easiest)
- copies of worksheet certificate
- bulletin board

*G*ratitude is

not only the

greatest of

virtues, but

the parent

of all others.

**— Cicero
(Marcus Tullius)**
Roman orator

PROCEDURE:

Discuss what it means to be caring and compassionate. (For a listing of the components of caring behavior, see definitions of the Six Pillars at the beginning of this book.)

Introduce the "caring camera." Say: *Now that we know how to show this kind of behavior, I thought it would be nice for us to document, as well as celebrate, the caring and compassion we show to one another each day. This camera is to be cared for and shared by all of us.* Discuss appropriate sharing behavior.

Ask the students if any of them is familiar with the TV show "Candid Camera." Discuss the concept of this show, then tell them that the "caring camera" will be used in much the same way: to catch people in the act when they don't know they're on camera.

Have the students take turns being "caring camera operators." Secretly designate a student to take three or four pictures in a predetermined amount of time (depending on how long you want to conduct this activity). Tell him or her to try to secretly take pictures of other students engaging in caring acts. Inform them that you will be keeping track of which pictures the students took. (You will probably want to keep a log for this purpose.)

Have the film developed and share the photos with the class. Discuss what kind of respectful, caring action is taking place in each photo. Then display them on a bulletin board. Present each child captured on the "caring camera" with a copy of the handout certificate.

Inspired by an idea in Lesson Plans for Character Education, *by Sharon Fincham, et al. (Manhattan, KS: The MASTER Teacher, Inc., 1998).*

Certified Caring

in action

was displayed by:

_____

_____

IDEA #60

Collecting Duffle Bags for Foster Children

OVERVIEW: Students are encouraged to appreciate aspects of their lives that they may take for granted. They show caring by organizing a duffle-bag-and-stuffed-animal drive for foster children.

PREPARATION / MATERIALS:
- empty duffle bag or suitcase (optional)

PROCEDURE:

Hold up an empty duffle bag or suitcase. Ask the students what purpose it serves and what kinds of items are often carried in it. List answers. Ask how people acquire a duffle bag or suitcase.

Ask how a homeless person would acquire a duffle bag. Discuss why owning one might mean a lot more to them. Also mention to them that many foster children who have to move frequently don't have duffle bags to move their possessions. Discuss what possessions many of us take for granted — not only all the items that we own, but the backpacks and bags we use to move them around. Tell the students that they can do something to help homeless people and foster children keep their possessions with them.

Indifference

is the essence

of inhumanity.

— **George Bernard Shaw**
20th-century Irish dramatist

Share one girl's success story: When nine-year-old Makenzie Snyder of Maryland heard that many foster children who are forced to move frequently use trash bags to transport their few possessions, she decided to do something about it: collect used suitcases and duffle bags and donate them to young people in need. So far, 1,000 kids in the area around Washington, D.C. have received suitcases (with a nice note and a stuffed animal inside) from Makenzie's brainchild, "Children to Children." The program recently received a grant to fund the purchase of duffle bags — and Makenzie was invited to the White House.

After the discussion, help the students organize a duffle-bag-and-stuffed-animal drive for foster children. After you have collected the bags and stuffed animals, have the students write letters to the young people and include one in each bag. Finally, contact Children to Children to arrange a pick-up or drop-off.

Children to Children
Attn: Makenzie Snyder
3262 Superior Lane, PMB #288
Bowie, MD 20715

Visit the Children to Children website at www.childrentochildren.org.

IDEA #61

Random Notes of Kindness

> **OVERVIEW:** Children offer a note of appreciation to a fellow classmate's guardian after discussing random acts of kindness.
>
> **PREPARATION / MATERIALS:**
> - envelopes (one addressed to each student's guardian)
> - paper; pencils or pens

PROCEDURE:

Have the students sit down in two or three rows and perform "the wave" by standing and sitting in sequence. After they have successfully performed it, say: *At sporting events like football and baseball games, it's common for the specta-tors to do "the wave." At first it may just be a few people, but eventually almost everyone catches on and joins in. It's like a chain reaction. One person does it, and then another, and another, and so on.*

Doing nice things for other people can work the same way. You might say that kindness is contagious. You treat someone with kindness, they feel hap-pier, and then they treat someone else nicely. When have you seen this hap-pen? Solicit responses and cite examples.

Next, ask the students to define the word "random." When they understand this word, ask them for examples of *random acts of kindness*. List their answers.

Show them the envelopes addressed to their guardians. Explain that once a week, you will randomly select an envelope, and each of them will write a brief note describing one nice thing they noticed about the student whose guardian will receive the envelope through the mail. (They do not have to sign their names.)

Pick one envelope and begin the process. Provide a few examples of the kind of appreciative words they might say in their notes.

Inspired by an idea from Larry Miller, Tennessee's state coordinator of National Random Acts of Kindness Week. His idea is posted on www.edmktsol.com/rak, one of several Random Acts of Kindness websites.

*M*en can

starve from a

lack of self-

realization as

much as they

can from a

lack of bread.

— **Richard Wright**
20th-century American novelist

IDEA #62

History's Heroic Citizens

> **OVERVIEW:** Students discuss various historical figures and explain why these people can be considered "heroic citizens."
>
> **PREPARATION/MATERIALS:**
> - slips of paper with names of historical figures on them
> - a hat
> - paper; pencils or pens

PROCEDURE:

If men were angels no government would be necessary.

— James Madison
18th-century American Founding Father; 19th-century U.S. president
(from the *Federalist Papers*)

Ask the students to define a "hero/heroine." Field and list answers. Then ask the students to define "good citizen." Compare the similarities between the traits involved in each definition. Discuss what famous people in history could be considered "heroic citizens" and why.

Divide the class into groups. Pull out the hat with slips of paper in it. Explain that each slip of paper contains the name of a historic citizen on it. Instruct each group to agree on and list three traits that prove the person was heroic. Make sure they explain why. When everyone is finished, have each group play charades to describe their figure's heroic traits.

Afterward, have each group read their actual answers.

Instruct them to research and write about the heroic citizens to more thoroughly prove their claims.

Submitted by Nat Cooper, director of the Center for Character Development at Lubbock Christian University (Lubbock, Texas).

IDEA #63

Community Calendar

OVERVIEW: Students discuss community membership and work together to create a calendar focusing on good citizenship. This calendar might be printed and sold for school fundraising, emphasizing a commitment to the school community.

PREPARATION / MATERIALS:
- legal-sized paper; pencils; markers; crayons;
- rulers
- paints and other art supplies (optional)

PROCEDURE:

Discuss the importance of caring for one's community, and the different needs of communities. Suggest that one of the communities students need to be responsible for and care about is their own school community. Have the students list ways these needs are met: by whom, how, etc. Mention the fiscal responsibilities associated with meeting all these needs. Ask students what improvements they would like to see at their school. Settle on an issue (by popular vote, if necessary) that the class will focus on to improve the school community.

Explain that the class is going to show their commitment to the school and make a calendar about good citizenship that can be sold to help raise money to support your school improvement project.

Divide the students into groups and have each group come up with a list of at least 10 things residents can do to improve the community. Develop a comprehensive list and divide these items evenly among the small groups.

Assign each a particular month (or months) of the calendar to create. Distribute several sheets of legal-sized paper to each group. Make sure they save one sheet for their final draft.

Have them place the paper vertically and divide it in half. Explain that the top half will display artwork that represents good citizenship, and the bottom half will display the calendar. (You might want to give them a sample page from a calendar to use as a model.)

Tell each group to incorporate the community-improvement tips from their list

This country will not be a good place for any of us to live in unless we make it a good place for all of us to live in.

— Theodore Roosevelt
19th/20th-century American adventurer and politician; Nobel Prize-winning U.S. president

in the boxes of the calendar. Have them show you a rough draft before they finish.

Compile all the groups' work and piece together the calendar. You can either photocopy it or make arrangements with a printing company to produce a large quantity to be sold to the entire school and community.

Use the funds you raise from the sale of these calendars to carry out your school-improvement project.

Inspired by the "Garden of Virtues" calendar by Christina Bondurant Keffler and Rebecca Ott Donnelli from Homegrown Inc. (www.virtuescalendar.com).

Without civic morality communities perish; without personal morality their survival has no value.

— Bertrand Russell
20th-century English mathematician and philosopher

IDEA #64

Shared Symbols and Values

OVERVIEW: Children reflect on and discuss the power of symbols and how they can be used to bring people together.

PREPARATION/MATERIALS:
- paper; pencils or pens

PROCEDURE:

Introduce the subject of symbols and the functions they serve. Say something like: *It would be hard to function efficiently as a society without signs and symbols. They represent values we share as a group. We are members of various groups — some very large like the nation, some very small like a club. Some symbols remind us of rules we are expected to know and follow. Some proclaim the authority of a particular office or government department (e.g., presidential seal, law-enforcement badge). Other signs, like product logos, are designed so that we remember a product and associate it with some positive feeling or characteristic. Religious communities have symbols that remind the faithful of their beliefs. And there are political symbols, like the flag of a country or a state.*

Ask: *What are some signs and symbols that you can think of?* (Write students' responses on the board; you might find it useful to organize these into categories.) Say: *What do these symbols and signs represent? What are the values they suggest?*

Then ask: *What about the Six Pillars of Character? What are those? Is there a symbol for those?* Draw on the board or otherwise display the CHARACTER COUNTS! logo:

Discuss how symbols can be used to unite a people. Discuss both the positive and negative effects of this. You might cite the example of the Tibetan flag, which the Chinese government has outlawed because this symbol legitimizes the idea of an independent Tibet.

A nation, as a society, forms a moral person, and every member of it is personally responsible for his society.

— **Thomas Jefferson**
18th-century American Founding Father, third U.S. president

Discuss citizenship as it relates to national symbols. Introduce the words *patriotism* and *jingoism*, which may involve blind allegiance to a national symbol such as a flag. Try to explain in simple terms the differences between these two words. Compare these with *citizenship* and *civic virtue*, which connote a deeper and more meaningful commitment to helping a community — even a global community.

Direct the students to create a symbol for good citizenship. When they are done, ask them to share their good-citizenship symbols with the whole class. Display these for all to see.

Art, like

morality,

consists of

drawing

the line

somewhere.

—G.K.
Chesterton
19th-century
English essayist
and poet

IDEA #65

Solution-Hero

OVERVIEW: Students analyze the decision-making skills of their favorite comic book superhero before creating their own.

PREPARATION / MATERIALS:
- paper; pencils, crayons and/or markers
- comic books (for students unable to acquire any)

*W*e cannot do everything at once but we can do something at once.

—Calvin Coolidge
20th-century U.S. president

PROCEDURE:

Introduce the topic: *Today we are going to discuss comic book superheroes. Who are some of your favorite superheroes?* List answers. *Why?* Discuss and list reasons. *Even though most of you suggested in one way or another that you liked these superheroes because they saved people from harmful individuals, I would like you to think about the ways they did that. What are some of the most common ways?* Again, list answers. Point out that many used violence or fighting to help others. Ask: *Why does this kind of action lack character?* Emphasize the long-term negative effects and consequences that can result from the choice to solve a conflict with violence.

Discuss how other people not involved in the fighting could have been affected. Ask what could happen as a result. Suggest that violent solutions have a domino-effect: violence begets more violence. Discuss the steps people can take to make good decisions without utilizing violence. Have the students jot down the core ideas:

1. Treat people the way you want them to treat you.
2. Make sure that when making a decision on how to act, these values are the primary consideration: *trustworthiness, respect, responsibility, fairness, caring* and *citizenship*. These should come before any other value.
3. Choose the action that offers the greatest good to the most people.

Next, instruct the students to analyze the character and decision-making skills of their favorite comic book superhero. Instruct them to list the values the superhero models. Then have them describe a particular action their superhero took that did not show any of the Six Pillars. Ask what the superhero could have done to demonstrate one or more of the Six Pillars. How could he or she have used the three keys to good decision making?

Once the students have completed the written task, instruct them to create their own superhero — a "solution-hero" — one with special "Six-Pillar powers" that exemplify good decision-making. Invite them to draw these solution-heroes and explain their Six-Pillar powers.

IDEA #66

Acronyms of Attributes

OVERVIEW: To reinforce the attributes of a person with good character, students create acronyms made up of words associated with the Six Pillars.

PREPARATION / MATERIALS:
- paper; pencils; markers or crayons
- copies of worksheets (one for each small group)

*P**arents**

wonder why

the streams

are bitter,

when they

themselves

have poisoned

the fountain.

— John Locke
17th-century
English
philosopher

PROCEDURE:

Define *acronym* for the students. Offer examples, such as: "T.R.U.S.T." for "To Respect Us Show Trust." Explain how each letter in the character trait is the first letter of each word in the saying. Make it clear that the saying and the acronym both encourage positive behavior.

Have the students help you create a couple of other acronyms from words related to the Six Pillars (don't use the same words as those that appear on the worksheet).

Then, divide the students into groups. Distribute an acronym worksheet to each group. Have them work together to create sayings for the acronyms and write them in the spaces provided. Tell them to see how many of the Six Pillars they can incorporate into each acronym.

Once you've reviewed their acronyms, instruct them to select one and make a poster of it to hang in the hallway.

Afterward, invite students to share their acronyms with the rest of the class.

_____

Inspired by a greeting card created and distributed by Keep Coming Back (Del Mar, CA).

IDEA #66 Worksheet: Acronyms of Attributes

S.H.A.R.E.

K.I.N.D.

J.U.S.T.

L.O.Y.A.L.

IDEA #67

Steps to Non-Violent Behavior

OVERVIEW: Students discuss nonviolent behavior and learn to solve conflicts without resorting to violence.

PREPARATION/MATERIALS:
● copies of worksheets (one for each student)

PROCEDURE:

Discuss why choosing not to fight can be difficult for some students. Then ask why it is important to avoid fighting. List answers. Invite the students to suggest ways people can avoid being violent. Again, list answers.

Next, distribute the worksheet and review the seven steps to help students handle violent behavior. You might want the students to write down the steps as you go over them to help them retain the information.

Have the students complete the worksheet. Once everyone has completed it, divide them into groups. Have them share their answers with each other and write down the answers they felt were best based on consensus. Inform them that they will have to share their group answers with the class

Afterward discuss how these steps may have helped them in past situations and how they will use them in the future.

Adapted from a lesson in Developing Character When It Counts: A Program for Teaching Character in the Classroom (Grades 6-8), by Anne L. Steele (Torrance, CA: Frank Schaffer Publications, 1999). This booklet is available from the **CHARACTER COUNTS!** national office, (800) 711-2670.

If there is anything we wish to change in the child, we should first examine it and see whether it is not something that could better be changed in ourselves.

— Carl Jung
20th-century Swiss founder of analytical psychology

IDEA #67 Worksheet: Non-Violent Behavior

1. **Don't lose your temper.**

2. **Learn to recognize "triggers" for fights.**
   List words or phrases that can start fights:

3. **Keep calm, and say to yourself: "The person is upset about something, and he or she is trying to use fighting to solve the problem."**
   List things you could do to avoid fueling this person's anger:

4. **Remember that part of this person is a decent person.**

5. **Try to talk calmly to the "decent side" of the other person.**
   List things you could say to this person:

6. **Recognize that sometimes you have to walk away.**

7. **Decide if the fight is really over.**
   List other people who could help settle this without violence if the fight isn't over:

Reprinted from Developing Character When It Counts: A Program for Teaching Character in the Classroom *(Grades 6-8)* *(Torrance, CA: Frank Schaffer Publications, 1999).*

THE SIX PILLARS OF CHARACTER

TRUSTWORTHINESS

- Be honest.
- Don't deceive, cheat or steal.
- Be reliable — do what you say you'll do.
- Have the courage to do the right thing.
- Build a good reputation.
- Be loyal — stand by your family, friends and country.

RESPECT

- Treat others with respect; follow the Golden Rule.
- Be tolerant of differences.
- Use good manners, not bad language.
- Be considerate of the feelings of others.
- Don't threaten, hit or hurt anyone.
- Deal peacefully with anger, insults and disagreements.

RESPONSIBILITY

- Do what you are supposed to do.
- Persevere: keep on trying!
- Always do your best.
- Use self-control.
- Be self-disciplined.
- Think before you act — consider the consequences.
- Be accountable for your choices.

FAIRNESS

- Play by the rules.
- Take turns and share.
- Be open-minded; listen to others.
- Don't take advantage of others.
- Don't blame others carelessly.

CARING

- Be kind.
- Be compassionate; show you care.
- Express gratitude.
- Forgive others.
- Help people in need.

CITIZENSHIP

- Do your share to make your school and community better.
- Cooperate.
- Stay informed; vote.
- Be a good neighbor.
- Obey laws and rules.
- Respect authority.
- Protect the environment

GOOD IDEAS

to Help _11- to 13-Year-Olds_ Develop Good Character

IDEA #68

What's the News?
Articles of Deception

OVERVIEW: Students analyze a current event involving some form of deception, and contemplate the far-reaching and long-term effects of dishonest behavior.

PREPARATION / MATERIALS:
- copies of current news articles about an event in which some form of deception was involved (one article for each group of five or so students)
- paper; pencils or pens

PROCEDURE:

Divide the students into groups and distribute a news article to each group. Instruct students to read the headline and first paragraph of their group's article. Then have them list questions and thoughts that come to mind based on the information just read. Share questions. List some of the better questions on the board.

Instruct them to discuss the questions listed on the board. Also, have them answer and discuss the following questions: *What motivated the accused to be dishonest? How did the accused carry out their dishonest actions? What resulted? Who was affected? How?*

Regroup as a class. Share and synthesize the answers, listing them on the board. Ask the students to explain what readers of this article can learn about honesty and why.

Then assign each group to monitor this story over the next several days to document and explain: *Who in the long run will be affected by the accused's behavior and what kind of impact will it have on society?* Have the students cut out or photocopy any articles that they read to answer these questions. Also, inform them that they will be presenting their answers to the rest of the class.

(You also could instruct the students to research a historical event involving dishonest behavior, having them explain the incident, answer questions and present his or her research to the class.)

Inspired by an idea posted on The New York Times *Learning Network (www.nytimes.com/learning).*

Courage is being scared to death — and saddling up anyway.

— Francis Marion (John Wayne)
20th-century
American actor

IDEA #69

Dishonesty: Clues and Consequences

OVERVIEW: Students discuss the kinds of dishonest behavior that their peers might display outside of school and then create hypothetical "whodunit" crime scenes of dishonesty. After the mysteries are solved, the students discuss the consequences of the crimes for all stakeholders (persons who were affected).

PREPARATION/MATERIALS:
● paper; pencils or pens

B e as you

wish to seem.

— **Socrates**
Greek
philosopher

PROCEDURE:

Ask the students to list types of crimes that occur in their community. Share answers. Then ask students to list types of crimes that young people often commit. Again, share answers.

Then suggest that another, less newsworthy type of infraction that occurs regularly: *dishonesty*. Ask the students to share examples of dishonest behavior. Have them explain what makes one act of dishonesty worse than another. Discuss the effects and consequences of the lies on the liar and on the ones being deceived.

Divide the students into groups of three. Instruct them to write an imaginative "whodunit" tale involving dishonesty. When they have finished, the rest of the class will have to figure out which character was dishonest. Instruct them to leave clues throughout their story that can help the other students identify the dishonest person. Remind them of the examples of dishonest actions you discussed earlier; these might be useful in helping them create scenarios.

On a separate sheet of paper, have them list who the liar is, how he or she was dishonest and why he or she acted that way. Also, have them list ways the dishonest behavior could have been avoided. Tell them that everyone in the group must contribute to the story.

Collect all the stories and redistribute them to different groups. Have each group do the following:

● Solve the caper and identify the dishonest culprit.
● Explain how the group arrived at its conclusions.
● List how events might have unfolded if the liar had been honest.

- Offer ways that characters in the story could have helped the liar be honest.

After collecting and reviewing the stories and responses, have each group share their "crime" and its solution.

(Optional) Have a law-enforcement official speak to the class about the types of consequences for certain dishonest actions. Have the speaker discuss methods that are used to help keep the individuals from repeating these offenses.

Inspired by the lesson plan "Fingerprint Detective" posted on the AskERIC Lesson Plans website (www.ericir.syr.edu/Virtual/Lessons/Interdisciplinary/INT0021.html).

Silently and imperceptibly, we grow strong or weak, and at last some crisis shows us what we have become.

—Bishop Westcott

IDEA #70

Myths Worthy of Trust

> **OVERVIEW:** After reading and discussing the myth of Phaethon, students create their own myth to teach a lesson about character.
>
> **PREPARATION / MATERIALS:**
> - paper; pencils or pens
> - crayons or markers (optional)

PROCEDURE:

Define a myth. Discuss the purpose myths serve. Explain that one of the reasons cultures create myths is to provide a code by which people can live. Suggest that myths serve to impart lessons about right and wrong.

Ask the students to share their knowledge of myths. Have them name gods and goddesses, describe stories, etc.

Share the myth of Phaethon with them, reading all or parts of the myth aloud. In this story, the sun god Helios has a son named Phaethon who wants to drive his father's fiery chariot across the sky. Helios had promised his son anything he wanted, and the father realizes that making this offer was a mistake: flying the fiery chariot is dangerous and Helios fears for his son's safety.

Still, he does not want to renege on the promise he made to his son. He warns Phaethon of the dangers. Phaethon listens to his father, and Helios trusts that his son will be cautious and fly safely.

As Phaethon flies the chariot into the sky, he encourages the horses to go dangerously fast until they begin to career out of control. He failed to heed his father's warning. The chariot races toward the stars and then dives toward the earth and sets it afire. To save the world, Zeus strikes Phaethon down with a thunderbolt and kills him and the horses.

After reading the myth, discuss what lessons this teaches about trustworthiness: *If his son had lived, would Helios been likely to trust Phaethon in the future? Who were the "stakeholders" in Phaethon's choice to fly recklessly through the sky (i.e., who suffered the consequences of his behavior)?* The stakeholders include: Helios, who lost a son; the horses, who were killed in the accident; Zeus, who was forced to strike Phaethon down; and those who were

The greatest of faults is to be conscious of none.

— **Thomas Carlyle**
19th-century
Scottish historian

injured or lost property as a result of the fire on the earth. Ask the students to suggest ways the fatal outcome could have been prevented.

Have the students create a myth of their own to teach a lesson about trustworthiness. As part of this assignment, you might have them research myths from different cultures that teach lessons about trustworthiness. Also, you might have them draw illustrations to accompany their stories, and then compile all of their work into a book.

*N*o one

ever became

extremely

wicked

suddenly.

— **Juvenal**
Roman writer

*I*n times of

stress, be bold

and valiant.

— **Horace**
Roman poet

IDEA #71

Objects of Diversity

OVERVIEW: Based on a Native American tradition, students share objects from various cultures in a circle discussion.

PREPARATION/MATERIALS:
- one object/photo from a specific culture (for each group)
- resource materials about a particular culture (optional)

An overdose of praise is like 10 lumps of sugar in coffee; only a very few people can swallow it.

— Emily Post
20th-century
American etiquette
advisor

PROCEDURE:

Ask students what defines a social group or a "culture." Mention customary beliefs and shared attitudes, values, goals, rituals and traditions. Then ask them to list various cultures from around the world. Field answers, and ask: *What makes each different and unique?* Solicit answers. Next, ask: *Do some individuals show a <u>lack</u> of respect for these cultural differences? How? Why? How can we properly show respect for cultural differences? Why is this important?* List answers on the board. Discuss ways to encourage respect for cultural diversity.

Present several objects (or photos of objects) from a particular culture (e.g., a Native American arrowhead, Jewish menorah, Greek or Turkish "worry beads"). Explain the significance of these objects to the particular culture being discussed.

Divide the class into groups. Ask them to sit in a circle. Distribute an object to each group. Say: *Each of you is to hold the object. While you are doing this, speak your mind about what the object means to you. What does it make you think of? How does it make you feel? The other participants in the group will model respect by listening carefully. No one is allowed to criticize, bicker, laugh or make other comments while the designated person speaks.*

Once everyone has had a chance to speak, discuss what the individuals learned from others in the group. Compare different points of view. Have the students suggest ways to use their knew knowledge to foster respect.

Adapted from an idea submitted by Tommy E. Laughlin, a counselor at Crystal Boarding School in Navajo, New Mexico.

IDEA #72

Bully Busting

OVERVIEW: Tolerance, respect and proactive behavior are modeled when students work to create a plan of action to eliminate the conflict between school bullies and their victims.

PREPARATION/MATERIALS:

A good resource for helping young people learn about and deal with bullying is How to Handle Bullies, Teasers and Other Meanies, *by Kate Cohen-Posey (Highland City, FL: Rainbow Books, 1995).*

- paper; pencils or pens
- Bullies Are Pains in the Brains, by Trevor Romain (Minneapolis, MN: Free Spirit Publications, 1997) or another book or article about bullying

PROCEDURE:

Ask the students to offer examples of common conflicts that arise in school (without using specific names). Ask and list on the board how these issues are best resolved. Have the students identify how these issues involve a lack of *respect*. List their answers on the board.

Introduce Bullies Are Pains in the Brains. Say: *One particular issue I would like to spend more time discussing is bullying.* Ask the students to help you define bullying. Then have them offer reasons why this behavior takes place between students. Ask: *What makes bullies pick on others?* List their answers. Be sure to mention these points:

- Bullies are often the victims of other bullies.
- Bullies pick on others because they feel strong and respected when they are putting others down. This may be their way of trying to regain the respect they lost when they were victims of another bully.
- People who tease others may do this because they feel like others ignore them; making others angry is their way of getting attention.
- Sometimes people act mean because they are angry, hurt or afraid.
- It may be hard to like someone who bullies and teases, but showing them respect and kindness may help them learn how people should be treated.

Next, read Bullies Are Pains in the Brains (or similar book on bullying). Instruct them to note suggestions the book makes for handling the issue. Afterward, go through each item and discuss ways to effectively combat bullying. Also discuss and promote solutions that offer positive outcomes for both parties.

Half the harm that is done in this world is due to people who want to feel important....They are absorbed in the endless struggle to think well of themselves.

— T.S. Eliot
20th-century Nobel Prize-winning American poet

Divide the students into groups. Instruct them to create a plan to discourage and resolve bullying issues in the school community. Explain that the solution must be *positive for the bully and his or her victim*. Have them explain in detail who would be involved in the solution, all the steps needed to actually implement it at the school, ways to enforce it, and how everyone involved would be affected.

Once everyone has completed the assignment, have each group present their bully-busting solutions. Take a class vote as to which seems most effective. Have the class work together to redefine the plan and prepare a detailed step-by-step plan for implementation. You may want to actually have the students work with faculty and administration to initiate the solution.

Inspired by How to Handle Bullies, Teasers and Other Meanies, *by Kate Cohen-Posey (Highland City, FL: Rainbow Books, 1995) and by ideas posted on www.familyeducation.com.*

We are the

people are

parents

warned us

about.

— Jimmy Buffet
20th-century
American
songwriter

IDEA #73

Respect Discussion Points and Survey

OVERVIEW: Students learn to examine aspects of respect as they discuss real life issues.

PREPARATION: none

PROCEDURE:

Review with students the do's and don'ts of respect at the front of this section. Ask students some or all of the following questions:

- *Are put-downs, name-calling, trash-talking, insults, or other verbal or non-verbal conduct ever appropriate in sports? When?*

- *Is it ever appropriate to cheer when an opposing team makes a mistake?*

- *How should we respond after a victory? After a loss?*

- *What is the difference between respecting and liking someone?*

- *How do you feel when someone judges you without knowing you or giving you a chance? How do you feel when someone calls you a name?*

- *How do you feel if you treat someone with respect and that person responds with rudeness? If someone insults you, should you insult that person in return?*

- *Do you think that people in our society are respectful enough? Why?*

- *Do you consider yourself to be a respectful person? Why, or why not? In what ways do you show respect to others?*

- *What are the benefits of people treating each other with respect?*

Direct students to conduct a survey in your school or community, asking questions such as: Do you think people are respectful enough? What are some disrespectful acts that annoy you? What are some respectful acts that you appreciate? Compile the results into a report.

All paths lead to the same goal: to convey to others what we are.

— **Pablo Neruda**
20th-century Nobel Prize-winning Chilean novelist

Adapted from the discussion points and group activities ideas in the discussion guide for "In Search of Character," a video series produced by Elkind + Sweet Communications in association with **CHARACTER COUNTS!**. *Please see www.goodcharacter.com for more ideas from "In Search of Character."*

IDEA #74

Seeing More Than the Tip of the Iceberg

OVERVIEW: Students discuss various facts and circumstances surrounding the Titanic disaster to better understand the importance of foresight and the role it plays in being responsible.

PREPARATION / MATERIALS:
- video and/or resource materials about the sinking of the Titanic (scenes from the James Cameron film "Titanic" may be useful, but the language and sexually explicit nature of some scenes may be inappropriate for younger viewers)
- paper; pencils or pens

PROCEDURE:

A dversity

introduces

a man to

himself.

—Anonymous

Ask students to define "foresight." Field and list answers. Emphasize that "foresight" requires *thoughtful preparation for the future.* Then discuss and list what is required to "thoughtfully prepare" (e.g., listening, researching, observing, considering causes and effects of actions). Think of an example relevant to students' lives (e.g., doing schoolwork, protecting your health, planning social events) and ask students to list the consequences of having and not having foresight. Discuss why having foresight plays an important role in being responsible.

Say: *One of the most famous examples of a lack of foresight is the sinking of an enormous ship called the "Titanic."* Briefly describe this historical event.

(If you will be showing excerpts from the video "Titanic") Say: *We are going to watch a few excerpts from the film "Titanic." But first I am going to divide you into groups and give each group the name of a character from the film. As you watch the film, it is your responsibility to look for examples of how your character showed foresight or a lack of foresight. List your examples on a sheet of paper. When we're finished watching the film, each group will share its observations.* Play excerpts and monitor the groups' efforts. (Pause the film to discuss scenes as necessary.)

Invite each group to share their examples. Then discuss the specific situations leading up to the sinking of the ship and how these could have been handled differently to avoid the disaster. Further research can be assigned on the topic.

Adapted from an idea submitted by Diane Young, a teacher at Gaithersburg Middle School in Gaithersburg, Maryland.

IDEA #75

Bill of Responsibilities

OVERVIEW: Reviewing the Bill of Rights, students name responsibilities that accompany these rights and then compose a "Bill of Responsibility."

PREPARATION/MATERIALS:
● paper; pencils or pens

What we call failure is not the falling down, but the staying down.

— **Mary Pickford**
20th-century American actor and entrepreneur

PROCEDURE:

Explain the Bill of Rights and its historical basis: The Bill of Rights is the first 10 amendments to the U.S. Constitution, which were adopted as a single unit in 1791. These amendments guarantee individual rights and place limitations on the power of federal and state governments. Forerunners to the Bill of Rights include England's Magna Carta (1215), the English Bill of Rights (1689) and Virginia's Declaration of Rights (1776). The Bill of Rights has binding legal force; the Supreme Court may void congressional acts or state initiatives if they conflict with the Bill of Rights.

Read through the amendments (see next page). As you go over each right, have students discuss the following:

1. *Who can enforce the right?*
2. *Toward whom is the right directed? How are they affected?*
3. *What responsibilities do the enforcers have to ensure the right? How?*
4. *What responsibilities do the citizens have to ensure the right? How?*
5. *What responsibilities can you take to ensure the right is not jeopardized?*

After you have covered each amendment and shared and listed answers to the above questions, ask the students to clarify the difference between a *right* and a *responsibility* for that right. List observations.

Divide the students into 10 groups (or five groups, if you don't have enough students). Assign each group an amendment (or assign two amendments to each of five groups). Have them list and discuss the key responsibilities individuals and good citizens can take to help ensure the right. Instruct them to write a "responsibility amendment" for a class "Bill of Responsibilities."

Collect each group's finished product and type up a final draft listing all of the "responsibility amendments." Copy and distribute to the class. (Depending on the quality of the finished product you may want to distribute it school-wide, or invite other classes to participate in drafting a Bill of Responsibilities for the school.)

Inspired by an idea in "Keeping the American Promise," Vol. 3, Issue 2, p. 2, (Los Angeles, CA: The American Promise, 1999).

IDEA #75 Handout: The U.S. Bill of Rights

Amendment I. Congress shall make no law respecting an establishment of religion, or prohibiting the free exercise thereof; or abridging the freedom of speech, or of the press; or the right of the people peaceably to assemble, and to petition the Government for a redress of grievances.

Amendment II. A well regulated Militia, being necessary to the security of a free State, the right of the people to keep and bear Arms, shall not be infringed.

Amendment III. No Soldier shall, in time of peace be quartered in any house, without the consent of the Owner, nor in time of war, but in a manner to be prescribed by law.

Amendment IV. The right of the people to be secure in their persons, houses, papers, and effects, against unreasonable searches and seizures, shall not be violated, and no Warrants shall issue, but upon probable cause, supported by Oath or affirmation, and particularly describing the place to be searched, and the persons or things to be seized.

Amendment V. No person shall be held to answer for a capital, or otherwise infamous crime, unless on a presentment or indictment of a Grand Jury, except in cases arising in the land or naval forces, or in the Militia, when in actual service in time of War or public danger; nor shall any person be subject for the same offence to be twice put in jeopardy of life or limb; nor shall be compelled in any criminal case to be a witness against himself, nor be deprived of life, liberty, or property, without due process of law; nor shall private property be taken for public use without just compensation.

Amendment VI. In all criminal prosecutions, the accused shall enjoy the right to a speedy and public trial, by an impartial jury of the State and district wherein the crime shall have been committed, which district shall have been previously ascertained by law, and to be informed of the nature and cause of the accusation; to be confronted with the witnesses against him; to have compulsory process for obtaining Witnesses in his favor, and to have the assistance of counsel for his defence.

Amendment VII. In Suits at common law, where the value in controversy shall exceed twenty dollars, the right of trial by jury shall be preserved, and no fact tried by a jury, shall be otherwise reexamined in any Court of the United States, than according to the rules of the common law.

Amendment VIII. Excessive bail shall not be required, nor excessive fines imposed, nor cruel and unusual punishments inflicted.

Amendment IX. The enumeration in the Constitution, of certain rights, shall not be construed to deny or disparage others retained by the people.

Amendment X. The powers not delegated to the United States by the Constitution, nor prohibited by it to the States, are reserved to the States respectively, or to the people.

IDEA #76

Monitoring Negativity

OVERVIEW: Made aware of the power of negative thoughts, students become more responsible for the effects that emotion has on their actions. (<u>Note</u>: If you want to incorporate a journal-writing activity into this assignment, be aware that sensitive information may be conveyed — and may require your responsible intervention.)

PREPARATION / MATERIALS:
- paper; pencils or pens

PROCEDURE:

Inform students that the class is going to figure out ways to avoid negative thinking in difficult situations. First discuss how thoughts and feelings influence actions.

Explain that thoughts and feelings are not *done to* us; each individual is *responsible* for his or her own outlook. Say: *It's our <u>responsibility</u> to be aware of what we think and feel, because thoughts and feelings are powerful. Of course, we have to be careful, because our thoughts and feelings influence our words and behavior.*

Part of being responsible is exercising self-control — not just over what we do, but over what we think and say. Unfortunately, many people don't know that, or they often forget it when their emotions get the best of them.

Discuss how we are responsible for our attitudes and behavior, and for cleaning up our environments by getting rid of negativity, in thought and word. Say: *It's not bad or wrong to be angry or have a negative thought about some situation or person, but the best way to deal with that is to confront the situation or person respectfully and directly. Don't let these thoughts eat away at you and cause you to treat others unkindly.*

Next, have the students highlight and discuss possible ways to constructively combat negative feelings in specific situations. Here are some quotes you might use to enrich and enliven the discussion:

"Anger is never without a reason, but seldom a good one." — Benjamin Franklin

*Y*ou can tell the size of the man by the size of the thing that makes him mad.

— **Adlai Stevenson II**
20th-century American politician

"Anyone can become angry. That is easy. But to be angry with the right person, to the right degree, at the right time, for the right purpose, and in the right way — this is not easy." — Aristotle

"You can tell the size of a man by the size of the thing that makes him mad." — Adlai Stevenson

"I shall allow no man to belittle my soul by making me hate him." — Booker T. Washington

Direct the students to make more of an effort to notice persistently negative thoughts or feelings that they have, what prompts them, and how they react to them. Instruct them to seek out constructive ways to deal with anger and other negative feelings, such as keeping a daily journal to monitor their negative emotions: what affects them, when, why and how they can turn them into positive thoughts (see note in overview).

We tend to think that being unhappy leads people to complain, but it's truer to say that complaining leads to people becoming unhappy.

— Dennis Prager
20th-century American radio host and author

IDEA #77

Through the Eyes of Another

> **OVERVIEW:** The children read a story with a situation that involves an issue that various characters might perceive differently. They reflect on and discuss the importance of seeing an issue from all sides before making a judgment.
>
> **PREPARATION / MATERIALS:**
> - copy of a short story that teaches a moral lesson (the story should involve several characters who might have different perspectives, but it should be told from the perspective of one character)
> - paper; pencils or pens

PROCEDURE:

Present this scenario: *A student is playing catcher in a softball game. Another student on the opposite team runs to home plate after his teammate hits the ball. As the runner slides into home plate, the catcher catches the ball and tags him. The runner says he is "safe." The catcher says he is "out." Fans sitting on one side agree with the runner. Those on the other side agree with the catcher. Who is correct?*

Solicit answers. Then explain: *Either of the players might be correct because they saw the throw from different points of view.* Ask the students to help you define "point of view." Then ask: *How could each player act more fairly if he had considered that everyone has a different point of view?* Field answers. Suggest: *The players might have been more willing to accept the other's opinion. Or they could have decided to have the hitter bat again.*

Say: *Everyone has his or her own view of things. Sometimes things are clearly right or wrong, but it is important to learn as much as possible about an issue and look at it from all angles before making a judgment.* Tell them you are going to read a story that is told from one point of view, then say: *Afterward, I am going to ask you to write the same story from the point of view of another character in story.*

Read the story aloud and then discuss what was learned from the experience. Decide who was treated most fairly and why. Discuss what was right and what was wrong in the story.

Next, instruct each student to write the same story from another's point of view. Tell them to explain what the character learned from the experience. Invite students to share their stories with the rest of the class.

Until he extends his circle of compassion to all living things, man will not find peace.

— **Albert Schweitzer**
20th-century Nobel Prize-winning German mission doctor and theologian

● read up and reach out at www.charactercounts.org ●

IDEA #78

Mediation Matters

> **OVERVIEW:** Students learn and role-play a mediation procedure to learn about resolving conflicts fairly.
>
> **PREPARATION / MATERIALS:**
> - paper; pencils or pens
> - copies of handouts (one for each student)

PROCEDURE:

If we are

to reach real

peace in this

world, we

shall have

to begin with

the children.

— Mohandas Gandhi
20th-century Nobel Prize-winning Indian civil rights leader

Ask the students to explain the purpose of medicine. List answers. Say: *Medicine can make people feel better, but it is not the only way to heal them. What are some other ways people can be healed?* Again, list answers.

Write the word *mediation* on the board. Have the students help you define the word. (To help them out, you might think of some sentences using this word.) Explain that mediation is a process by which one party helps other parties who are in conflict resolve their differences. Ask the students to cite examples.

Distribute the handouts. Explain that the handout is a step-by-step guide to mediating. Read it aloud together. Ask students what they notice about these steps. Suggest that the process requires good listening, fair opportunities to voice opinions, compromise, signed contracts, and follow-up to see if people are adhering to the bargain. Ask the students how this type of problem-solving might be more fair than other ways. List answers. Discuss how mediation can help prevent future conflicts.

Divide the students into groups of three. Have two students in each group portray characters from a popular book or movie who have a conflict needing mediation. (They can also role-play scenarios that arise in the school setting.) Have the third person act as the mediator. Instruct the groups to script their mediation process and perform it in front of the class. Invite the rest of the class to offer feedback about resolutions.

Adapted from ideas in "Conflicts and the Story of Our Lives," a teaching unit by Barbara Stanford (University of Arkansas at Little Rock, Teacher Education Department, 1996) posted on www.ualr.edu/~coedept/bs/AHCLIT.html.

IDEA #78 Handout: Mediation Matters

Use the following guidelines for mediating conflicts:

(The mediator and both parties must understand and agree to these three conditions if the mediation process is to be productive.)

1. The mediator will make sure **both** parties want to solve their problem.

2. The mediator will make sure **both** parties listen carefully and stand in the other's shoes.

3. The mediator makes sure **both** parties are willing to explain what they want the other to do differently.

*(The mediator needs to help the parties offer **positive** language and solutions throughout the rest of the steps.)*

4. The mediator asks one person to explain what he or she wants the other person to do differently.

5. Once this person has finished speaking, the mediator asks the listener to summarize the speaker's explanation.

6. The mediator then follows the same two steps for the other party.

7. The mediator then has each party come up with solutions to the problem. *(Keep them practical and realistic)*.

8. Discuss what compromises each party must make, and try to reach an agreement. Once an agreement has been reached, write it out and have both parties sign it.

9. The mediator reminds the parties that there is often no quick fix to disputes, and changes in behavior take time.

These steps based in part on ideas in "Conflicts and the Story of Our Lives," a teaching unit by Barbara Stanford (University of Arkansas at Little Rock, Teacher Education Department, 1996) posted on www.ualr.edu/~coedept/bs/AHCLIT.html.

IDEA #79

Fair Game: Playing by the Rules

*W*hen

things go

wrong, don't

go with them.

— **Elvis Presley**
20th-century
American
entertainer

*E*ndurance

is nobler than

strength and

patience than

beauty.

— **John Ruskin**
19th-century
British critic
and author

OVERVIEW: After discussing the function that rules play in society, students create their own games with specific rules.

PREPARATION / MATERIALS:
- various small objects from your classroom or activity area (e.g., erasers, chalk, pens, paper clips, staplers, etc.). Note: these should be different for each group.
- paper; pencils or pens

PROCEDURE:

On the board list several types of games the students might play. Have the them explain the object of each game. Ask: *What helps you have fun while you are playing?* After soliciting answers, say: *One key element is a set of rules that all the players must follow.* Discuss the rules for one of the games. Ask: *How do these rules help?* List their answers. Say: *Rules allow everyone to start from the same place, so no one has an advantage. They also help promote a safe, orderly and respectful atmosphere enabling players to concentrate on having fun and winning. What happens when players don't follow the rules?* Have the students cite specific examples from the games you listed on the board. Discuss the conflict and disrespect that can result when players violate rules. On the board, list the effects of breaking rules (e.g., mistrust, resentment, fighting, winning unfairly, etc.).

Next, divide the students into groups. Distribute various objects to each group. Explain: *Rules are not created quickly. They involve careful thought and planning to be sure that everyone is treated fairly and has the same opportunities.*

Your task is to create a fair game using the objects in front of you. You must explain the object of the game and write down all its rules. Make sure to include penalties for the players who violate the rules. Have them title their game and prepare to teach the rest of the class how to play it.

After each group has shared its games with the class, have the students compare the function of their games' rules with the function of school and community rules. Ask the students to explain how they know when a rule is positive or unfair. Discuss how unfair rules can be changed.

Adapted from "Playing by the Rules" in <u>Character Education in America's Schools</u>, *by Terry Akin, et al. (Torrance, CA: Innerchoice Publishing, 1995). Used with permission.*

IDEA #80

Caring Artifacts From The 21st Century

OVERVIEW: Students view objects in their daily lives as instruments of a caring society. They discuss compassion and how they can display it.

PREPARATION / MATERIALS:
● paper; pencils or pens

PROCEDURE:

Ask the students to define *artifact* (something created by humans usually for a practical purpose; an object remaining from a particular period). Discuss what people can learn about cultures from artifacts. Next, ask students what kinds of objects are lying around their bedrooms (books, snacks, shoes, etc.). Ask them to define their uses. List answers.

Next, suggest that the listed objects are useful in a different way: as instruments of *caring*. Ask the students how this is possible (e.g., a comic book can be read to a younger sibling). Encourage them to be more specific than simply saying, "You can share it."

Then say: *Sometimes we are so used to seeing objects in one way that we forget they have other uses. Some of the most helpful ideas in society origi-nated from individuals who took the time to see things in a different way.* Cite examples.

Next introduce the task. Say: *Pretend a thousand years have passed. You are an alien who has discovered five present-day "artifacts" from your room in a box labeled "Care Kit." Write an essay explaining what the objects are and how they might have been used to show caring and compassion toward others. Remember, the alien will not know the meaning of caring or compas-sion until you explain these terms.*

When they are done, invite the students to share their essays with the class.

Provision for others is the fundamental responsibility of human life.

— Woodrow Wilson
20th-century U.S. president

● read up and reach out at www.charactercounts.org ●

IDEA #81

Caring Situations

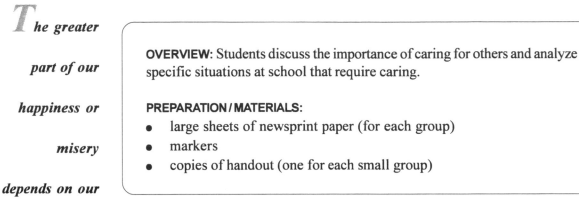

*T*he greater

part of our

happiness or

misery

depends on our

dispositions,

and not our

circumstances.

**— Martha
Washington**
18th-century U.S.
First Lady

OVERVIEW: Students discuss the importance of caring for others and analyze specific situations at school that require caring.

PREPARATION / MATERIALS:
- large sheets of newsprint paper (for each group)
- markers
- copies of handout (one for each small group)

PROCEDURE:

Discuss the importance of caring for others, noting that all people want to know that others care about them. You might say: *We not only want to know others care, we want them to show they care.*

Explain that caring consists of two aspects: being concerned about something and doing something about it. Explain that everyone sometimes needs support and assistance. Emphasize that people who help *just because they want to* do so because of their caring nature.

Divide the class into groups. Instruct them to designate a "chairperson," "recorder" and "spokesperson." Distribute the handout listing "caring situations" to each group. Inform them that the activity will challenge how they decide to handle specific situations at school that call for caring. Instruct them to avoid mentioning actual people who are involved in similar situations in their own lives. Assign three or four of the situations to each group. Give them 15 minutes to decide as a group how they should respond. Have them write down their caring responses with a marker on the newsprint paper so that they can show the rest of the class.

*S*haring

money is what

gives it value.

— Elvis Presley
20th-century
American
entertainer

Have each group present its responses. Then post their newsprint paper in the front of the room. Ask the rest of the class to offer comments on the group's caring solutions. Once every group has shared its responses, congratulate the students for acting in a caring manner by working well together. Invite the students to turn to one other person in the room and tell them what they will do in the next week to be more caring in school. Finally, ask students to share their commitment to more caring behavior with the whole class.

Reprinted from "Exercising Character in School," developed by the Louisiana Cooperative Extension Service (Louisiana State University Agricultural Center, 1999). Visit their website at www.agctr.lsu.edu/wwwac.

IDEA #81 Handout: Caring Situations

Describe what a <u>caring</u> person would do in the following situations. (Remember, an <u>ethical</u> person tries to make his or her behavior reflect <u>all</u> of the "Six Pillars of Character" — trustworthiness, respect, responsibility, fairness, caring and citizenship.)

1. A new student has started school and doesn't know anyone.

2. One of your teenage friends uses drugs or drinks alcohol.

3. One of your classmates didn't make a school team and feels bad.

4. One of your fellow students has been upset for several days.

5. Your friend's boyfriend or girlfriend is secretly dating someone else.

6. Someone vandalized the school, and you know who did it.

7. One of your classmates is always left out of social activities.

8. A friend's uncle died recently.

9. It is the holiday season and parents of some fellow students have been out of work for a long time because a local factory closed down.

10. A fellow student has a serious disease.

11. You hear some students gossiping and putting down other people.

12. One of your teachers is upset and sometimes cries during class. You have heard that she and her husband are getting a divorce.

13. A classmate must pass the next math test to pass for the year.

IDEA #82

Harmful Words

> **OVERVIEW**: Students discuss angry feelings underlying the hurtful statement "I hate you!" They discuss how these words can have harmful consequences and offer solutions for making more productive, caring statements.
>
> **PREPARATION / MATERIALS:**
> ● paper; pencils or pens (optional)

Values are like fingerprints, Nobody's are the exactly the same, but you leave 'em all over everything you do.

— Elvis Presley
20th-century American entertainer

PROCEDURE:

Present a scenario that models a conflict causing one of the angry participants to utter "I hate you!" Example: A mother refuses to let her daughter go to a party at her friend's house. The daughter gets angry and yells this hurtful phrase. The words harm the relationship.

Ask the students to offer other classroom-appropriate examples of when people say "I hate you" without really thinking. List these examples on the board. Then ask them to think about what feelings these people might have been experiencing when they said this. Note these feelings next to the corresponding situations on the board.

Ask: *How do you think the people on the receiving end of these words felt?* Go through the list of examples and note the students' answers. Next, ask the students to help you explain what the people who said the hurtful words really meant to say when they blurted out the uncaring remarks. Again, list their answers on the board. Suggest that anger is not a *wrong* feeling, but that impulsive outbursts (like "I hate you!") have consequences. Ask them to share some possible consequences and suggest that there is no real benefit for the person who says this. Then say: *If the people in these examples had chosen more accurate words to communicate the reasons they were angry, they might have helped the situation and been less hurtful.* Present several ways that the daughter in your opening example could have done this (e.g., "I am upset that you won't let me go to the party," etc.).

Divide students into groups. Assign one of the situations on the board to each group. Instruct them to come up with at least five ways the person who said the hurtful words could have spoken more accurately, and caringly, about his/her feelings. Inform them that they will have to share how the situation could have been avoided if the parties had told each other about their feelings prior to the heated exchange. Reiterate the need to understand why we are angry and the importance of choosing positive, precise words to communicate those feelings.

Inspired by "I Hate You!" an article by Elizabeth Pantley posted in the "Experts' Advice" section of the ParentsTalk website (www.parentstalk.com). This article was excerpted from Perfect Parenting: The Dictionary of 1,000 Parenting Tips (NTC/Contemporary Publishing Group, 1999).

IDEA #83

Safety by the Dozens

OVERVIEW: Students compare their experience of trying to keep an egg from breaking with the fragility of maintaining a healthy community.

PREPARATION / MATERIALS:
- drop cloth or large piece of plastic
- one egg for each team of four students
- 25 straws for each team of four students
- masking tape

PROCEDURE:

Ask the students to define and list the characteristics of an egg. Compare those qualities to a community. The goal is to suggest that an egg is fragile and requires care and support to keep it from breaking so that it can provide life (or nourish our bodies). Then ask them to explain how a community can be fragile and why we should care about it. Next inform them that they are going to practice the skills of saving a community by saving an egg.

Divide the class into teams of four with a designated work area. Give each group an egg. Explain that the egg represents a member of their community. Say: *Each member of a community needs to be protected, but that can be difficult. How do communities protect individual members?* Solicit responses and discuss.

Inform each team that they have seven minutes to create a device to keep the egg safe when it is dropped from a designated height (say, the height of your waist). They can only use the resources provided. Distribute the straws and masking tape.

After each team explains their finished product, one person from the team drops their egg from a designated height onto their egg-catching device. (Place a drop cloth under the device in case it doesn't manage to keep the egg intact.)

Afterward, discuss what challenges they faced keeping the eggs safe. Ask: *What challenges would you face keeping your community safe? What responsibility do you have to the community? How and why?*

Education makes a people easy to lead, but difficult to drive; easy to govern, but impossible to enslave.

— **Omar N. Bradley**
20th-century American general

Adapted from an idea submitted by Mary Jo Williams, a 4-H youth development specialist (4-H Youth Program, University Extension, University of Missouri System). This is based on an idea that originally appeared in <u>Adventures in Peacemaking: A Conflict Resolution Activity Guide for School-Age Programs</u>, by William J. Kreidler and Lisa Furlong (Hamilton, MA: Project Adventure, 1996).

IDEA #84

Character Maps

> **OVERVIEW:** Honing research skills and geographical knowledge of our nation, students create maps displaying town names associated with the Six Pillars.
>
> **PREPARATION / MATERIALS:**
> Students should have access to a library or the World Wide Web to conduct research.
> - drawing paper; pencils and markers
> - a map of the United States
> - atlas or almanac

PROCEDURE:

*Y*ou can

never solve

a problem

on the level it

was created.

— Albert Einstein
20th-century Nobel Prize-winning Swiss physicist and mathematician

Explain that good citizenship involves awareness of our environment. Have the students help you list ways they can become more aware of their national environments (e.g., reading newspapers, watching the news on TV, learning about the country's history, its voting process, etc.). Then suggest that gaining geographical knowledge is also a way to learn about a community. Ask the students to explain how and list their answers.

Display a map of the United States. Have the students point out the elements that make up a map. Ask where someone could find information to put on a map (the World Wide Web, maps in a library, etc.). Show them how to find specific places using the index in an atlas or almanac.

Divide them into groups. Instruct each group to create a map of a specific state or of the United States. Explain the exercise: *Not only are you going to become more knowledgable citizens, but you are going to encourage good citizenship with these maps. Each will display the geographical location of towns whose names are somehow related to the Six Pillars of Character — trustworthiness, respect, responsibility, fairness, caring and citizenship. Also, you may identify on your map towns, streets or other landmarks that share the names of people whose actions can be associated with the Six Pillars.* Cite an example such as: *Lincoln, Nebraska, can be associated with trustworthiness because Abraham Lincoln is known for having a great deal of integrity.* Designate a specific amount of time to complete the "character maps."

Once the maps are completed display them in a prominent location.

Inspired by <u>All Over the Map</u>, by David Jouris (Berkeley, CA: Ten Speed Press, 1994), a collection of maps based on themes and word groups.

IDEA #85

And the Survey Says . . .

> **OVERVIEW:** Students prepare and conduct a survey about a community issue, then send the results to the person or agency connected with the issue.
>
> **PREPARATION / MATERIALS:**
> - paper; pencils or pens
> - copies of activity sheets (one for each small group)

PROCEDURE:

Discuss with the students an issue at school or in the community. Then pose a related question to them, giving them the option to agree, disagree or declare that they are undecided by raising their hands. Count the number of hands raised for each answer. Draw a table on the board to display the totals for each option. Then calculate the percentages for each response (optional).

Explain that they have just participated in a survey. Ask them to explain what a survey is, what purpose it serves and who takes surveys. List answers to these questions on the board.

Explain that they too can take surveys. Say: *As a responsible citizen, you take interest in issues that can help or hurt the community. A survey is one way for you to find out information about a particular issue in the community: how people think and feel about it, and what they would like done about it. While you may not agree with the results, you can use the information to help you figure out what kind of action you need to take to make sure the community's best interests are served.*

Divide students into groups of three. Distribute and explain the activity sheet. Tell them to use this as a model for their assignment.

Have each group pick an issue in the community they are concerned about and create a survey of four or five related questions. Help each group fashion respectful, objective questions. Tell them that they will create a table charting the results in percentages after they have polled people.

Explain the importance of safety and accuracy; specifically, be sure to discuss: acquiring proper permission to be in certain areas, being safe (not entering respondents' houses if going door-to-door; taking a supervisor along), asking questions

*T*he true *test of* civilization is not the census, nor the size of cities, nor the crops – no, but the kind of man the country turns out.

— Ralph Waldo Emerson
19th-century American essayist, public philosopher and poet

respectfully, bringing enough supplies, and remaining calm and polite if people object to or disagree with any part of the survey.

After all groups have analyzed and shared their results, have them locate and send their survey results to an agency or individual who can use the information to constructively act on the issue in question. (Of course, the students' surveys will not be "scientific" or statistically sound, and you should explain this to them. Make them aware that statisticians do a great deal of work to ensure that their methodologies are legitimate and that their results are representative of a specific community or demographic.)

Adapted from "Power Surveys," an activity in The Kid's Guide to Social Action *by Barbara A. Lewis (Minneapolis, MN: Free Spirit Publishing, 1998, pp. 52-53). Used with permission.*

No great

deed is done

by falterers

who ask for

certainty.

— **Mary Ann Evans (a.k.a. George Eliot)**
19th-century English novelist

IDEA #85 Activity Sheet: And the Survey Says . . .

<u>Survey Goal</u>: To find out how people feel about the town offering recycling bins to accompany trash disposal and pick up for homeowners.

<u>Number of Adults Surveyed</u>: 75

<u>Possible Answers</u>:   **SA** – Strongly Agree
                    A – Agree
                    D – Disagree
                    U – Undecided
                    SD – Strongly Disagree

<u>Opinion Survey Questions</u>:

_____ 1. Currently, I recycle most of my glass, paper and plastic products.

_____ 2. Currently, I don't recycle most of my glass, paper and plastic.

_____ 3. If the town provided a recycling basket along with the trash cans for waste pickup, I would recycle more of my glass, paper and plastic.

_____ 4. If I had to pay more to the city government to receive a recycling basket with my waste pickup, I *would not* mind.

_____ 5. If I had to pay more to the city government to receive a recycling basket, I *would* mind, but I would still recycle more of my glass, paper and plastic.

	SA	A	U	D	SD
1	10%	20%	15%	50%	5%
2	20%	48%	12%	12%	8%
3	60%	20%	10%	6%	4%
4	15%	33%	27%	15%	10%
5	54%	22%	16%	7%	1%

What do these results suggest? Why?

IDEA #86

Popular Songs

OVERVIEW: Students share and discuss popular songs that contain positive messages and then create their own lyrics focusing on one of the Six Pillars.

PREPARATION / MATERIALS:
- portable CD/tape player, CD or tape with a popular song containing a positive message
- paper; pencils or pens

PROCEDURE:

*W*ith our

thoughts

we make

the world.

— **Buddha**

Ask students to explain why they listen to music. Field answers and discuss how various types of songs affect people's emotions.

Say: *Now I am going to play a popular song for you.* Share the title and artist. (Try to pick a song that will appeal to the students.) *While it is playing, I want you to listen for and jot down any words you hear that are related to the Six Pillars of Character: trustworthiness, respect, responsibility, fairness, caring and citizenship. Also note how the song makes you feel.* Before playing the song, have them write the six words on a paper, with enough room under each word to list appropriate song lyrics.

Play the song. Then collect students' papers and, based on student responses, list key words and phrases on the board.

Then ask students to share how they felt after listening to the song. Ask the students to suggest ways music can encourage constructive behavior.

As a homework assignment, instruct the students to select a popular song that offers a positive message related to one or more of the Six Pillars. Have the students bring the song to class, share it, and explain which of the Six Pillars is (are) promoted in the song and what positive messages are conveyed. Then have them offer examples of constructive behavior that could result from listening to the song.

Once everyone has shared his/her song, divide the students into groups of three or four. Instruct them to pick a song and create new lyrics for it, focusing on one of the Six Pillars of Character. Invite them to share their creations with the class.

Adapted from an idea submitted by Danette Townsend, adolescent and family director at the Mountainside YMCA in Albuquerque, New Mexico.

IDEA #87

Problem Solving Contest

OVERVIEW: Groups of students work together as a team to solve problems and then "perform" their solutions in front of parents and peers, highlighting good character traits that are required.

PREPARATION/MATERIALS:
Each group of students decides what materials are needed.

PROCEDURE:

Ask students to define *cooperation* (people working together for common benefit). Next, ask them what skills are necessary for cooperation to take place. List these on the board. Then ask them what skills are necessary to solve problems effectively (e.g., respect, responsibility, fairness, deduction, sharing, listening, planning, etc.). List these also. Have the students explain why these skills help build character.

Divide the students into groups. Explain that they will have to solve a particular problem in an allotted amount of time. (This contest can take as long as you feel is necessary for them to produce a solution.) Present several challenging scenarios. Allow them to choose one to solve. Some examples might be: students must find a way to mail an egg so that it arrives without being broken; students figure out a way to determine whether their class is getting the recommended daily allowance of a specific vitamin; students create and describe a type of creature that can best survive on a newly discovered planet where the wind constantly blows in excess of 180 miles per hour at a temperature below freezing; students determine the quickest walking route with the least amount of steps from one specific destination to another (that you determine).

Once the contest deadline arrives, the groups set up, demonstrate, or present their solutions to peers and parents. Each group is interviewed by you or a committee of teachers to explain what character skills were needed in the process to figure out a solution. The best solution should be judged on the cooperative effort considered and displayed in the process of discovering their solution.

Inspired by "Cooperative Contests" by Marlynn Clayton. This was the "Article of the Month" (January 1999), posted on The Responsive Classroom website (www.responsiveclassroom.org).

The question for the child is not 'do I want to be good?' but 'who do I want to be like?'

— **Bruno Bettelheim**
20th-century German/ American child psychologist

IDEA #88

The Six Mistakes of Man

> **OVERVIEW:** Young people think about and discuss mankind's shortcomings — and what to do about them.
>
> **PREPARATION / MATERIALS:** none

PROCEDURE:

Introduce Cicero to the students. Explain that he was a Roman statesman, philosopher and lawyer who lived during the final civil wars that destroyed the Roman Republic (b: 106 B.C., d: 43 B.C.).

Point out that Cicero famously reduced the folly of man to six mistakes. List on the board these "Six Mistakes of Man":

Criticize by creation, not by finding fault.

— Cicero (Marcus Tullius) Roman orator and statesman

1. The delusion that personal gain is made by crushing others.

2. The tendency to worry about things that cannot be changed or corrected.

3. Insisting that a thing is impossible because we cannot accomplish it.

4. Refusing to set aside trivial preferences.

5. Neglecting development and refinement of the mind, and not acquiring the habit of reading and studying.

6. Attempting to compel others to believe and live as we do.

Ask the students if they think these points are still relevant today. If not, ask them to explain why. Ask what "mistakes," if any, are missing from this list.

Have the students choose two of Cicero's mistakes that they agree are still a problem today and write a report showing evidence of these mistakes in action. Invite them to include photos and other art or to make a video to accompany their findings. As part of their research, they might investigate what other philosophers have thought of mankind's biggest errors or character flaws.

The student reports — due in two weeks to one month (depending on the creativity and resources of the class and your schedule) — should have a concluding section on what students would do to "solve" or lessen the effects of their two chosen "mistakes."

IDEA #89

Creating a Code for Coaches

OVERVIEW: Students create a code of conduct for coaches. As part of this activity, they analyze the values, privileges and ideals of participating in team sports and see that trust is built when clear rules are adhered to.

PREPARATION / MATERIALS:

● paper; pencils or pens

PROCEDURE:

Say: *Playing sports professionally and even in college has become quite lucrative for athletes today. What does "lucrative" mean?* Solicit and list answers. Then say: *Playing a sport can be valuable for other reasons besides the fact that it makes someone wealthy. In what other ways is participation in team sports valuable to both professional athletes and each of you?* Again, list answers. List the Six Pillars of Character on the board and associate benefits of team sports with each character trait.

Have the students offer examples of ways that players sometimes jeopardize the joy of the game and the character-building experience (e.g., bad-mouthing opponents, fighting, cheating, etc.).

Ask what role coaches play to make participation in team sports valuable. List answers. Have the students offer examples (e.g., modeling honesty, watching out for students' safety, showing good sportsmanship, etc.). Say: *As we've pointed out, coaches, just like students, need to realize that participation in team sports is a privilege that requires responsibilities. And one of the best ways for people to conduct themselves properly is to teach them how to do that. Today I want you to create a code of conduct for coaches. While you won't be presenting this to them, it will help you realize what actions you can model for the coaches. How will that help them?* After soliciting answers, suggest that good attitudes and admirable behavior are contagious.

Divide the class into groups. Have them create a code of conduct with at least six specific rules for coaches to follow — one for each of the Six Pillars of Character. They must cite the reasons for each rule. Encourage them to be creative.

When they've finished, have students share their codes with the rest of the class. Highlight or list the most prevalent ideas.

Freedom is not procured by a full enjoyment of what is desired, but by controlling that desire.

— Epictetus
Greek historian

Discuss strategies the school or community could use to encourage good sportsmanship and character development in sports activities.

Suggest the students try to note their own attitudes and the attitudes of others now that they have completed these codes. At a later date discuss their observations and experiences.

"Standards of Conduct for High School and Middle School Coaches" and "Standards of Conduct for Student Athletes" are available from the **CHARACTER COUNTS!** *national office. Call (800) 711-2670 or visit www.charactercounts.org.*

To many people virtue consists of repenting faults not avoiding them.

— Georg Christoph Lichtenberg

THE SIX PILLARS OF CHARACTER

TRUSTWORTHINESS

- Be honest.
- Don't deceive, cheat or steal.
- Be reliable — do what you say you'll do.
- Have the courage to do the right thing.
- Build a good reputation.
- Be loyal — stand by your family, friends and country.

RESPECT

- Treat others with respect; follow the Golden Rule.
- Be tolerant of differences.
- Use good manners, not bad language.
- Be considerate of the feelings of others.
- Don't threaten, hit or hurt anyone.
- Deal peacefully with anger, insults and disagreements.

RESPONSIBILITY

- Do what you are supposed to do.
- Persevere: keep on trying!
- Always do your best.
- Use self-control.
- Be self-disciplined.
- Think before you act
  — consider the consequences.
- Be accountable for your choices.

FAIRNESS

- Play by the rules.
- Take turns and share.
- Be open-minded; listen to others.
- Don't take advantage of others.
- Don't blame others carelessly.

CARING

- Be kind.
- Be compassionate; show you care.
- Express gratitude.
- Forgive others.
- Help people in need.

CITIZENSHIP

- Do your share to make your school and community better.
- Cooperate.
- Stay informed; vote.
- Be a good neighbor.
- Obey laws and rules.
- Respect authority.
- Protect the environment

GOOD IDEAS

to Help _Teenagers_ Develop Good Character

IDEA #90

Keeping News Trustworthy

OVERVIEW: Students keep a news media log to analyze and prompt discussion on how newspapers, magazines, radio and TV portray daily life and events.

PREPARATION/MATERIALS:

- Special "media literacy" resources for teachers and students include:
  - Center for Media Literacy: www.medialit.org, (323) 931-4177
  - Media Awareness Network (Canada): www.media-awareness.ca/eng/med/class/
  - Media Literacy Online Project (at the University of Oregon College of Education): http://interact.uoregon.edu/MediaLit/HomePage
  - New Mexico Media Literacy Project: www.nmmlp.org
  - Links to media literacy sites: www.ci.appstate.edu/programs/edmedia/medialit/links.html

PROCEDURE:

Explain that news and entertainment are powerful forces and that they influence how we perceive ourselves and the world.

Suggest that what we watch on television and the way a show presents a story or event can affect our opinions about it. Point out that this is why TV shows have to offer equal time to political opponents running for the same office. Ask the students why this is important. Present an example of how a newscast can influence viewers' perspectives of an event or issue:

A news program begins with a report of a "violent" crime. The reporters explain that a woman's purse was stolen, and she was knocked down in front of a store. The program presents pictures of people crying hysterically at the crime scene. Another newscast on at the same time starts its show with several reports on the stock market and then talks about the purse-snatching event. They don't show any videotape of the scene, nor do they label it as "violent."

Ask students to explain how the two shows covered the same story differently (one lead with a story, the other didn't; one labeled it "violent," the other didn't; one showed specific video footage, the other didn't; etc.).

Next, explain that media (television, newspapers, etc.) are businesses too. Note that in order for them to earn money, they have to get companies to advertise. First,

*B*e

honorable

yourself

if you

wish to

associate

with

honorable

people.

— Welsh proverb

ask why companies would want to advertise in a certain magazine or on a certain television show. Then, ask students to explain how that might affect what content we read or see and why. Together, list ways a story or event may be presented and why. Then inform the students that they are going to learn to analyze (or *deconstruct*) what the media presents.

Invite the students to list various questions that can help them better understand the content of a story in the media. Include: *How realistically do sitcoms portray relationships, the workplace and family life? How do social, political and economic factors influence what is reported, and how?* Ask students how critical analysis can help maintain the public's trust in the media. Again, list key answers.

Explain to them that everything they see and read is the result of an editing process, which is necessary in order to tell a story. Refer back to your original example and have the class help you answer the following questions:

What was said or shown? What wasn't? Why? What effect does the way the story was presented have on your feelings and on the way you think about what occurred?

After this class discussion, pass out the "Media Log" handouts and instruct students to analyze one daily newspaper or magazine or a television news program for the next week (one sheet per day). You might have students report their findings to the whole class or collect the completed assignments and assess them as a class. Discussion topics can include: impartiality, timeliness, relevance, magnitude, surprise, impact, fame, strangeness, conflict, continuity of coverage (follow-up stories), negativity, solutions, emotions, diversity and politics.

Finally, introduce the term "media literacy" to students. Explain to them that being literate in the language and methods used by the media does not mean being cynical. It means being responsible for our own perceptions — and, through criticism, for helping to keep the media (especially the news) worthy of our trust.

*I*t is a

hard man

who is only

just, a sad

one who is

only wise.

— **Francois Marie Arouet de Voltaire** 18th-century French philosophe

IDEA #90 Media Log Handout: Keeping News Trustworthy

Periodical or program name: _____

Date of publication or airing: _____

Lead story (+ description): _____

Length/duration: _____

Other major stories:
(note length of each and which feature graphics, photos and on-site or field reporters)

1 _____

2. _____

3. _____

4. _____

5. _____

ANALYSIS

What percentage of space/time did the periodical/program spend on:

Local news? _____

National news? _____

International news? _____

Sports? _____

Commercials? _____

Crime? _____

Celebrities? _____

Developed from the "Media Logs" exercise in "Keeping the American Promise," Vol. 4, Issue 1, p. 11 (Los Angeles, CA: The American Promise, 1999). Keeping the American Promise, Box 514989, Los Angeles, CA 90051 (www.americanpromise.com).

IDEA #91

Courage in the Movies

Courage finds its own eloquence.

— Plautus
Roman
statesman

> **OVERVIEW:** Teens examine the decisions and behavior of movie characters through the prism of integrity and courage to encourage better awareness of their own ethical decision making in difficult situations.
>
> **PREPARATION/MATERIALS:**
> - television, VCR
> - videotapes of movies (see suggestions below)

PROCEDURE:

Engage the students in a discussion about *integrity* (being true to your <u>best</u> self) and how that requires courage and unselfishness. You might say: *One of the key elements of trustworthiness is living a life of integrity — being true to yourself so people know they can trust you. What could be simpler, right? But, of course, we know it isn't that easy. Integrity requires courage — to do the right thing and be true to your best self. It is one of the toughest requirements of the ethical life because courage requires us to face down those things that we fear. And fear is powerful. When faced with conflict and paying a price we might not want to pay, it's easier to compromise your values, go with the flow or not stand up for someone or something that's right.*

If you let fear of consequence prevent you from following your deepest instinct, then your life will be safe, expedient and thin.

— Katherine
Butler Hathaway

Explain that the class will watch a movie (or movies, depending on your schedule) and discuss the value of courage and integrity as it is exhibited — or not exhibited — by the characters. Tell the students to focus on key decisions made by the characters. Pick a movie you think is age- and content-appropriate, such as *Death of a Salesman, Schindler's List, Dead Poet's Society, Mr. Holland's Opus, My Bodyguard, etc.*

(<u>Note</u>: Some of these movies may have violent or graphic content. These elements may be judged historically accurate or important to the story, but as with any movie you choose to show students, you should screen the films first, as some families may object to young people being shown certain movies.)

After the movie, refocus the students' attention on to the issues of trustworthiness. Give the students one week to write a one- to two-page argument showing that one character's specific actions were ethically courageous or not. Make sure they can back up their claims with examples and explanations.

IDEA #92

Go Figure: Your Credit Is Built on Trust

OVERVIEW: Teens understand that credit and money markets are based on trust and that an honorable person honors his debts and protects his reputation.

PREPARATION / MATERIALS:

● Worksheet for each student (master provided — you may want to block out answer section before photocopying and distributing)

PROCEDURE:

Ask students how credit cards work. After getting responses, you might say: *Credit cards offer convenience. But they are not free or easy money; there are costs to using them. They are a form of borrowing and all borrowing is based on trust. If you give people reason to believe that you will not honor your debts, they will not trust or extend credit to you in the future. Having a clean credit history is important in our society — and is another reason to build and maintain a good reputation. When people trust you, you can more easily leverage your time and resources.*

Explain that by using a credit card, users enter into a contract with the credit card company. Different credit card companies have different terms, and it is the user's responsibility to understand them. For instance, if you don't pay off what you owe each month, you will be charged a fee based on a percentage of what you owe; this is called a finance charge. Point out that the method used to calculate this fee makes a difference in how much the user pays. Pass out copies of the handout on the following page and give students 10 minutes to see how this works and answer the questions. While they are working you might want to write on the board some or all of the following terms to discuss:

T rust that man in nothing who has not a conscience in everything.

— **Laurence Sterne**
18th-century
English novelist

● **Annual Percentage Rate (APR).** The cost of credit expressed as a yearly rate.
● **Periodic Rate.** The rate the card issuer applies to the balance to figure the finance charge for each billing period (the annual rate divided by 12).
● **Variable Rate.** Some card issuers change the APR on the account when specific interest rates (like the prime rate) change. Rate changes raise or lower the amount of the finance charge you pay on your account (if you carry a balance from month to month).

● **Grace Period.** The period of time the credit card company does not charge interest on a new purchase — as long as the entire balance is paid before the due date.
● **Annual Fees.** A fixed amount charged each year for the privilege of using a card.
● **Transaction Fees and Other Charges.** Fees for cash advances, late payments or over-limit.
● **Balance Computation Method for the Finance Charge.** How your card issuer figures how much interest to charge you if you don't pay your balance off in full.

Information derived from the Federal Trade Commission's "Facts for Consumers" (www.pueblo.gsa.gov/cic_text/money/credit-card/credcard.htm)

IDEA #92 Worksheet: Go Figure: Your Credit Is Built on Trust

To figure Average Daily Balance (including new purchases):
Multiply the previous balance by the number of days until payment is received, add to new balance multiplied by number of days until new purchase is made, add to balance for remainder of period multiplied by the number of days remaining in period; divide this resulting sum by 30 days (the billing period)

To figure Average Daily Balance (excluding new purchases):
multiply the previous balance by the number of days until payment is received, add to new balance multiplied by number of days remaining in the billing period; divide this resulting sum by 30 days (the billing period)

	Average Daily Balance (including new purchases)	Average Daily Balance (excluding new purchases)
Monthly rate	1½ %	1½ %
APR	18 %	18 %
Previous Balance	$400	$400
New Purchases (on 18th day)	$50	$50
Payments (on 15th day) new balance = $100	$300	$300
Average Daily Balance	#1 _____	#2 _____
Finance Charge	#3 _____	#4 _____

Answer 1: $270
$$\frac{(\$400 \times 15 \text{ days}) + (\$100 \times 3 \text{ days}) + (\$150 \times 12 \text{ days})}{30 \text{ days}}$$

Answer 2: $250
$$\frac{(\$400 \times 15 \text{ days}) + (\$100 \times 15 \text{ days})}{30 \text{ days}}$$

Answer 3: $4.05   1½ % x $270

Answer 4: $3.75   1½ % x $250

Tips for Maintaining Good Credit — and a Good Financial Reputation

- Don't spend more than you earn.
- Pay off the balance due each month; don't just make the minimum payment.
- Pay bills promptly to keep finance charges as low as possible; avoid late payments and over-the-limit fees.
- Don't have more than one card.
- Make sure you understand the terms of a credit card plan before you accept the card.

- Keep copies of sales slips and compare charges when your bills arrive.
- Draw a line through blank spaces about the total when you sign receipts.
- Sign your card so no one else can use it.
- Don't lend your card to anyone, even to a friend.
- Keep your account information private. Never give out your credit card number or expiration date over the phone unless you know whom you're dealing with.

Information derived from the Federal Trade Commission, Bureau of Consumer Protection and other sources.

IDEA #93

Respectful Interview

OVERVIEW: Students focus on respect as they hone their listening and interviewing skills with residents of a senior citizen community center.

PREPARATION / MATERIALS:
- copy of magazine interview
- paper; pencils or pens
- video camera, VHS tapes and a VCR (optional)
- microcassette recorder (optional)

SETTING: classroom and senior citizen community center

A most insidious form of fear is that which ... condemns as foolish and futile the small, daily acts of courage which help preserve man's self-respect.

— Aung San Suu Kyi
20th-century Nobel Prize-winning Burmese civil rights leader

PROCEDURE:

Offer an example of an informative interview from a television news program or a magazine article. Afterward, ask the students to list what makes a good interview. In addition to discussing the substance of the interview, be sure to mention the process of conducting the interview: a good interviewer shows respect by being prepared and by being a good listener and not interrupting.

Next, introduce the project by telling the students that they are going to be reporters and are going to interview residents at a local senior citizen community center or retirement home. Say: *The subject of these interviews will be respect. Focus on how we can be more respectful as a society.* Instruct them to ask the elderly people they interview how society has changed in this regard, how they were taught to be respectful, and what parents and teachers should do differently (if anything) to encourage more respect.

Divide the students into pairs and match the pairs up with a resident of the senior citizen center or retirement home. (Of course, you will have to schedule these meetings in advance with the senior center or residence.) Try to arrange for these interviews to be videotaped so that the students can present them to the class. If this is not possible, try to secure a microcassette recorder so that they can record and transcribe their interviews. Tell the students that each person should have the opportunity to ask questions while his/her partner videotapes or records the conversation.

After watching the interviews, discuss what they learned from the process and from what the senior citizens had to say.

Adapted from an idea submitted by Teresa Edwards, a teacher at Sapulpa Middle School in Sapulpa, Oklahoma.

IDEA #94

Exhibiting a Respect for Work

Life is not so short but that there is always time enough for courtesy.

— **Ralph Waldo Emerson**
19th-century American essayist and poet

OVERVIEW: Acknowledging the effects of others' hard work on their community, students create a photo and text exhibit that examines the careers of individuals in the community whose work they respect.

PREPARATION / MATERIALS:
- paper; pencils or pens
- camera, ability to get photos developed

PROCEDURE:

Write the following questions on the board: *What does work mean to us as individuals? As a society? How does work shape our values? Our lives?* Have the students copy the questions down, then discuss them. List answers to the questions. Suggest that the work we do for ourselves and our families also affects others. Have the students cite examples such as: If someone works hard and is proud of his or her work, it fosters respect from those who directly benefit from it, as well as from those who simply witness it. This respect, in turn, can inspire others to be more responsible and committed in their work.

Discuss what makes a job worthy of respect. Discuss concepts like prestige, esteem, authority and power, and how these influence the way we perceive workers. Be sure to emphasize the importance of respecting all persons who contribute to society, regardless of how much money they earn or how much authority or status they wield.

Introduce the project. Say: *To foster respect for working people in the community and to display our appreciation for these people, we are going to showcase them.* Tell the students that their assignment is to seek out, interview and photograph a worker whom they respect. Also inform them that once everyone has completed these tasks, the group will create an exhibit of the photographs, including descriptions of each photo.

Assign each student the following tasks (by a certain date):

1. Interview a particular individual about his or her job. Ask the same questions that were discussed at the beginning of class.
2. Take a photo of the worker (at his/her job).
3. Write a brief essay highlighting the worker's answers to questions, explaining why this person was chosen. (This will accompany the photo.)

Have the students plan, prepare and construct the exhibit after they have completed the tasks above. You might get the exhibit started by including a sample photo and caption of a worker whom you admire.

Also, you might have the students add quotes on work and respect to their exhibit. Here are some samples:

"Every man is to be respected as an absolute end in himself; and it is a crime against the dignity that belongs to him as a human being, to use him as a mere means for some external purpose." — Immanuel Kant

"Hard work spotlights the character of people: some turn up their sleeves, some turn up their noses, and some don't turn up at all." — Sam Ewig

"Never look down on anybody unless you are helping him up." — Jesse Jackson

"The credit belongs to the man who is actually in the arena, whose face is marred by dust and sweat and blood; who strives valiantly; who errs and comes short again and again, who knows the great enthusiasms, the great devotions, and spends himself in a worthy cause; who at best, knows the triumph of high achievement; and who, at the worst, if he fails, at least fails while daring greatly, so that his place shall never be with those cold and timid souls who know neither victory nor defeat." — Theodore Roosevelt

"The real measure of your wealth is how much you'd be worth if you lost all your money." — Unknown

"Don't say you don't have enough time. You have exactly the same number of hours per day that were given to Helen Keller, Pasteur, Michaelangelo, Mother Teresa, Leonardo da Vinci, Thomas Jefferson, and Albert Einstein." — H. Jackson Brown

"The true measure of an individual is how he treats a person who can do him absolutely no good." — Ann Landers

L̶ife's most persistent and urgent question is: What are you doing for others?

— Martin Luther King, Jr.
20th century Nobel Prize winning American civil rights leader

---

Adapted with permission from the Bread and Roses Cultural Project (330 West 42nd St., 7th floor, New York, NY 10036; 212-631-4565; www.breadandroses.com). A version of this activity is posted on the Southern Poverty Law Center's Teaching Tolerance website (www.splcenter.org/teachingtolerance). Quotes were culled from a variety of sources, including the Josephson Institute's "QuoteUnquote" library of quotations, available at www.josephsoninstitute.org.

IDEA #95

The Great Privacy Debate

OVERVIEW: Students research privacy issues and stage a formal debate. (The official national high school debate topic for the 2000-2001 school year is "the right of privacy.")

PREPARATION / MATERIALS: none

PROCEDURE:

There is no witness so terrible, no accuser so powerful as the conscience which dwells within us.

— Sophocles
Greek dramatist

Introduce the subject of privacy by saying something like: *This is a complex society with a lot of wants and expectations. We want to feel safe from crime and harassment. We want ever-greater convenience and comfort. We want easily available information.* Ask students for their ideas of the trade-offs and costs. Say: *A lot of consumer-driven prosperity, as well as our desire for security, is accomplished through surveillance, investigation and monitoring — by government, media, employers and merchants. Arguably, we have relinquished some privacy in search of greater openness and convenience and efficiency. Not a bad thing. Yet forces we have entrusted with personal information might mismanage this information, putting us at risk. Not a good thing.*

Ask students: *What is privacy?* Write on the board the classic definition given in 1928 by Justice Louis D. Brandeis: "the right to be let alone — the most comprehensive of rights, and the right most valued by civilized men." Ask students what they think about that definition, weighing the meaning of its components ("comprehensive," "civilized," etc.).

Create debate teams of four members each. You might borrow or adapt the national high school debate topic for the 2000-2001 school year — "Resolved: That the United States federal government should significantly increase protection of privacy in one or more of the following areas: employment, medical records, consumer information, search and seizure."

If debate is not your class's strong suit, you might have students write essays (of 2,000 words or so) on the debate topic above, choosing the pro or con position. Whether in debate or in writing, students should address some fundamental issues, with plenty of examples, data and reasoning to back up their positions:

• Are contemporary privacy concerns overstated? Understated?
• What does privacy have to do with the value of respect? Are other values involved?

- Is privacy the same thing as secrecy? What is the difference?
- What are the dangers, if any, of so much information so readily available to so many people with so many motivations?
- Who owns information about you?
- Is information knowledge? What's the difference? If you have enough data about a person, can you judge or predict that person's behavior?

When somebody lies, somebody loses.

— **Stephanie Ericsson**
20th-century
American author

The intention makes the crime.

— **Aristotle**
Greek
philosopher

IDEA #96

Peace Partners

> **OVERVIEW:** Students research the similarities of historically conflicting cultures and then negotiate and write a peace agreement to promote them.
>
> **PREPARATION / MATERIALS:**
> - copies of handouts (for each student)
> - news reports of ethnic conflicts

PROCEDURE:

Discuss the nature of many of the world's ethnic conflicts. Explain that many stem from ancient hatreds, passed from generation to generation. Ask students to come up with examples, which might include: Hutus vs. Tutsis in and around Rwanda, Kosovars vs. Serbians, Catholics vs. Protestants in Northern Ireland, Sinhalese vs. Tamil in Sri Lanka, Kurds vs. Turks (or Iraqis or Iranians), Turks vs. Greeks, Armenians vs. Azerbaijanis, Israelis vs. Palestinians, etc. Write these on the board.

Ask students what form these conflicts might take. Answers might range from petty insults and caricatures to genocidal wars ("ethnic cleansing"). At your discretion, distribute media reports of such conflicts. Discuss underlying issues such as: competition for political spoils and land, racism, religious intolerance and tribal identity.

Point out that while cease-fires have sometimes maintained an uneasy peace over these conflicts, lasting peace has not been secured by outside force (or a gun). Suggest that lasting peace comes from within the communities in conflict, through mutual respect and understanding. Ask the students to help explain what this means.

Emphasize the importance for different cultures to learn about others' points of view. You might say: *It takes courageous, long-term commitment to resolve ethnic prejudices. And it takes a fresh perspective, either from individuals who can put aside the past or from those without too much invested in the past — the kind of perspective that youth provides.*

Explain that in this exercise, students in pairs will be assigned "rivaling" ethnic identities (not their own), which they will research with particular attention to belief systems, cultural values and historical "enemies." Explain that each student will then be paired with the "enemy" of his or her ethnicity (use examples in first paragraph). The "enemies" will be partners in finding ways to promote peace through the discussion of each other's grievances and exploration of common values (ethical and otherwise). Each pair will then write a statement of values, later presented to the class.

Divide students into pairs and designate ethnicities (or allow them to choose from your list on the board). Distribute copies of handout #1. As you conclude the exercise, distribute and discuss handout #2, "The Bostonian Agreement."

Politeness is the art of choosing among one's real thoughts.

— Adlai Stevenson II
20th-century American politician

IDEA #96 Handout #1: Peace Partners

My assigned ethnic identity is _____ .

My peace partner's ethnicity is _____ .

Here are some of the things our two cultures have in common, which we have discovered through research and discussion.

Foods	Sports	Music	Cultural Values	Ethical Values

Here are some of our ideas for increasing awareness of what our two cultures share in common:

IDEA #96 Handout #2: Peace Partners
"The Bostonian Agreement"

Forsan Hussein and Michael Bavly are best friends, which is not remarkable except that Hussein is a Palestinian and Bavly is an Israeli. Their people have a history of violent confrontation with each other; cross-cultural friendships are unusual. Having met as students at Brandeis University in Massachusetts, these friends work to bring their peoples together by promoting knowledge of their similarities rather than dwelling on their differences. They do this by organizing interfaith campus dialogues and hosting a radio program that focuses on shared values. Operating on the belief that *lasting* peace between nations may involve governments but ultimately must rest on understanding between peoples, the two drafted "The Bostonian Agreement." "It stresses education," Hussein told *Hope* magazine. "Coexistence is a long process. If you tell a child that one plus one is two, he will believe it. It's the same thing with peace. If you tell the same child that Palestinians or Israelis are your friends and neighbors, he will also believe it." Here is a section from Article III of The Bostonian Agreement:

The parties realize that the hearts and minds of people from both sides are infected with hate, fear and ignorance; therefore, the required change is educating all people about statutes of peace: tolerance, respect, acceptance and trust. Mutual re-education uproots hatred, fear and contrary ideologies.

The parties realize the importance of education as a means to achieve peace. Education materials that promote hostility must be modified to promote coexistence and peace. In addition, it is necessary to create and implement in both communities education programs that teach the history, literature and religion of the other.

From "The Bostonian Agreement," Article III (Confidence-Building Measures), by Forsan Hussein, a Palestinian, and Michael Bavly, an Israeli. Reprinted from Hope magazine (Fall 1999). Reprinted here with permission from Bavly and Hussein, who may be reached at mbavly@brandeis.edu and forsan@brandeis.edu.

IDEA #97

Student-Led Parent Conferences

OVERVIEW: Instead of visiting school periodically to listen to teachers explain how their children are doing, parents are directly guided through this process by students themselves. Everyone benefits: students learn responsibility and presentation skills; parents get a new perspective on how their children are performing; and teachers escape the tedium of assembly line-like recitation. The key is preparation.

PREPARATION/MATERIALS:
● three-ring notebooks for students

PROCEDURE:

At the beginning of the school year or grading period, explain to students the importance of parent conferences. Tell students they will be responsible for preparing a portfolio of their work and direct them to set aside a binder in which to file their assignments and special projects.

A week before the conference, send an invitation letter to parents. Three days before the conference, direct the students to prepare their presentations, which should include at least one quiz, one homework assignment and one lesson from which they feel they learned the most. Instruct students to complete the handout on the following page to serve as a cover sheet for their presentation materials. (You might also encourage students to talk about what they learned in terms of the Six Pillars of Character, as appropriate.) The day before the conference, practice presentations with the students by assuming the role of the parent, then by assuming the role of the student while the students pretend to be parents. In their presentations, students should cover: the purpose of assignments; what was learned; the grade received, and why. Finally, students should help prepare the conference room(s) by cleaning, setting up refreshments, etc.

During the conference, visit with each family, pointing out students' strengths. If coordinating this activity with other teachers in a "team teaching" environment, make sure that parents know each teacher on the team is available for discussion. Direct those students whose parents can't attend to hold their conferences at home; these students should return to you a form (designed by you) signed by their parents, signifying the home conference has taken place.

The best place to find a helping hand is at the end of your own arm.

— Swedish proverb

Adapted from "Letting Students Lead Parent Conferences" by Laura Hayden, a teacher at Derby Middle School in Derby, Kansas. Her article is posted on the National Association of Elementary School Principals website (www.naesp.org/comm/mmf98b.htm).

IDEA #97 Handout: Student-Led Parent Conferences

> These are the areas I will cover in my conference:
>
> - the purpose of assignments
> - what was learned
> - the grades earned, and why

■ These are my thoughts on my grades:

■ These are my thoughts on my study habits:

■ These are my thoughts on my behavior in class and toward my classmates and teachers:

■ These are my academic goals for the rest of the year:

■ These are my personal goals for the rest of the year:

IDEA #98

Writing a Grant Proposal

OVERVIEW: Limited school and government budgets can't always stretch to accommodate a mural project, an experimental garden or new band uniforms. Yet this funding challenge is itself an opportunity. Students generate and write a grant proposal to raise money from charitable, corporate or governmental sources, and learn the value of persistence and planning as they hone writing and researching skills.

PREPARATION / MATERIALS:

● typewriter/computer terminal and printer

Excellent Internet resources include:

- Foundation Center (www.fdncenter.org)
- WestEd: Tips on Preparing a Successful Proposal (www.wested.org/tie/granttips.html)
- Grantscape: Grantseeking 101 (www.grantscape.com/omaha/grants/services/101.html)
- The Paladin Group – Grant Mentors: Elements of a Grant Proposal (www.silcom.com/~paladin/promaster.html)
- Grantseeking in Minnesota: Writing a Successful Grant Proposal (www.mcf.org/mcf/grant/writing.htm)
- National Youth Development Information Center (www.nydic.org/funding.html)
- The Management Assistance Program for Nonprofits (www.mapnp.org/library/fndrsng/np_raise/np_raise.htm)
- Michigan State University Library (www.lib.msu.edu/harris23/grants/znonprof.htm)
- Chardon Press (www.chardonpress.com)
- Raising More Money (www.raisingmoremoney.com)

PROCEDURE:

It's important to know before starting this project that fundraising can be a slow and painstaking process. The young people involved in this grant-seeking activity may not be around when, and if, the funds come through. But the goal of the activity is not so much to focus on the money but on the process involved in thoroughly conceptualizing a problem-solving idea and then working as a team to make it a reality. Securing funding can mean writing many grant proposals, to many potential funders. Because of this long-term outlook — and because money and ongoing fiduciary responsibilities are involved — you should coordinate this activity with the

*N*ot in time,

place or

circumstance

but in the man

lies success.

— James Joyce
20th century Irish
novelist

*F*all seven

times, stand

up eight.

**— Japanese
proverb**

administration of your school or organization. Ideally, you and your students, along with your administration, will set up a process to involve future students in managing the newly funded project.

Ask the students to list the greatest needs of their school (or organization) and, separately, of the community at large. Depending on the size of the class, you might divide the students into groups of six or so and let them discuss these needs; assign them this task as a homework-research assignment. Have them reassemble the next week as a whole class and consolidate lists. Then, hold a vote to select the best fundable project.

A grant proposal tells a story. Elements of a successful "Six Pillars" proposal include: goals; objectives; and an explanation of how the grant will help students make one or more of the Six Pillars stronger at school, in the community and in their own lives.

*W*ealth

consists not in

having great

possessions,

but in having

few wants.

— Epicurus
Greek sage

At large corporations there is usually one person in charge of corporate giving. Find out who this person is and what the company's guidelines are. Address that person and follow the guidelines with a compelling and clearly written proposal, stressing why your activity merits sponsorship. Follow up with polite inquiries about the application's status. Remember:

- Be realistic about what can be accomplished.
- Be factual (not emotional). Be specific; don't make statements in your proposal you can't substantiate.
- Use clear English (no abbreviations, jargon or slang).
- Get approval from your school or district; collaborate, if necessary, with other pending proposals. You should know if matching funds are available.
- Follow grant guidelines closely and completely.
- Be clear about the amount of work required and who will do it.
- Do your homework; know the cost of all project materials and expenses (including labor) called for in your proposal.

Whether or not the grant is received, direct the young people to write thank-you notes for the opportunity to apply. The group leader/teacher also should write a thank-you note. If a grant is received, give credit to the donor by sending a press release to local newspapers.

Looking for a good idea that might get funding? Here are some leads:

Students at Boone Grove High School in Valparaiso, Indiana, wrote a successful grant proposal to fund a center for senior citizens at their school called Project CARE. Contact: Maureen Maher, Project CARE Coordinator, at (219) 462-1966.

Also, Kraft Foods in partnership with the National 4-H Council offers grants of $500 to $2,500 to local teams promoting youth and adult involvement in such solutions as food banks, outreach and public awareness. Contact: 4-H Council (www.fourhcouncil.edu) or Kraft Foods.

IDEA #99

Achieving Self-Control Through Anger Management

OVERVIEW: Young people realize that they are responsible for their own well-being and that only they can control their feelings. This exercise is not an examination of the causes of anger, but rather its effects.

PREPARATION / MATERIALS:

● copies of handouts (one for each student)

PROCEDURE:

Start a discussion about anger and its consequences. Say something like: *We all get upset sometimes. What are some of the things you get angry about?* List responses, which might include people being hurtful, people breaking rules like cutting in line or cheating, people being slow to understand, etc. Discuss why these things make the students angry.

Next, say: *What are some of the ways we express anger?* Write down responses, which might include: keeping anger in and "venting" it later; keeping it in and never expressing it; seeking revenge, such as spreading gossip about someone or not sharing information the adversary needs; calling names, mocking; sarcasm; getting physical, etc.

Ask students to help you explain what it means when we say someone or something "makes" us angry. Discuss how this can happen. After student responses, ask: *Is it really true that other people have control over our emotions? Is anger like a witch's spell or a curse that gives other people power over us and makes us unable to do anything about it?*

Suggest: *We can't control what other people do and say. But we can control ourselves. Our anger is our own problem, a problem we alone can solve. There is no way to live a happy, constructive life — a life of good character — without self-control, and that means controlling our anger.*

Say: *Anger does not give you energy. It does not keep people from taking advantage of you. Anger is a response to fear, psychologists say. You have to learn to deal with that fear to be free of it.*

We make problems worse when we react in anger. You need to deal with problems calmly, without making them worse by destroying your well-being and relationships. It does not help you get your own way. It makes you suffer. You almost always lose more than you gain when you get angry, regardless of the way it seems to you at the moment.

*A*nyone can become angry — that is easy. But to be angry with the right person, to the right degree, at the right time, for the right purpose and in the right way — that is not easy.

— **Aristotle**
(Nicomachean Ethics)
Ancient Greek philosopher

The weak

can never

forgive.

Forgiveness is

the attribute

of the strong.

— **Mohandas Gandhi**
20th-century Nobel Prize-winning Indian civil rights leader

Direct the students to come up with a plan to recognize and deal with anger (including responding to other people's anger). Instruct students to write down a list of challenges and ideal ways to respond; a list of excuses for getting angry; and ways to take responsibility for our feelings. Encourage them to creatively write about dealing with anger in such forms as: poetry, acronyms, advertising slogans, etc.

In his book *4 Downs to Anger Control*, author Tom Letson uses football terminology to reach his audience. He makes the distinction between "offensive" thinkers and "defensive" thinkers. In football, defense players are trained to view yardage gained as a personal attack, but, he says, this doesn't work off the gridiron. He suggests people view themselves (in life) as offensive players moving the ball against a tough defense, not reacting to problems, but anticipating them. He terms his "four downs" to anger control **A.S.A.P.**: 1. **A**ssess the problem; 2. **S**trategy development; 3. **A**ssess strategy successes; and 4. **P**unt the failing strategy. He also came up with **T.I.M.E.**: **T**hink! (about your anger); **I**ntercept! (angry thoughts); **M**ove! (out of the area); and **E**xit! (the premises completely).

In his book *Winning Every Day*, Notre Dame football coach Lou Holtz came up with **F.A.I.L.U.R.E.** to explain how *not* to deal with anger: **F**rustration (you don't have any answers); **A**ggression (misdirected); **I**nsecurity (you fear you can't cut it anymore); **L**eadership (you abandon it); **U**ndisciplined (you stop practicing fundamentals); **R**esentment (you assume the victim's role); **E**xcuses (it's everyone's fault but your own).

It is important for the students to come up with something that works for them. (It can be simple, but it should show evidence that thought has been invested in the topic.) After the assignments are turned in, share student ideas. In closing, distribute and discuss copies of the handout.

Special Resources:

- *Anger Kills: 17 Strategies for Controlling the Hostility That Can Harm Your Health,* by Redford Williams, M.D. and Virginia Williams, Ph.D. (New York: Times Books, 1993)
- *4 Downs to Anger Control,* by Tom Letson (Finish Line Press, 1998)
- *How to Keep People From Pushing Your Buttons,* by Albert Ellis, Ph.D. and Arthur Lange, Ed.D. (Carol Publishing Group, 1994)
- *Letting Go of Anger: The 10 Most Common Anger Styles and What to Do About Them,* by Ron Potter-Efron, M.S.W. and Pat Potter-Efron (New Harbinger Publications, 1995)
- *What to Do When You're Angry,* by E. Dean Bevan, Ph.D. (Highland City, FL: Rainbow Books, 1994)
- American Psychological Association (www.apa.org/pubinfo/anger.html)
- Anger Management Resource List (www.christophers.org/anger_resources.html)

Act

in haste,

repent

in leisure.

— **William Congreve**
18th-century English playwright

Handout adapted from <u>What to Do When You're Angry,</u> *by E. Dean Bevan, Ph.D. (Highland City, FL: Rainbow Books, 1994).*

IDEA #99 Handout: Manage Anger and Gain Self-Control

We all have problems with people sometimes. But getting angry only makes problems worse, and you will suffer further distress in the bargain. So get smart and get in control. Deal with conflict calmly and rationally. Here's how, according to E. Dean Bevan of Baker University in Kansas.

1. **Name and "own" the feeling.** Admit it to yourself if you are angry — not "stressed" or "hassled" or "depressed" or "upset" or "abused." And don't say someone "made" you angry.

2. **Be civil.** Ironically we often treat strangers better than the people we know; so treat those closest to you at least as well as you treat strangers.

3. **Don't raise your voice.** Yelling at others does not release pressure, it adds to it — and it turns off the person you're trying to communicate with. It doesn't "clear the air," it poisons it. How do you feel when someone yells at you? Resentful, at best. In a disagreement, remain calm and say, with a smile if possible, "I don't agree." If this feels odd or unnatural, it doesn't make you a phony. You're trying something new that takes getting used to ... so get used to it.

4. **Don't get physical.** Acting out your anger (from slamming doors to hitting) is like throwing gasoline on fire: it doesn't quench the anger, but makes it leap to another level, with potentially serious repercussions.

5. **Listen.** Angry people tend to argue, usually pointlessly, with people they are around the most (friends and family). Because we feel we know the other person, we have their argument all worked out in our head beforehand — meaning we don't have to listen to what they are actually saying. If you are listening to people, you should be able to repeat what they are saying.

6. **Don't exaggerate.** Be specific about a problem you are trying to solve and the true frequency of its occurrence. Avoid saying "always" and "never" or phrases like "I've told you a million times," etc.

7. **Avoid absolutes.** See #6. If your adversary hears you saying he is "always" this or "never" that, what chance do you think he'll agree with you?

8. **Stick to the facts.** If you are upset about someone not being considerate and inviting you along for lunch, say so (if only to yourself). Don't think, or say, something like, "you never think of me." Naming the exact problem, like naming anger itself, is a step toward a calmer perspective. Also, don't character-ize a problem ("your work is a mess"); use specifics ("you made these three errors on these two pages"). Feelings are not facts, but your feelings are legitimate. So name your feelings *about the facts*. Say: "You told a story about me to other people that embarrassed me."

9. **Don't call names.** This only produces more anger and makes it hard for the other person to back down. Once harsh words leave your mouth, they can't be taken back. Relationships can heal after an argument, but personal attacks can leave scar tissue. Even after the argument or conflict is over, your relationship with the person you called derogatory names will probably never be the same.

10. **Don't mock.** What good can come of belittling someone by caricaturing his behavior or by using an exaggerated tone to distort her words? Of course it's rude and disrespectful, but it also does you no good.

11. **Memorize your escape.** If an argument escalates and you feel you can't continue calmly, smile and say, "Let's stop and talk about this another time." Then stop talking; resist the temptation to have the final word (this doesn't mean punishing the other person with the "silent treatment").

12. **Don't take hostages.** If someone wants to leave an argument, let him. Don't block his exit.

13. **Say "you may be right."** You may not believe it, but saying this sends the message that you have an open mind. (Of course, the idea here isn't to be phony; do your best to be *genuinely* open-minded.)

14. **Don't make major decisions when you're angry.** Making a decision to spite someone else will only hurt you. If you're upset, give yourself a few days before making any major decisions. Wait until you can rationally ask yourself how you will benefit from your decision.

IDEA #100

Media Coverage

Never doubt that a small group of thoughtful, committed citizens can change the world; indeed, it is the only thing that ever has.

— **Margaret Mead**
20th-century American anthropologist

OVERVIEW: Teens research news coverage using magazines, newspapers, television and the Internet to make the case that a particular *local* topic is not getting the fair attention it deserves.

PREPARATION / MATERIALS:
- access to library, news reference database

PROCEDURE:

Ask students where they get their information about current events (newspapers, magazines, television news programs, the Internet). You might say: *There's a lot of information out there, isn't there? And yet a lot of important issues probably aren't getting the attention they deserve — and because of that these issues may remain problems longer than they have to.* Ask students why this might be true. Possible answers: these issues are being ignored by the media; people are apathetic and don't care to stay informed; there's so much information out there that we have trouble prioritizing the importance of what we read, watch and hear.

Tell students they will each research a local issue that they think has been inadequately covered in the news. Explain that a "local" issue is either one that only concerns the local community or is a local expression of a larger issue or problem (like homelessness for example). Ask the students to help you define "inadequate" coverage: reporting on an issue without balance (fairness to all sides of the issue) or just not covering an issue as much as other stories. Inform students that they must back up their assertions with research from the library (or the Internet) to find out how much coverage there has been.

Reports are due in two weeks. Check in with students at least once a week to make sure they're making progress. You may want selected students to make a class presentation on their findings as well as explain what they are willing to do to raise awareness of the neglected issue.

As a follow-up exercise, you might instruct students to write reports on the neglected topics and then submit them — with a letter explaining the project — to local media organizations. This can be an individual or group exercise.

IDEA #101

Teen Court

OVERVIEW: While reflecting on the virtues of the democratic jury system, students participate in a mock trial and hone critical thinking and communication skills to reach a fair, unanimous judgment. Alternately, this exercise can be used to judge the specific action or behavior of a historical or literary figure.

PREPARATION/MATERIALS:
- chairs for "jurors"

*I*t is

reasonable

that every

one who asks

justice should

do justice.

— Thomas Jefferson
18th-century American Founding Father, 19th-century U.S. president

PROCEDURE:

To set the stage, you might say: *Any society needs a system of justice to decide if the rules that define and protect the society have been broken — and, if they have, what to do about it. The perceived fairness of this system lends legitimacy to authority and order in that society. In the United States, we employ the ancient right of being judged by a "jury of one's peers."*

Inform the class that you are going to hold a mock trial. Choose one student to play the defendant, one the prosecutor, one the defender and 12 students to be jurors. You will be the judge.

Tell the students the facts of the case: The defendant, Phil, is a 17-year-old junior who was caught stealing school supplies and a pair of sneakers for his little brother at Wal-Mart. Phil has never shoplifted before, but was teased for not having basic stuff that other kids have. His mother, a single parent, works all day in a minimum-wage job and doesn't have much time or money for her children, whom Phil usually cares for after school (he doesn't have time for a job). Several months before this incident, he was caught shoplifting in the same store, but the store clerk simply asked Phil to return the goods and then let him go. Lastly, when he was younger, the store clerk who caught Phil used to shoplift with Phil's older brother (Phil knows this).

Tell the jurors that they are to decide a *just* punishment or remedy to the criminal actions presented. After a designated amount of preparation time, the prosecutor will make a five-minute opening statement about what he/she feels the defendant's actions should warrant (with reasons given for his/her arguments). Next, the defender has five minutes to rebuff prosecutorial comments and pose his/her own remedy to the crime. Then, each juror asks the defendant one or two questions. After all the jurors' questions have been asked (the defendant answers directly), the jurors must unanimously reach a fair remedy or punishment to the crime, write it out, and present it to the rest of the class.

Once the remedy is shared, discuss why it was chosen and what might result. Highlight its rehabilitative nature (or lack thereof). Lastly, ask the jurors to discuss what skills they needed to reach a fair judgment and how these skills can be applied to everyday life.

End with this statement: *Do you think that young people could never sit in judgment on a <u>real</u> case? Think again. Students at Wilson High School in Los Angeles act as jurors to listen to first-time offenders under the supervision of a Superior Court judge. The jury asks questions and the defendant must explain his or her actions. The sentences typically run to community service (say, 50 hours for vandalism, curfew violation, assault). The student jurors decide what's fair. Those who are judged guilty also must return to serve on a jury themselves.* <u>Contact</u>: Wilson High School, 4500 Multnomah St., Los Angeles, CA 90032

N o man chooses evil because it is evil; he only mistakes it for happiness, the good he seeks.

— Mary Wollstonecraft
19th-century
English novelist
("Frankenstein")

IDEA #102

Fair Opportunities: Teaching Disadvantaged Youngsters

OVERVIEW: Teens establish a tutoring program for disadvantaged youngsters and meet regularly to compare notes and share teaching ideas and successes. You may want to make this an elective exercise, however, for it involves a serious commitment from your students.

PREPARATION/MATERIALS:
- student notebooks for journal-keeping
- Resources include (check www.charactercounts.org for more):
  - Boys & Girls Clubs of America
  - Big Brothers Big Sisters
  - YMCA
  - "School on Wheels," a nonprofit, trademarked, Los Angeles-based tutoring program for homeless youth (310) 589-2642

SETTING: Tutoring can be done in any public place, such as a library or at a shelter (but not in a private living space).

PROCEDURE:

Inform students that not all young people have a home life that is conducive to studying. Some parents are working or absent or unable to help with schoolwork. Suggest that inconsistent parenting and schooling can be a particular problem for youth who live in foster care or who move from shelter to shelter. Ask students to help explain how and why this can harm the futures of these individuals. Point out that homeless children in particular are forced to move frequently and need someone to help them with their studies.

Tell the students that they can help address this fundamental injustice by becoming tutors and mentors. Give students a list of local tutoring/mentoring resources and tell them they have three weeks to get involved in an approved group. They can choose to help someone younger, as a mentor, or another teen, as a peer. Emphasize that good tutors/mentors, stick with it (after their own assignment ends). You might relay that helping a homeless child simply to fulfill a class assignment does not model genuine good character.

Instruct students to keep a journal of their tutoring sessions and report back to the class every month about problems they are encountering and solutions they've found. At the end of the term, have students write a 2,000-word report, exploring how the experience challenged and changed them.

The intention makes the crime.

— **Aristotle**
Greek philosopher

IDEA #103

Seniors Prom

OVERVIEW: Students develop and promote cooperation, commitment and community caring through the planning of a senior citizen prom.

PREPARATION / MATERIALS:
● art supplies, decorations, refreshments, music

SETTING: cafeteria or community center activity room

M en are

only great as

they are kind.

— Elbert Hubbard
19th/20th-century American entrepreneur and publisher

PROCEDURE:

Discuss why students have a prom. Discuss and list all the preparation required to execute a prom. Ask students to explain how these various responsibilities incorporate the Six Pillars — in particular, the trait of caring. Discuss the positive feelings students gain from producing and attending a prom. Have them explain how the experience can promote character growth.

Next, have them discuss why this activity should or shouldn't be limited to high school students. Then, ask the students to consider the possibility of having a prom for true "seniors"— senior citizens — at a retirement home or center. Discuss the responsibilities involved as well as how such an activity would benefit the attendees.

Assign or designate responsibilities to pairs or groups of students such as:

• contacting the center's administrative staff to arrange date and time
• acquiring art supplies to make decorations
• obtaining refreshments and refreshment supplies
• finding music and music equipment
• coordinating the actual prom set up and execution
• formulating a budget (based on funds and resources)
• planning possible fundraiser events

At the event, students serve as hosts and hostesses, dance partners, etc. After the prom, students can again discuss how the prom provided opportunities to express and develop the trait of caring. As a summary project, you might have students write about the misconceptions young people have about the elderly (and vice versa), suggesting how a project like this can foster understanding.

Inspired by "Senior (Citizen) Prom" activity posted on the Cooperating School Districts website (www.info.csd.org/staffdev/chared/newcec/newhigh.html).

● **read up and reach out at www.charactercounts.org** ●

IDEA #104

Running a Blood Drive

> **OVERVIEW:** Students take responsibility for organizing a blood drive, working as a team with field representatives of the American Red Cross. The Red Cross representative will also provide promotional and collateral material.
>
> **PREPARATION / MATERIALS:**
> - brochures, posters, fliers and promotional items (available and designed to educate and encourage students to donate blood). For the American Red Cross representative in your area, call (800) 491-2113 or visit www.redcross.org.
>
> **SPECIAL SETTING:** Auditorium

Compassion is the basis of all morality.

— Arnold Schopenhauer
19th-century German philosopher

PROCEDURE:

Have a talk with students about the importance of a secure supply of blood in health care. The community blood supply is everyone's responsibility, and by letting them know they have the power to save lives, they will feel as if they can and do make a difference. You might say: *Sometimes it's hard to see ourselves as heroes. But every day, you have the power to save lives.* Point out that blood is a matter of life and death to someone needing a transfusion. Yet of the Americans who could give blood, less than three percent do. For every unit of blood that is donated, up to three lives can be touched when the blood is separated into its components of red cells, plasma and platelets.

Ask students to share experiences that they may have had with someone who gave or received blood. Putting a face on the need for blood makes a powerful statement.

Contact an American Red Cross representative to help the students coordinate a blood drive. Create a student committee responsible for distributing posters and fliers, placing an article in the school and local newspapers, volunteering on the day of the drive and, most importantly, recruiting donors. According to the Red Cross, the primary reason people don't give blood is that no one asks them to give.

After the blood drive, the committee should thank donors by creating a large poster, placing a thank-you ad in the school newspaper or creating cards for donors.

Special thanks to Julie Juliusson, communications manager, American Red Cross Blood Services, Southern California Region.

IDEA #105

A Thousand Words

OVERVIEW: To make students more aware that compassion involves a commitment to understanding and engaging in another person's life, they view images of other people's lives and take the time to creatively interpret what they see.

PREPARATION / MATERIALS:

- photo(s) cut out from various magazines (be sure these have no headlines, captions or associated articles describing the scene)

There are two ways of spreading light: to be a candle or the mirror that reflects it.

— Edith Wharton
19th/20th-century American novelist

PROCEDURE:

Choose one or more photos (the amount is up to you) that provoke some sort of emotional response from the viewer. The photo should feature at least one person. Try to choose images where the emotions of the person in the photo are not displayed overtly (screaming, crying, laughing, etc.), but where their mood or situation is ambiguous.

To begin, you might say: *There is an old saying: "A picture is worth a thousand words." We are going to look at a picture and describe it in a thousand words. But before we perform this task, we need to ask ourselves what a person has to do to feel compassion for another person and why.* Solicit and list answers. Point out that part of caring involves empathy — seeing another's perspective and feeling what he or she is going through. Then say: *Our purpose here is to look at the people in the photo with compassionate eyes. Imagine their lives, their thoughts, their dreams, their fears. Invent a story for them. To do that, you have to care about them.*

Distribute the photo(s) and then display them for everyone to see. If you have more than one photo, direct the students to choose only one to write about. Encourage them to pretend that they are the figure in the photo(s), or that they are the photographer. Invite them to think about: what the person/photographer sees, hears, tastes, smells, touches and feels in the captured moment; why the figure in the picture is happy, scared, bored or sad; where he/she has come from and where he/she is headed; and why the photographer cares enough about him/her to take a picture. Once the stories are complete, invite students to share them. Lastly, suggest that taking the time to figure out a person's feelings is the essence of empathy and compassion, key elements of caring. Ask them to help you explain why.

Adapted from "Keeping the American Promise," Vol. 4, Issue 1, p. 2 (Los Angeles, CA: The American Promise, 1999). Also inspired by the "What They Were Thinking" photo feature of <u>The New York Times Magazine</u>.

IDEA #106

Opportunity in Crisis

OVERVIEW: Somewhere in the world a community is facing a crisis — an earthquake, flood, tornado, the "Jerry Springer Show." The next community, the next crisis, could be yours. Learning to prepare yourself and others is a noble — and prudent — thing to do. It is an act of good citizenship. With the threat, if not fact, of crisis and breakdown comes opportunity, an opportunity to *research and reflect on* the essential needs of self, family and community. This exercise encourages young people to explore how their complex society is put together, how people are interdependent, and how it shows good character to be prepared and to share information and resources with others.

PREPARATION / MATERIALS:
Research a crisis that you think is relevant to your class and your area (extreme weather, etc.). For assistance, you might contact the American Red Cross: (800) 491-2113 / www.redcross.org/youth/hip/disaster.html.

PROCEDURE:

Define relevant terms such as: *hurricane, earthquake, crisis, catastrophe, environmental, disaster*, etc.).

Point out to students the interdependence of human societies, making the whole vulnerable when one part is damaged. This is increasingly true in our highly complex modern world, where almost everything depends on artificial power: water and sewage systems; electric generators (which deliver power to everything from hospitals to grocery stores to homes to airports); data storage (banks, the government, etc.).

Say something like: *As human needs and wants have grown, so has the complexity of the systems and institutions we have created to satisfy those needs and wants. But crisis happens, not just to individuals, but to whole communities.* Discuss various kinds of crises. Then say: *Crises shake us up, but that's life. You need to prepare for what life can throw at you and the communities you are responsible for — just like you have to prepare to take care of yourself by maintaining your health, studying hard and saving money and staying out of debt. Hopefully, you will never need to deal with a major catastrophe. But you need to prepare, so you take care of yourself and others.* Select a specific community crisis and tell the students that you will be focusing on this type of crisis.

Security is mostly superstition. It does not exist in nature, nor do the children of men as a whole experience it. ...To keep our faces toward change and behave like free spirits in the presence of fate is strength undefeatable.

— Helen Keller
20th century Nobel Prize-winning American social activist and author

Say: *In preparing for crisis, you need to think about your needs and the needs of your family and community.* Use a visual aid like a chalkboard or a large piece of paper taped to a wall and make two columns: "NEEDS" and "WANTS."

If you have a small group, solicit their opinions about daily needs and wants. If you have a large group, break it up into smaller groups of six or so each, giving the groups 15 minutes to come up with their lists. Then collect the lists and write them up on your board, eliminating redundancies. The NEEDS should come down to true essentials: clean water, food (including for pets), shelter, warmth, dry clothes, means of shedding light (batteries, flashlights, candles, matches), means of preparing/storing unrefrigerated food. Everything else is usually a want. (As a side benefit, this discussion may encourage students to recognize that many of the things we take for granted or feel entitled to are luxuries, extraneous to what is really important in life.)

Ask the whole group if they have enough of these essentials in their household to take care of family needs for a given period of time (say, two weeks) if outside services (such as gas, water and electrical power) are not available. Ask them how much food and water they think they and their family consume each day. If they don't know exactly, ask them how they could find out.

Now divide the students into small groups to create an "action plan" for their families. If their families were to designate a special area for emergency supplies, what would be stored there? (Look for answers such as canned/dried food, bottled water, manual can-opener, matches, candles, etc.) What would be the first thing the family would do? The second? What about the neighbors? Consolidate the reports from the groups and create a general action plan.

Ask the students how they could spread the word about preparation to their families and neighbors. (Another activity would be to have students design and write a brochure or flier about the essentials for the home — with a reminder for everyone to be calm and considerate of others in a stressful situation.)

Conclude by discussing these points as a whole group:

- Discuss the character traits that are most valued and needed in times of crisis. Again, you might want to list these on the board. Talk about the need to think clearly and creatively and to be courteous to others.

- Talk about the need to show a good example to other people who may be panicking or acting irresponsibly (grabbing and pushing at grocery stores, etc).

- Talk about the need to get information from the media, but to be aware of the occasional tendency of the deadline-driven, competitive and entertainment-minded media to inspire fear and paranoia rather than helpfulness.

If we only wanted to be happy it would be easy, but we want to be happier than other people, which is almost always difficult.

— **Charles-Louis de Secondat Baron de Montesquieu**
17th/18th-century French jurist and philosopher

IDEA #107

Budgeting Priorities

OVERVIEW: Students discuss how the people's representatives decide how to allocate funds, then role-play decision makers and learn about budgeting and deliberation. The goal of the exercise is to realize that communities have many demands for spending tax dollars and that interests must compete for limited funds.

PREPARATION / MATERIALS:
● paper; pens or pencils

The final test of a leader is that he leaves behind him in other men the conviction and will to carry on.

— Walter Lippmann
20th century American journalist

PROCEDURE:

Start a discussion about the different roles and responsibilities of government. Draw boxes on the blackboard to represent the federal government's major administrative functions and divisions: defense, social security, justice, commerce, energy, health, education, agriculture, treasury, state (foreign affairs), transportation, etc. Include major regulatory agencies such as the Federal Communications Commission, Federal Trade Commission, Food and Drug Administration, etc. Discuss what each department does, as necessary.

Explain what is at stake with government budgetary decisions, such as people's jobs and fortunes. If an army base is closed, for instance, it saves money, but people are put out of work. Cutting back on agriculture subsidies may mean some farmers go bankrupt. Naturally, people will see themselves as winners and losers with almost any decision. Therefore, there will often be conflict, even bitter arguments.

In a democracy, everyone has a say, even if this means the decision making process is drawn-out, clumsy and noisy. Discuss the virtues and drawbacks of this system. Pick some students to be lobbyists (advocates) for certain interest groups (e.g., business/industry, environmental, labor, military, peace movement).

Give your class a budget (say $500 billion) and divide them into small groups. Have each group allocate its money to each of the departments on the blackboard. Tell them to be ready to defend their decisions. The lobbyists can circulate among the groups to advocate for their cause.

Write down societal categories on the board: elderly, middle age, students, children, etc.; very rich, well-off (affluent), middle-class, poor; race, religion, etc. After decisions are made assign students to certain categories of your (or their) choosing: e.g., poor, religious immigrant. How do students in these categories view the budget choices made? How would they re-order priorities?

Inspired by the "Candy Store" exercise posted on The American Promise (www.americanpromise.com/ ap3510.html).

IDEA #108

School Safety Survey Project

> **OVERVIEW:** Students discuss possible safety issues in their school environment, then create, conduct and assess a school-wide survey about them. They present findings with possible solutions to the school board/administration.
>
> **PREPARATION / MATERIALS:**
> - paper; pencils or pens
> - access to resources (for student research)
> - access to a photocopier

*M*ore dangers have deceived men than forced them.

— **Francis Bacon**
16th-century
English essayist

PROCEDURE:

Relay an appropriate personal incident in which you felt fearful. Write the word "fear" on the board. Ask the students to think about a time or place in which they felt fearful. Ask them to articulate how feeling afraid affected their behavior. Suggest that even if nothing happens, fear can be damaging. Say: *It can preoccupy a person and keep people from being able to give their best and stay focused on a task or responsibility at hand.* Explain how this can have a domino-effect. Offer a school-related example involving a safety issue. Invite students to offer ways this situation could be made less fearful. Say: *Providing an environment that people feel is safe can take away a lot of that damaging fear.* Ask the students to explain how this might apply to their school, citing examples. List their answers on the board.

Explain that they are going to have to find out more accurately what safety concerns their school community has through a survey project. Ask them to explain why you would have them do this. Reiterate the role of a good citizen and the responsibility that they have to make their community a better, safer, less fearful, place for it to be its most productive.

Next, assign them the task of each looking up articles about school safety. Have them summarize their findings in a chart form appropriate to the class level. (The chart or graph they include should reinforce the processes and critical thinking skills needed to analyze and convert data into accurate percentages.)

Have the class brainstorm to create survey questions and write them down. Clarify who the survey participants will be and decide if they accurately represent the makeup of your school community. Together select and edit the questions that will be on the survey.

Decide how and when to conduct the survey and assign specific students to specific tasks.

Once the data have been collected, instruct the students to convert this information into charts that can be distributed and analyzed by the whole class. Assign certain students to assess the numbers for designated questions on the survey. Have them summarize what the numbers signify. Inform them that they will present their findings to the class.

Once the findings have been presented and discussed, have the class figure out possible, practical solutions that students, faculty and administration could carry out to alleviate fears and increase confidence in school safety. Assign the same groups who analyzed certain survey data to write out a step-by-step implementation strategy for one of the solutions proposed.

Finally, gather all the survey information and plans for solutions and compile it into a binder for presentation to the school administration or board.

Reiterate the role awareness plays in our ability to be good citizens.

Inspired by an idea in "Safety" from <u>What Teens Need to Succeed</u>, by Peter L. Benson, Judy Galbraith and Pamela Espeland (Minneapolis, MN: Free Spirit Publishing, 1998, p. 88).

Zeal will do

more than

knowledge.

— **William Hazlitt**
18th-century
English essayist
and literary critic

IDEA #109

The Ideal Parent

OVERVIEW: It's not easy being a good parent, especially to a teenager who is simultaneously looking for direction and for independence. What do teens themselves think they need from parents — and how would *they* be a good parent to a teen? This exercise finds out.

PREPARATION / MATERIALS:

● paper; pens or pencils

The art of living lies not in eliminating but in growing with troubles.

— Bernard Baruch
20th-century American financier and statesman

PROCEDURE:

Say: *What makes a good parent? Today we are going to create a code of behavior for parents — the kind of parents we would like to be one day.*

Write the following questions on a board for all to see, or create a handout using the questions and distribute a sheet to each pupil. Give the students time to write down brief answers. Then go down the list of questions, writing down volunteered answers. Encourage the students to write down whatever responses they like so they can add them to their own initial responses. After 15 minutes, direct the students to write their own code, based on the answers they like best. Tell the students to write the code as a series of declarative statements (e.g., "the good parent sets clear rules and enforces them consistently," or "good parents never do anything they say is bad for kids," etc.). Finally, encourage the kids to discuss their codes with their parents.

QUESTIONS

1. What should parents do when they are angry?
2. What effect do parents' personal habits have on their kids?
3. How strict should parents be about rules (homework, chores, curfew, etc.)?
4. What should parents do when kids break the rules?
5. Should parents try to act more like kids (in the way they talk, dress or dance)?
6. How tough should parents be when a kid is caught lying, stealing or being cruel?
7. Should parents give kids everything they want? How should they say no?
8. Which is more important to being a good parent: honesty or kindness?
9. What do good parents say or do when kids do something right or good?

Inspired by a "Dear Abby" column, printed in the <u>Los Angeles Times</u>, Sept. 29, 1999.

IDEA #110

Pursuing Victory With Honor: The All-Character Team

OVERVIEW: Teens select athletes with winning character and honor them with awards.

PREPARATION/MATERIALS:
- copies of certificates (master provided)

PROCEDURE:

To introduce the exercise, you might say: *Athletes are honored for their on-field and on-court achievements by being named to "All" teams, like All-Pro, All-Star, All-American, etc. You are going to nominate and award athletes to an "All-Character" team.* Explain that the criteria for selection is the athlete's demonstrated commitment to pursuing victory with honor. This means that he or she demonstrates the Six Pillars of Character in his or her life. It doesn't matter what sport the athlete plays; coaches can also be nominated.

Each student chooses a nominee and writes a one-page profile of that athlete (or coach) extolling his or her virtues. Instruct the students to submit these nominations in two weeks, with oral presentations in front of the class explaining why their nominees should be chosen. Then have the students vote on the athletes by secret ballot. The top ten athletes will be the "winners" of certificates.

Instruct the teens to look for:

- demonstrated, outstanding commitment to the community
- behavior toward teammates, opponents, coaches, referees and fans

You might take this a step further by actually sending the certificates to the winning athletes and writing (with the students) a press release announcing your awards and the recipients.

Energy and persistence conquer all things.

— Benjamin Franklin
18th-century American Founding Father, inventor and statesman

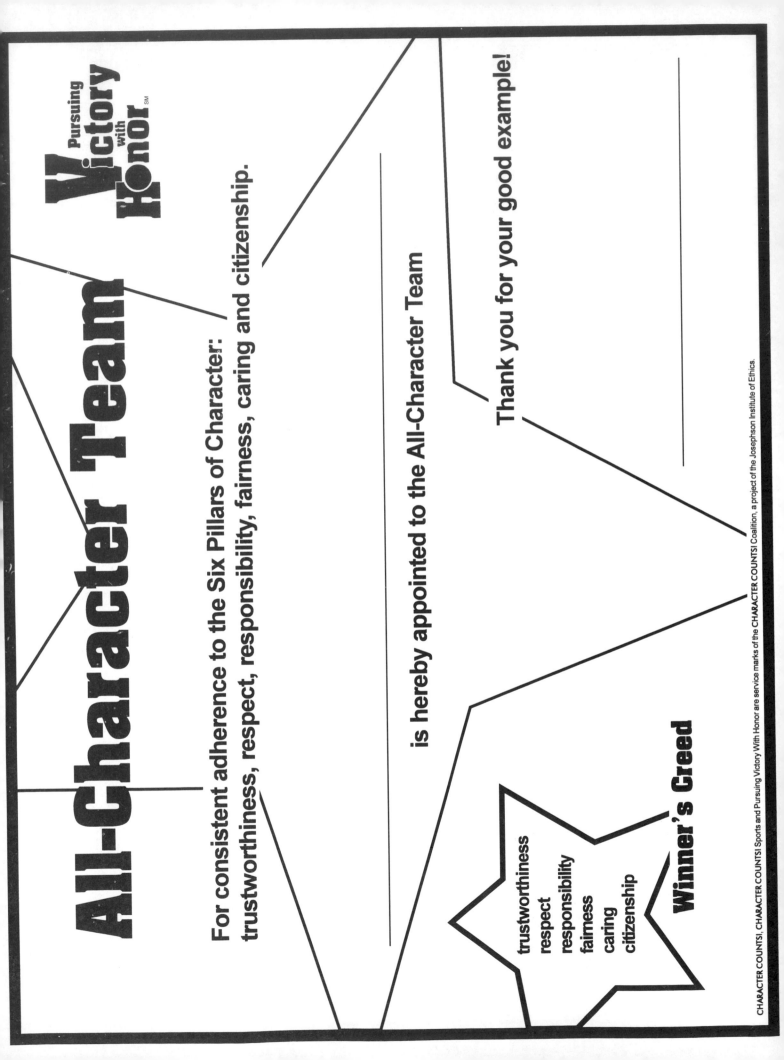

All-Character Team

For consistent adherence to the Six Pillars of Character:
trustworthiness, respect, responsibility, fairness, caring and citizenship.

is hereby appointed to the All-Character Team

Thank you for your good example!

Pursuing Victory with Honor℠

Winner's Creed

trustworthiness
respect
responsibility
fairness
caring
citizenship

IDEA #111

Writing Vir-Ku (Virtue Haiku)

*A*n aim

in life is the

only fortune

worth finding.

— **Jacqueline Kennedy Onassis**
20th-century American First Lady and celebrity

OVERVIEW: Teens write haiku, a Japanese form of poetry, using one or more of the Six Pillars of Character (trustworthiness, respect, responsibility, fairness, caring and citizenship) or other "virtue" words.

PREPARATION / MATERIALS:
- paper; pens or pencils
- other resources:
  - *The Haiku Anthology*, edited by Cor van den Heuvel, with over 800 English-language haiku (Norton, 1999)
  - *The Haiku Handbook* by William S. Higginson with Penny Harter (Kodansha, 1992)

PROCEDURE:

Explain that haiku is a centuries-old Japanese poetry form which makes a simple, sometimes profound or oddly moving observation about a moment in time. Provide some background by saying something like: *Haiku is usually about nature. The haiku we'll be writing will suggest something positive about* <u>human nature</u>, *using one or more of the words that reflect ethical values known as the Six Pillars of Character: trustworthiness, respect, responsibility, fairness, caring and citizenship.* You might write the Six Pillars on the board and ask students to add other "virtue" words to the list (e.g., courage, honor, compassion, honesty, etc.).

Explain the structure of haiku: It contains 17 syllables in three lines (five, seven, five); has a nature theme; and is written in the present tense about a single moment.

Explain that haiku poets make close observations about nature and *think small*. Focusing on a single tree or leaf or petal, for example, often works better in haiku than trying to take in the whole forest. The idea is to create a word picture, not to tell a story. (If the syllable count is off a bit, that's OK.)

Here is a sample "vir-ku" (virtue haiku) you might share with students:

Kindness in his words, / the tutor explains the task / the young pupil smiles

Tell the students that their haiku will be collected and shared with everyone in the class. Put together an anthology of student work by compiling a binder of work for everyone to view. You might choose some of the better efforts and ask the poets to read their work aloud to the class.

*H*e is poor

who does not

feel content.

— **Japanese proverb**

Some haiku explanation from <u>Scholastic Instructor</u> *(March 2000).*

IDEA #112

The C.Q. Test

OVERVIEW: Teens answer hypothetical challenges to their character. (This quiz is the work of an editor, not a psychologist, and should not be seen as a comprehensive or scientific test of someone's character. It is meant to be an engaging way to start a discussion about how to be successful in life — and what success really means.)

PROCEDURE:

Introduce the subject of "emotional intelligence," which involves many valuable skills, from anger management and politeness to planning for the future. You might say: *Psychologists and educators now widely recognize that there is more than one kind of intelligence. We can be "smart" in one thing, "dumb" in another. We can excel in certain endeavors but habitually do and say things that turn others away from us or thwart us from true happiness — things that are untrustworthy, disrespectful, irresponsible, uncaring or unfair (or on a really bad day, all of the above).*

Draw attention to *Emotional Intelligence*, the best-selling work of psychologist Daniel Goleman, according to whom the basics of emotional intelligence include:

- Knowing your feelings and using them to make decisions you can live with.
- Being able to manage your emotional life, not being controlled by it — not being paralyzed by depression or worry, or swept away by anger.
- Persisting through setbacks; pursuing your goals.
- Reading other people's emotions without their having to tell you what they are feeling (i.e., being empathetic).
- Handling feelings in relationships with skill and harmony — being able to articulate the unspoken mood of a group, for example.

Say: *Because these skills often involve anticipating others' needs and weighing consequences when making choices, we might call a measurement of one's emotional intelligence a test of one's "character quotient" — let's call it our C.Q.*

Distribute copies of the following quiz or project it with an overhead onto a screen or wall. Add or delete questions as you see fit. Tell the students the quiz is not a scientific test of their character, but just a fun way to see what it takes to be successful in life (and what success really means). Say: *There are not always right and wrong answers to these questions, but if you're stumped it helps to remember the Golden Rule of treating others the way you want them to treat you. That can usually take a person pretty far in life.*

1 What would you do if you were fired from a job?

a. ☐ Not worry about it. There are plenty of other jobs out there.

b. ☐ Reflect on why you were dismissed and create a specific plan of action to do better next time (whether or not you were at fault).

c. ☐ Write a scathing letter to your former boss and bad-mouth him to your friends and family. What a jerk!

2 What would you say to a very good friend who wants your help in cheating on a test? The person is very upset and desperate and will fail the class and maybe not get into college if the test is failed. (This friend has helped you out a lot.)

a. ☐ "I'm really sorry, but you're on your own. I can't jeopardize my future because you thought other things were more important than studying."

b. ☐ "Of course, I'll help. We're buds!"

c. ☐ "Can I help you find a way to approach the teacher about a make-up exam?"

d. ☐ "Uh, can I get back to you on that?"

3 What would you say to someone whose appearance has changed in some way you don't think is attractive (weight gain, bad haircut, skin problems, etc.)?

a. ☐ "Are you pregnant?" (if the friend is heavier ... and female)

b. ☐ "I love your new look!"

c. ☐ "Wow, what the heck is *happening* to you?"

d. ☐ Nothing. Talk about it only if the friend brings up the subject.

4 Your friend is furious about something that happened to him/her. You:

a. ☐ Say, "Calm down. It's not that bad."

b. ☐ Are sympathetic, but try to change the subject.

c. ☐ Show solidarity by joining your friend in his/her rant.

d. ☐ Tell him/her about a time something like this happened to you and how you felt just as mad, but later realized you didn't know the whole story.

e. ☐ Nothing; wait for the storm to pass.

5 You're in a group of popular kids. You want them to like you. One of them makes a cruel remark about someone who is not there (and definitely *not* considered a candidate for coolness). Everyone laughs. You:

a. ☐ Laugh too. (Hey, it's *funny*.)

b. ☐ Scowl and say, "I don't think that's right."

c. ☐ Just smile and say nothing.

d. ☐ Say nothing at the time, but plan to later tell each person in the group about the ridiculed person's good qualities.

e. ☐ Walk away, deciding this is not a group you want to be part of.

6 You're trying to get on a team, but you've been cut twice in a row. You:

a. ☐ Call it quits.

b. ☐ Assess qualities in yourself that may be undermining your ability to make the cut, and create a step-by-step strategy to make the team the next time.

c. ☐ Consider another sport/activity.

All bad precedents begin as justifiable measures.

— Julius Caesar
Roman leader

7 You were planning to get an A in a course, but just got a C on the midterm exam (making that A very tough to get now). What do you do?

a. ☐ Develop a plan to improve your grade.

b. ☐ Resolve to do better in the future.

c. ☐ Tell yourself it really doesn't matter *that much* how you do in the course, and resolve to concentrate on classes where your grades are higher.

d. ☐ Go see the teacher and try to talk her into giving you a better grade.

Based in part on and inspired by Emotional Intelligence, by Daniel P. Goleman (New York, NY: Bantam, 1995) and Raise Your Social I.Q., by Michael Levine (Secaucus, NJ: Citadel Press, 1998).

Fame is a vapor, popularity an accident, riches take wing. Only character endures.

— **Horace Greeley**
19th-century American journalist

— Answers —

1. B is best. It's grown-up time, folks.

2. C. You need to be a supportive friend but maintain your own honor and integrity at the same time; you'll be a more valuable friend in the long run.

3. D. Even though this a trusting relationship, candor isn't necessarily called for if it involves gratuitous judgments about one's appearance. Unless you are seriously concerned about your friend's mental or physical health, say nothing unless your friend invites comment. And then be tactful and supportive.

4. B is best. This is a tricky one (D may also be appropriate), but sometimes it is best to help divert an angry's person's attention away from the source of his/her wrath so he/she can gain perspective. This question was adapted from a question developed by Daniel Goleman, who cites data on rage and how to calm it. He shows the effectiveness of distracting the angry person from the focus of his/her rage, empathizing with his/her feelings and perspective, and suggesting a less anger-provoking way of seeing the situation. To say nothing might be called for in some instances.

5. Another tricky one. Certainly "B" is an option (and is admirable in the courage it requires) — but that scowl part, what's up with that? That's a little over the top and may show that you don't know how to communicate effectively and persuasively with others. "D" is tempting, but isn't it a little too easy to rationalize your cowardice with the promise to do something *later*, when it's *safe*? While it doesn't mandate direct confrontation, perhaps "E" is best; at least you have some class.

6. B or C. Come on, stick with it! But be smart about it; if you're not good enough make an effort to turn it around. Or find another outlet for your energy — that's fine too. Just don't quit.

7. A is better than B because it involves an actual plan. Good intentions often lead nowhere and the smart thing to do is to plan and execute.

GOOD IDEAS

BOOKS AND OTHER CHARACTER EDUCATION RESOURCES

Books and Other
Character Education Resources

BOOKS

Adrienne, Carol
The Purpose of Your Life: Finding Your Place in the World Using Synchronicity, Intuition, and Uncommon Sense (New York, NY: William Morrow and Company, Inc., 1998)

Akin, Terry; Dunne, Gerry; Palomares, Susanna; and Schilling, Dianne
Character Education in America's Schools (Spring Valley, CA: Innerchoice Publishing, 1995)

Allman, Barbara (for grades K-1 and 2-3 booklets); and Steele, Anne (for grades 4-5 and 6-8 booklets)
Developing Character When It Counts (Torrance, CA: Frank Schaffer Publications, 1999)

Almeder, Robert
Human Happiness and Morality: A Brief Introduction to Ethics (Amherst, NY: Prometheus Books, 2000)

Andrews, Sharon Vincz; Martin, Donna M.
Teaching Kids to Care (Jefferson City, MO: Scholastic, Inc., 1987)

Bauer, David G.
The Teacher's Guide to Winning Grants (San Francisco, CA: Jossey-Bass Inc., 1999)

Bennett, William
The Book of Virtues (New York, NY: Simon & Schuster, 1993)

Benson, Peter L.
All Kids Are Our Kids: What Communities Must Do to Raise Caring and Responsible Children and Adolescents (San Francisco, CA: Jossey-Bass, Inc., 1997)

Benson, Peter L.; Galbraith, Judy; and Espeland, Pamela
What Teens Need to Succeed: Proven, Practical Ways to Shape Your Own Future (Minneapolis, MN: Free Spirit Publishing Inc., 1998)

Berson, Robin Kadison
Young Heroes in World History (Westport, CT: Greenwood Press, 1999)

Bevan, E. Dean
What to Do When You're Angry (Highland City, FL: Rainbow Books, Inc., 1994)

Billings, Henry and Billings, Melissa
Stories of Fairness (San Diego, CA: Young People's Press, 1995)

Boyer, Ernest L.
The Basic School: A Community for Learning (Princeton, NJ: The Carnegie Foundation for the Advancement of Teaching, 1995)

Britzman, Mark J.
The Lives and Legacies of Everyday Heroes (Bloomington, IN: Unlimited Publishing, 2000)

Brock, Gillian
Necessary Goods: Our Responsibilities to Meet Others' Needs (Lanham, Maryland: Rowman & Littlefield Publishers, Inc., 1998)

Brolin, Donn E.
Life Centered Career Education (Reston, VA: The Council for Exceptional Children, 1993)

Brooks, B. David
Lessons in Character (San Diego, CA: Young People's Press, 1993)

Brooks, B. David and Goble, Frank G.
The Case for Character Education: The Role of the School in Teaching Values and Virtue (Northridge, CA; Studio 4 Productions, 1997)

Byrnes, John Carroll
A Book of Values (Baltimore, MD: John Carroll Byrnes, 1995)

Chappelle, Sharon and Bigman, Lisa
Diversity in Action (Covington, GA: Project Adventure, Inc., 1998)

Cohen-Posey, Kate
How to Handle Bullies, Teasers and Other Meanies (Highland City, FL: Rainbow Books, 1995)

Colby, Anne; James, Jacquelyn; and Hart, Daniel
Competence and Character Through Life (Chicago, IL: The University of Chicago Press, 1998)

Coleman, Sally and Anderson, David S.
Charting Your Course: A Life-Long Guide to Health and Compassion (Notre Dame, IN: University of Notre Dame Press, 1998)

Connolly, Theresa; Dowd, Tom; Criste, Andrea; Nelson, Cathy; and Tobias, Lisa
The Well-Managed Classroom (Boys Town, NE: The Boys Town Press, 1995)

Davitz, Lois Leiderman and Davitz, Joel R.
20 Tough Questions Teenagers Ask: And 20 Tough Answers (Mahwah, NJ: Paulist Press, 1998)

Deal, Terrence E. and Peterson, Kent D.
Shaping School Culture: The Heart of Leadership (San Francisco, CA: Jossey-Bass, 1999)

Delisle, Deb and Delisle, Jim
Growing Good Kids: 28 Activities to Enhance Self-Awareness, Compassion and Leadership (Minneapolis, MN: Free Spirit Publishing Inc., 1996)

Dellabrough, Robin; Hollister, Ben; Marlin, Alice Tepper; Swaab, Emily; Rose, Jonathan; and Will, Rosalyn
Students Shopping 4 a Better World (New York, NY: Council on Economic Priorities, Inc., 1992)

Dinkmeyer, Don and McKay, Gary D.
Raising a Responsible Child (New York, NY: Simon & Schuster, 1973)

Durst, Mose
Principled Education (Hayward, CA: The Principled Academy, 1998)

Elias, Maurice J.; Tobias, Steven E.; and Friedlander, Brian S.
Emotionally Intelligent Parenting: How to Raise a Self-Disciplined, Responsible, Socially Skilled Child (New York, NY: Harmony Books, 1999)

Ender, Steven; Newton, Fred; and Caple, Richard
Contributing to Learning: The Role of Student Affairs (San Francisco, CA: Jossey-Bass Inc., 1996)

Eyre, Linda and Eyre, Richard
Teaching Your Children Responsibility (New York, NY: Fireside Books/Simon & Schuster, 1984)

Eyre, Linda and Eyre, Richard
Teaching Your Children Values (New York, NY: Fireside Books/Simon & Schuster, 1993)

Fincham, Sharon, et al.
Lesson Plans for Character Education, Elementary Edition (Manhattan, KS: The MASTER Teacher, Inc., 1998)

Franquemont, Sharon
You Already Know What To Do: 10 Invitations to the Intuitive Life (New York, NY: Jeremy P. Tarcher/Putnam, 1999)

Freedman, Marc
The Kindness of Strangers: Adult Mentors, Urban Youth, and the New Voluntarism (San Francisco, CA: Jossey-Bass, 1993)

Freeman, Sara (grades K-1 booklet); Pearce, Q.L (grades 2-3 and 4-5 booklets); Inferrera, Gia and White, Kelly (grades 6-8 booklet)
Spotlight on Character: Plays That Show CHARACTER COUNTS! (Torrance, CA: Frank Schaffer Publications, 1999)

Goleman, Daniel P.
Emotional Intelligence (New York, NY: Bantam, 1995)

Gordon, Sol
A Friend in Need: How to Help When Times Are Tough (Amherst, NY: Prometheus Books, 2000)

Gough, Russell W.
Character Is Destiny: The Value of Personal Ethics in Everyday Life (Rocklin, CA: Forum, 1998)

Greer, Colin and Kohl, Herbert
A Call to Character (New York, NY: HarperCollins, 1995)

Guroian, Vigen
Tending the Heart of Virtue: How Classic Stories Awaken a Child's Moral Imagination (New York, NY: Oxford University Press, 1998)

Gust, John
Developing Character-Building Values: A Whole Language Approach (Morristown, NJ: Good Apple, 1995)

Hass, Aaron
Doing the Right Thing: Cultivating Your Moral Intelligence (New York, NY: Pocket Books, 1998)

Hall, Susan
Using Picture Storybooks to Teach Character Education (Phoenix, AZ: Oryx Press, 2000)

Holland, Gail Bernice
A Call for Connection: Solutions for Creating a Whole New Culture (Novato, CA: New World Library, 1998)

Howely, Rhonda
Building Character and Community in the Classroom, K-3 (Cypress, CA: Creative Teaching Press, 1997)

Humphrey, Sandra McLeod
If You Had to Choose, What Would You Do? (Amherst, NY: Prometheus Books, 1995)

James, Donna Walker and Jurich, Sonia
More Things That Do Make a Difference for Youth: A Compendium of Evaluations of Youth Programs and Practices, Vol. II (Washington, DC: American Youth Policy Forum, 1999)

Josephson, Michael and Hanson, Wes (eds.)
The Power of Character: Prominent Americans Talk About Life, Family, Work, and More (San Francisco, CA: Jossey-Bass Publishers, 1998)

Jouris, David
All Over the Map
(Berkeley, CA: Ten Speed Press, 1994)

Kirschenbaum, Howard
Kids With Courage: True Stories About Young People Making a Difference (Minneapolis, MN: Free Spirit Publishing Inc., 1992)

Kohn, Alfie
What to Look For in a Classroom...and Other Essays (San Francisco, CA: Jossey-Bass Inc., 1998)

Kreidler, William J. and Furlong, Lisa
Adventures in Peacemaking: A Conflict Resolution Activity Guide for School-Age Programs (Cambridge, MA: Educators for Social Responsibility, 1995)

Lamme, Linda Leonard; Krogh, Suzanne Lowell; and Yachmetz, Kathy A.
Literature-Based Moral Education: Children's Books and Activities for Teaching Values, Responsibility, and Good Judgment in Elementary School (Phoenix, AZ: Oryx Press, 1992)

LaMuth, John E.
The Ultimate Guide to Family Values (Lucerne Valley, CA: LaMuth Publishing Company, 1999)

LeGette, Helen R.
Parents, Kids & Character: 21 Strategies to Help Your Children Develop Good Character (Chapel Hill, NC: Character Development Publishing, 1999)

Levine, Michael
Raise Your Social I.Q. (Secaucus, NJ: Citadel Press, 1998)

Lewis, Barbara A.
The Kid's Guide to Service Projects: Over 500 Service Ideas for Young People Who Want to Make a Difference (Minneapolis, MN: Free Spirit Publishing Inc., 1995)

Lewis, Barbara A.
100 Ways to Enhance Values and Morality in Schools and Youth Settings, (Needham Heights, MA: Allyn & Bacon, 1995)

Lewis, Barbara A.
Being Your Best: Character Building for Kids 7-10 (Minneapolis, MN: Free Spirit Publishing, 2000)

Lewis, Barbara A.
The Kid's Guide to Social Action (Minneapolis, MN: Free Spirit Publishing, 1991)

Lewis, Barbara A.
What Do You Stand For?: A Kid's Guide to Building Character (Minneapolis, MN: Free Spirit Publishing, 1998)

Lickona, Thomas
Educating for Character (New York, NY: Bantam Books, 1991)

Loeb, Paul Rogat
Soul of a Citizen: Living With Conviction in a Cynical Time (New York: St. Martin's Griffin, 1999)

Los Angeles Unified School District
The Teaching of Values, An Instructional Guide (Los Angeles, CA: Los Angeles Unified School District, 1978)

Marx, Jeffrey A. and Gruberger, Risa Munitz
What's Right? What's Wrong?: A Guide to Talking About Values for Parents and Kids (Pleasantville, NY: The Reader's Digest Association, Inc., 1999)

McLaughlin, Milbrey W.; Irby, Merita A.; and Langman, Juliet
Urban Sanctuaries: Neighborhood Organizations in the Lives and Futures of Inner-City Youth (San Francisco, CA: Jossey-Bass, Inc., 1994)

Murray, Margo
Beyond the Myths and Magic of Mentoring: How to Facilitate an Effective Mentoring Program (San Francisco, CA: Jossey-Bass Inc., 1991)

Pearce, Q. L.
A Parent's Guide to Developing Character in Your Preschooler (Don Mills, Ontario, Canada: 2000)

Popov, Linda Kavelin; Popov, Dan; and Kavelin, John
The Virtues Guide: A Family Handbook, (Fountain Hills, AZ: Virtues Communications, 1995)

Postman, Neil
The End of Education: Redefining the Value of School, (New York, NY: Alfred A. Knopf, 1995)

Pritchard, Ivor
Good Education: The Virtues of Learning, (Norwalk, CT: Judd Publishing, Inc., 1998)

Reed, Bobbie
501 Practical Ways to Teach your Children Values (St. Louis, MO: Concordia Publishing House, 1998)

Reuben, Steven Carr
Raising Ethical Children (Rocklin, CA: Prima Publishing 1994)

Roufberg, William
Practicing Moral Decision Making (Kingston, NJ: Compass Editions, 1995)

Ryan, Kevin and Bohlin, Karen E.
Building Character in Schools: Practical Ways to Bring Moral Instruction to Life (San Francisco, CA: Jossey-Bass, Inc., 1999)

Sadlow, Sarah,
Advisor/Advisee: Lessons for Teachers and Counselors (Chapel Hill, NC: Character Development Group, 1998)

St. Romain, Philip
Building Character in Young People (Gretna, LA: Pelican Publishing Company, Inc., 1986)

Schiller, Pam and Bryant, Tamera
The Values Book: Teaching 16 Basic Values to Young Children (Beltsville, MD: Gryphon House, Inc., 1998)

Schulman, Michael and Mekler, Eva
Bringing Up a Moral Child (New York, NY: Main Street Books/Doubleday, 1994)

Shaw, Vanston
Community Building in the Classroom (San Clemente, CA: Kagan Publishing, 1992)

Sherwin, Byron L.
Why Be Good? Seeking Our Best Selves in a Challenging World (New York, NY: Daybreak Books, a Division of Rodale Books, 1998)

Sizer, Theodore R.
Horace's Hope: What Works for the American High School (New York, NY: Houghton Mifflin Company, 1996)

Steinberg, Laurence
Beyond the Classroom: Why School Reform Has Failed and What Parents Need to Do (New York, NY: Simon & Schuster, 1996)

Talkington, Audrey E. and Albers Hill, Barbara
To Save A Child (Garden City Park, NY: Avery Publishing Group, 1993)

Taylor, Richard
Good and Evil (Amherst, NY: Prometheus Books, 2000)

Templeton, Sir John
Golden Nuggets (Radnor, PA: Templeton Foundation Press, 1997)

Turley, Robert J.
The Choices are Yours: How Values-Driven Choices Change Lives (Highland City, FL: Rainbow Books, Inc., 1998)

Unell, Barbara C. and Wyckoff, Jerry L.
20 Teachable Virtues: Practical Ways to Pass on Lessons of Virtue and Character to Your Children (New York, NY: Perigree Books/The Berkley Publishing Group, 1985)

Unell, Barbara C.; Jerry L. Wyckoff
Twenty Teachable Virtues (New York, NY: Perigree Books/Berkeley Publishing Group, 1995)

Van Linden, Josephine A. and Fertman, Carl I.
Youth Leadership: A Guide to Understanding Leadership Development in Adolescents (San Francisco, CA: Jossey-Bass Inc., 1998)

Vincent, Philip Fitch (ed.)
Promising Practices in Character Education (Chapel Hill, NC: New View Publication, 1998)

Wattles, Jeffrey
The Golden Rule (New York, NY: Oxford University Press, 1996)

OTHER CHARACTER-EDUCATION RESOURCES

America the Beautiful Fund
1730 K St., NW, Suite 1002
Washington, DC 20006
www.america-the-beautiful.org
(contact regarding free seeds to start community garden)

The American Promise
P. O. Box 514989
Los Angeles, CA 90051-4989
www.americanpromise.com
info@americanpromise.com

"Boomerang!" Character Education Program (1998)
ISU Extension Distribution
119 Printing and Publications Bldg.
Iowa State University
Ames, IA 50011-3171
(515) 294-5247

Bread and Roses Cultural Project
330 West 42nd St., 7th Floor
New York, NY 10036
(212) 631-4565
www.breadandroses.com

Center for the 4th and 5th Rs
State University of New York College at Cortland
P.O. Box 2000
Cortland, NY 13045

Children to Children (group that collects duffle bags and stuffed animals for foster children)
3262 Superior Lane, PMB #288
Bowie, MD 20715
www.childrentochildren.com

"Exercising Character: Lesson Plans & Activities," by Peggy Adkins
CHARACTER COUNTS! Coalition
4640 Admiralty Way, #1001
Marina del Rey, CA 90292-6610
(310) 306-1868 • cc@jiethics.org
www.charactercounts.org

"Exercising Character in School"
Louisiana Cooperative Extension Service
Louisiana State University Agricultural Ctr.
P.O. Box 25100
Baton Rouge, LA 770894
(225) 388-4141

Hope magazine (Hope Publishing)
P.O. Box 160, Naskeag Rd.
Brooklin, ME 04616
(800) 273-7447

"In the Palm of Your Hand" activity (1998)
YMCA Earth Service Corps
(Y Care International, CreActivity)
www.mightymedia.com

Instructor magazine (Scholastic, Inc.)
555 Broadway
New York, NY 10012-3999
(212) 343-6400
www.scholastic.com/instructor

"It's Your Character That Counts!"(cassettes with songs, activity booklets), by Paul Tracey
CHARACTER COUNTS! Coalition
4640 Admiralty Way, #1001
Marina del Rey, CA 90292-6610
(310) 306-1868 • cc@jiethics.org
www.charactercounts.org

Kids for Character (activity booklet/videotape, 1996)
CHARACTER COUNTS! Coalition
4640 Admiralty Way, #1001
Marina del Rey, CA 90292-6610
(310) 306-1868 • cc@jiethics.org
www.charactercounts.org

"Learning for Life: A Partner in Education"
(curriculum booklet, 1995)
Boy Scouts of America
1325 West Walnut Hill Lane
P.O. Box 152079
Irving, TX 75015-2079

National Association for Humane and Environmental Education (the youth education division of The Humane Society of the U.S.)
P.O. Box 362
East Haddam, CT 06423-0362
(860) 434-8666
nahee@nahee.org

Points of Light Foundation
1737 H St., NW, Washington, D.C. 20006
(202) 729-8000
www.pointsoflight.org

"Reaching Today's Youth: The Community Circle of Caring Journal"
1252 Loesch Rd.
Bloomington, IN 47404

"Show-Me Character All Star Curriculum"
4-H Youth Program
University of Missouri System, Lincoln University,
210 Whitten Hall
Columbia, MO 65211
(573) 882-3226

State Farm Insurance Company
"Thought, Word and Deed" program
www.statefarm.com/educate/twdpage.htm

"Teaching Tolerance" (an educational project of the Southern Poverty Law Center)
400 Washington Ave.
Montgomery, AL 36104
Fax: (334) 264-3121

"Youth Leadership in Action: A Guide to Cooperative Games and Group Activities"
Project Adventure, Inc.
P.O. Box 100, Hamilton, MA 01936
(508) 468-7981
www.pa.org

RESOURCES ON SPORTS

BOOKS

Asinof, Eliot
Eight Men Out: The Black Sox and the 1919 World Series (New York, NY: Henry Holt and Company, Inc., 1963)

Bates, Bill
Shoot for the Star: An Inspiring Story of Beating the Odds to Fulfill a Lifelong Dream (Dallas, TX: Word Publishing, 1994)

Bowman, John
Sportsmanship (New York, NY: The Rosen Publishing Group, Inc., 1990)

Bradley, Bill
Values of the Game (New York, NY: Artisan, A Division of Workman Publishing Company, Inc., 1998)

Buzby, Jonathan H.
Coaching Kids: It's More Than X's and O's
(Bear, DE: Kids-n-Sports, 1998)

Byers, Walter
*Unsportsmanlike Conduct: Exploiting College
Athletes* (Ann Arbor, MI: The University of
Michigan Press, 1991)

Clifford, Craig and Feezell, Randolph M.
Coaching for Character (Champaign, IL: Human
Kinetics Publishers, Inc., 1997)

George, Gary R.
Winning Is a Habit (New York, NY:
HarperCollins Publishers, 1997)

Gibson, John H.
*Performance Versus Results: A Critique of
Values in Contemporary Sport* (Albany, NY:
State University of New York Press, 1993)

Golenbock, Peter
*Personal Fouls: The Broken Promises and
Shattered Dreams of Big Money Basketball at
Jim Valvano's North Carolina State* (New York,
NY: Carroll & Graf Publishers, Inc., 1989)

Gough, Russell W.
*Character Is Everything: Promoting Ethical
Excellence in Sports* (Fort Worth, TX: Harcourt
Brace College Publishers, 1997)

Holtz, Lou
*Winning Every Day: The Game Plan for
Success* (New York, NY: HarperCollins
Publishers, 1998)

Isenberg, Marc and Rhoads, Rick
*The Real Athletes Guide: How to Succeed in
Sports, School, & Life* (Los Angeles, CA: Athlete
Network Press, 1999)

Klatell, David A. and Marcus, Norman
Sports for Sale (New York, NY: Oxford
University Press, 1988)

Lapchick, Richard
*Five Minutes to Midnight: Race and Sport in
the 1990s* (Lanham, MD: Madison Books, 1991)

Lapchick, Richard E. and Slaughter, John B.
The Rules of the Game: Ethics in College Sport
(New York, NY: Macmillan Publishing, 1989)

Lee, Martin
Coaching Children in Sport (New York, NY:
Chapman & Hall, 1993)

Lupica, Mike
*Mad as Hell: How Sports Got Away from the
Fans and How We get it Back* (G. P. Putnam's
Sons, 1996)

Martens, Rainer; Christina, Robert W.; Harvey,
John S.; and Sharkey, Brian J.
Coaching Young Athletes (Champaign, IL:
Human Kinetics Publishers, Inc., 1981)

National Federation of State High School Associations
Citizenship Through Sports (Kansas City, MO:
NFSHSA, 1997)

Rosen, Roger and McSharry, Patra
Good Sports: Fair Play and Foul (New York,
NY: The Rosen Publishing Group, Inc., 1992)

Sack, Allen L. and Staurowsky, Ellen J.
*College Athletes for Hire: The Evolution and
Legacy of the HCAA's Amateur Myth* (Westport,
CT: Praeger Publishers, 1998)

Selleck, George A.
*How to Play the Game of Your Life: A Guide to
Success in Sports — and Life* (South Bend, IN:
Diamond Communications, Inc., 1995)

Summit, Pat
*Reach for the Summit: The Definite Dozen
System for Succeeding at Whatever You Do*
(New York, NY: Broadway Books, 1998)

Walton, Gary.
*Beyond Winning: The Timeless Wisdom of Great
Philosopher Coaches* (Champaign, IL: Human
Kinetics Publishers, Inc., 1992)